Lost in Mongolia

TAD FRIEND

LOST IN MONGOLIA

TRAVELS IN HOLLYWOOD
AND OTHER FOREIGN LANDS

NEW YORK

All rights reserved under International and Pan-American Copyright
Conventions. Published in the United States by AtRandom.com Books,
a division of Random House, Inc., New York, and simultaneously
in Canada by Random House of Canada Limited, Toronto.

ATRANDOM.COM BOOKS and colophon are trademarks of Random House, Inc.

The articles and essays in this book have been previously published in slightly
different form in the following periodicals: *Esquire, GQ, Harper's, The New
Republic, New York, The New Yorker, Outside, Spin,* and *Vogue.*

Library of Congress Cataloging-in-Publication Data

Friend, Tad.
Lost in Mongolia: travels in Hollywood and other foreign lands/Tad Friend.
p.   cm.
ISBN 978-0-8129-9155-0
I. Title.
AC8.F6968   2001
070.4′44—dc21   00-066489

Website address: www.atrandom.com

146470499

FOR MY PARENTS

Contents

PART III

FAR FROM HOME

Introduction

The creation of this, my first book, was so easy and enjoyable that I'd like to share the process. Boy, was I lucky! First, I spent a dozen years writing for magazines on topics completely unrelated to one another and totally unsuited for expansion into a book. I forget why I did this.

Next, I was sitting at home in my bathrobe minding my own business when an editor at Random House called. He indicated, rather disapprovingly, that the company's shareholders had voted to have some of my better pieces gathered into a book. Apparently the idea met with favor because it would have no effect whatsoever on the corporation's balance sheet, particularly as I was to be paid in brightly colored beads and chocolate coins.

Which articles to choose? I started reading through everything, beginning with the first article I ever wrote (*Scholastic* magazine: "Don't Run with Scissors!"). Pretty soon I had to go lie down. When I was able to take solid food and read on, I was pleased to see that the tone of reflexive sarcasm that stamped my earlier writings gave way, gradually, to a more assured and becoming tone of jokey smugness. Yet I noticed with dismay that throughout my career I have used a vocabulary of only about sixty words, placing an especially heavy reliance on "rueful," "peppery," and "frog-marched." Often those words were combined to striking effect. The sentence "The rueful, peppery fox frog-marched over the lazy dog" appeared at least five times, twice in the same short article about presidential tracking polls.

I set aside the few pieces that seemed relatively disaster-free. With an old bottle of Wite-Out in hand—just one of the technological marvels made possible by electronic publishing—I then blotted out the lapses that my editors should have saved me from years ago. (Most editors are notorious hopheads and dope fiends.)

Thereupon I divided the redacted pile into three smaller piles, each constituting a thematic section of the book. Collections must be divided into thematic sections, and mine are no lamer than anyone else's. Each section is also, I am proud to report, entirely chronological. The first part I call "Hollywood," because it is about Hollywood. I go out there from New York every few months to look around. For years I was careful to avoid being pigeonholed as an "entertainment writer," but everyone believes that he is careful and yet the hospitals are full of babies.

The second part is "America and Its Discontents." I have written a number of reported essays about American culture because I love it, and hate it, and want it to get better, and know that it won't, and can't resist trying to coax it along.

"Far from Home," comprising some of the pieces I've reported from abroad, concludes the book. I used to travel a lot, and have been to all seven continents, more than fifty countries, and forty-nine states. I have also visited five of our solar system's nine planets.

At last, when I had made my body of work look coherent enough to fool the untrained eye, I took a taxi to Random House, fought my way past the security guards, and handed in the book. The editors glanced up briefly from their hookahs and jugs of Ripple and slurred out, "Wan'shin. Nobyreeboo, b'wayluffsgun'shin." This I took to mean "Write an introduction. Nobody reads books, but everyone loves a good introduction."

After the deadline was well past, I did, reluctantly, sit down to write this brief introduction. I resist writing. I resist it for the very good reason that it makes me pace and sigh and gaze despairingly at myself in the mirror. I find writing so painful that my girlfriend is amazed that I am a writer at all. A writer herself, she sings a little song at her computer as her hands fly over the keys: "La la la, look at me go, I am writing and also singing. Whee!" I love her very much, most of the time.

I haven't told you much about why I became a writer, or why I never became an expert on one particular topic, preferring to roam the aisles of the world like a binge eater at the Piggly-Wiggly. My belief is that you'll find the answers to those questions by reading the articles themselves. Is that so much to ask? No, I think, is the only possible response. At least, that is the only response I ever hear from readers: No no; no, thank you; no. Later, perhaps, but not just now.

Enjoy.

PART I

HOLLYWOOD

SITCOMS, SERIOUSLY

A *Brady Bunch* dream the other night. I was a Brady kid, in the sunken living room with Greg, Marcia, Peter, Jan, Bobby, and Cindy. We were fighting over the lead in the school play, or who could drive the car—something, anyway—when Mike Brady lolloped in. Our father wore bell-bottoms and a totally boss Qiana shirt and was grooving to a Walkman. Scattered laugh-track chuckles, perhaps at the anachronistic personal stereo. We all shouted, "Hey, Dad, we've got a problem!" Mike bopped on.

KIDS: Hey, Dad!
MIKE: What?
KIDS: You can't hear us. You've got a Walkman on!
MIKE: What?
KIDS: You can't hear us. You've got a Walkman on!
MIKE: I'm sorry, kids, I can't hear you—I've got a Walkman on!

The laugh track roared, and I awoke, lunging out of the sheets. It's spooky to have a Brady dream, particularly one with a laugh track. Spookier still to have my sleep troubled by lame sitcom dialogue. Weren't there some deep-seated childhood conflicts to work out?

Since then I've come to realize that the Brady dream *did* express a childhood conflict. This was clarified for me one recent evening when I sat on the beach with a dozen friends, enjoying the stars, the salty tang of the incoming tide, the moon glowing over the white carpet of water. Inspired, we took turns naming *Brady Bunch* episodes and recalled 107 before someone was stumped. They only made 116.

By my own estimate I have spent eleven thousand hours of my life, many of them the golden afternoons of youth, watching television sitcoms. They were often idiotic; I loved them anyway. Nowadays, as more or less a grown-up, I view sitcoms with a mixture of irony, nausea—many of them really do suck—and, still, deep affection. So, I'm conflicted.

Something new has happened to the generations born since *The Goldbergs,* the first sitcom, aired on CBS forty-four years ago. Those of us under forty-five grew up whelmed in sitcoms as minnows are whelmed in the sea, in thrall to a new mass art form, a transcontinental, transsocietal in-joke that reaches up to thirty million people every half hour. We are cradled in sitcoms, rocked in their warm lap, nursed from what Harlan Ellison calls "the glass teat."

"Who needed friends when we had chums like Dobie and Maynard, Margie and Mrs. Odettes, Walter Denton and Eddie Haskell?" writes Rick Mitz in *The Great TV Sitcom Book.* TV has come to understand its role as wet nurse: whereas in the early 1960s *The Beverly Hillbillies'*s Granny mistook a television for a newfangled washing machine, now the opening credits of *The Simpsons, Dream On,* and *The Jackie Thomas Show* present their characters hungrily eyeing the set.

The sitcom is television's defining form. Although only one of the ten top-rated shows in 1952 was a sitcom and three of ten in

1972 were sitcoms, seven of the top ten in 1992 were sitcoms. Sitcoms are on the networks during prime time, on local channels early in the morning and late at night, on Turner Broadcasting, Christian Broadcasting, the Family Channel, and Nick at Nite. If you have cable in New York City, you can (try to) watch 32½ hours of sitcoms a day. Sitcoms have become our most pervasive, powerful, and cherished form of media output. They flow into every corner of our lives.

And what have we learned from electronic Mom? Not much, say "adults," who denounce sitcoms for turning us into Chance the Gardener. As long ago as 1961, FCC chairman Newt Minnow declared sitcoms "formula comedies about totally unbelievable families"; more recently Steven Spielberg, of all people, called *Cheers, Roseanne,* and *The Cosby Show* part of "a wasteland of homogenized milk." And certainly when I ponder how contentedly I watched *Hogan's Heroes*'s Sergeant Schultz shake his strudel-fed face and protest for the thousandth time, "I know *nuth*-ing," the suspicion occurs that he wasn't kidding.

The dismissive adult view of sitcoms is loudest espoused by highbrow cultural guardians like Neil Postman and the late Allan Bloom, who want to build a fire wall around the popular art forms they claim will destroy us with their damnable intent to cause pleasure and laughter. The adult view says that sitcoms fail to meet traditional highbrow standards: great art should kidnap its auditors, knock them on the head and drag them through the cobbled streets, shake the snowy globe of the world and let the flakes fall where they may.

Sitcoms don't have this effect. But so what? Those of us who've swum in the cathode sea since birth experience sitcoms in a new way and expect them to serve a different purpose from that of *Madame Bovary* and Schubert's Eighth Symphony—we expect them to show us our place in the world, not disturb it.

Sitcoms, like pop songs, seep into memory through reruns, filtering home while we think we're paying attention to something else.

Reruns, which collapse time into the eternal present, are how we best appreciate television; a show's early episodes can't be experienced as classics because we don't yet really know and love the characters—early episodes gain density over the years. Watching for the third time an encore episode of *The Wonder Years,* with its nostalgic emphasis on old TV and old Herman's Hermits and James Taylor songs, is the ur–sitcom experience.

The average American watches more than twenty-eight hours of television a week, and according to a 1989 study, even the Luddite 8 percent who insist they never watch average ten hours a week; TV, as Camille Paglia notes, is "a hearth fire in the modern home. . . . It is simply on all the time"—seeping in. So while velvet clown paintings and steamy drugstore novels trip a few cortical synapses and vanish forever, endlessly repeated songs like "Brandy (You're a Fine Girl)" and the entire *Sanford and Son* oeuvre remain in memory Ziploc fresh. Seep, I should note, is the process by which we discover that we're mired in complex family relations, that we're in love, or that we're getting flabby and short of breath. Seep is how we learn jugular truths.

It's important to make a distinction here that most critics omit as they blitzkrieg across popular culture, using *Three's Company* as the propaganda equivalent of the Reichstag fire. There are actually two basic sitcom varieties: high-concept comedies, like *Three's Company* and *Welcome Back, Kotter,* which feature farcical characters, absurd mishaps, and double entendres; and character-driven comedies, like *Seinfeld,* which seek to illuminate emotional truths.

It's hard to defend *Three's Company* too strenuously, because it is pure formula (four lame misunderstandings, eight pratfalls, twelve gay jokes, thirty-four boob and boinking gags). But it and shows like it have a certain limited worth; the pure sitcom formula, honed by generations of writers from the *I Love Lucy* and *Honeymooners* models, is valuably predictable, particularly for children. Love outweighs queasiness when I think about a bad high-concept comedy like *The Brady Bunch* for the same reason that love outweighs queasiness when I think about my old toy bunny. The cocoon of *The Brady Bunch*'s repetitive plots (Jan has allergies; Jan feels unloved; Jan's dream guy falls for Marcia; Jan's so depressed that she gets a wig; Jan's jealous of Marcia; Jan's too vain to wear glasses; Jan's worried how she'll look when she's old; Jan wants her siblings dead; Jan fails at ballet, tap dancing, and baton twirling, then can't get the lead in the school play—*but she perseveres and triumphs through foreseeable plot twists and robotic parental guidance*) conjured the world as a safe place, as warm and fuzzy and remote-controllable.

We feel affection for bad childhood sitcoms because we needed that message then, needed a cathode pacifier. We are also fond of them because we use sitcoms as triangulation points to chart our growth from the child who watched with wonder to the adult who watches with doting irony. Wed to that childhood moment, and to our changing perspective on it, we don't particularly care to see Bobby Brady in a wheelchair in the 1990 adult-oriented sequel, *The Bradys*, and we scoff at bad sitcoms that come along later—for me, at age thirty, the *Blossom*s and *Mr. Belvedere*s—because to an adult they proclaim the world not so much harmless as pointless.

On the other hand, the classic character-driven comedies—*The Honeymooners, The Dick Van Dyke Show, All in the Family, The Mary Tyler Moore Show, Taxi, Cheers, Roseanne, The Simpsons*—admit that life is too much for us. These shows face death and despair, combat them with man's best existential weapon—sharp wit—and suggest that in a cruel and possibly meaningless world, a soft bower awaits. Thus *Cheers* weaves maladjusted barflies into a charmed circle; and even a lesser show like *The Golden Girls* assures us we'll still have friends when we're old and our spouses have died. "A great half hour is like having a wonderful dinner with friends," says *Roseanne* and *Home Improvement* creator Matt Williams. "You have an afterglow—you feel glad to be part of the human race."

For me, now, even hearing *The Mary Tyler Moore Show* theme song on Nick at Nite is fiercely exalting. It's partly because the shows are weekly time capsules (remember Betty Ford's appearance?) and because they conjure up those family Saturday nights, watching *MTM* when I was freshly bathed, in my flannel pj's, and angling not to be sent to bed. And because I had a monster crush on Mary.

But it's mostly because *MTM* was so well written, well acted, and funny that it subconsciously schooled me through seep. I knew those people better than I knew anyone outside my family, and I understood them better than I understood most people *in* my family. So I believed that my friends, too, would get married and give birth in my apartment, that coffee sobers a drunk, that bald people are especially witty, and that women look sexy in flared slacks. Sadly, this information turned out to be false.

But *MTM* also taught me that loneliness, separation, divorce, and death can be borne and that life is a hard journey eased by love. If these sound like fairy-tale truths, they should: great character-driven sitcoms have become our fairy tales (whereas high-concept comedies and bad character-driven sitcoms—those that coerce us with sermons and life lessons—are our fables. I'll expand on this distinction later).

Just as a child insists on hearing fairy tales read the same way every night, so we delight in reruns. Like fairy-tale formulas and stock characters—the three wishes, the wicked stepmother—character-driven sitcom formulas and stock characters are deeply satisfying. A fairy tale, Bruno Bettelheim notes in *The Uses of Enchantment,* "simplifies all situations. Its figures are clearly drawn" and polarized: "One brother is stupid, the other is clever. One sister is virtuous and industrious, the others are vile and lazy. One is beautiful, the others are ugly."

And fairy tales, like great sitcoms, show us our place in life, in the family we'll grow into: they "provide the modern child with images of heroes who have to go out into the world all by themselves

and who, although originally ignorant of the ultimate things, find secure places in the world by following the right way with deep inner
confidence."

That perfectly describes Mary Richards, who set out in her car
toward Minneapolis in 1970 alone and uncertain and ended seven
years later clustered in a warm rugby scrum with her TV family—
Murray, Ted, Sue Ann, Georgette, Mr. Grant. In the final episode
Mary made explicit the message encoded in all great sitcoms: "I
thought about something last night. What is a family? And I think I
know. A family is people who make you feel less alone and really
loved. Thank you for being my family."

In the highbrow view, anyone who enjoys watching this scene
has debased standards and perhaps even debased morals. Viewing
"is a private act, an act that we perform by ourselves and with ourselves," Michael Arlen has written. "What it resembles most, I
think, is masturbation." Actually, *writing* about sitcoms most resembles masturbation. *Watching* them most resembles adoption.

We watch, in other words, to join a surrogate family. Yet our link
to these substitute families is uneasy, because we supply so much of
the love. "That song in *Cheers*—'Sometimes you want to go / Where
everybody knows your name'—is very comforting, but it's completely untrue," notes Andy Borowitz, co-creator of *The Fresh Prince
of Bel Air.* "We know *their* names, we know Sam and Woody and
Norm, but no one on the show knows *your* name. In fact, you're really all alone out there."

———

Probably without having thought about it much, we all know what
a sitcom is: a bunch of people who love one another, either a family or a familylike gang of co-workers and friends, and twenty-two
minutes of funny things that happen to them at work and at home.
Time has brought some changes: *All in the Family* introduced social issues and bedroom topics; and with *The Simpsons* and *Married . . . with Children,* Fox established a new pop-psych paradigm:

the dysfunctional family (loser dad teasing and being teased by his budding-loser children). Sitcoms have also increasingly incorporated purely dramatic moments, as on a recent *Wonder Years* about a Vietnam veteran's difficult readjustment at home—yet these plots are always balanced by a jokey subplot or leavened with cheer at the end.

Through all these thematic changes, the basic sitcom structure has remained remarkably constant. Its narrative arc is usually divided into two "acts" comprising three or four scenes each. A recent *Cheers* illustrates the armature:

> *Problem:* Cliff's old girlfriend, Maggie, is back in town.
>
> *Cliff-hanger near the act break:* She's pregnant, calls Cliff "Daddy."
>
> *Crisis moment early in the second act:* After taking "you stud" congratulations all around, Cliff confides to Sam that he never had sex with Maggie.
>
> *Increased jeopardy:* Maggie admits the child is really her ex-boyfriend Jerry's; Cliff says he'll marry her anyway.
>
> *Resolution:* Maggie calls Jerry to tell him, and he says he wants her back after all; Cliff's off the hook.
>
> *Denouement:* Turns out Maggie and Cliff did have sex once, only he was drunk and forgot. "You were great!" she assures him.

Classic sitcom structure "turns" the story every seven pages and has three jokes per page, or a joke at least every twenty-eight seconds. Characters *can* evolve over the years (Edith Bunker learns to stand up for herself; *The Bob Newhart Show*'s Howard Borden becomes more than just an absentminded dunderhead—he becomes a lonely and appealing absentminded dunderhead), but to maintain the show's core dynamic, most episodes, like the *Cheers* example above, must end where they started. If Roseanne inherits a million dollars, she must lose it; if Jethro meets a Bel Air babe, nineteen minutes later she's revealed as a gold-digger, maniac, or robot hermaphrodite.

"In real life, Alex Keaton is now doing pro bono work for women's rights groups," says *Family Ties* creator Gary David Goldberg, "but the audience would never have let us do that. They wanted purity, not real-life change. Michael [J. Fox] said to me, 'What do I care that Mallory talks on the phone? How can I still care?' And he was right—we did 180 *Family Ties* and the last 100 we were fighting the format."

But, as with the sonnet, a lot can be packed into a confining structure. Sitcoms have developed their own emotional shorthand: for instance, that we never see Buddy's wife, Pickles, on *The Dick Van Dyke Show;* Phyllis's husband, Lars, on *The Mary Tyler Moore Show;* or Norm's wife, Vera, on *Cheers* speaks volumes about those marriages. And most sitcoms ring changes on about ten plots. This has been decried as unimaginative; in fact, it's exemplary structural purity. Sitcom plots, after all, are really just vehicles allowing the characters to be vengeful, vexed, perplexed, conniving, or goofy—whatever they do best.

The characters who inhabit these story lines—the ensemble of lovable eccentrics—are as typical as Punch and Judy or commedia dell'arte figures. Among many other types there's the blond bimbo (Chrissy Snow, Elly May Clampett, Kelly Bundy); the crusty-but-lovable boss (Lou Grant, Mr. Mooney, Louie De Palma); the kooky-but-cuddly foreigner/alien (Latka, ALF, Mork); and the all-powerful servant (Benson, Mr. French, Ann B. Davis as Alice).

"The stupid guy, the wiseass, the sex maniac, the fat guy, the saucy wench, the bitch, the fop, and the distaff fop—that describes the cast of *Cheers,*" says Susan Borowitz, co-creator of *Fresh Prince.* "That one-line *TV Guide* blurbiness is necessary for people to recognize the show, to clearly understand what's going on." This singleness of intent is underscored by signature expostulations: *"Ayyy!"*; *"Dyn-o-mite!"*; "To the moon, Alice!"; "Stifle yourself!"; "Kiss my grits!"; "Oh, *Ro-o-ob!"*; and "Don't have a cow, man!"

The characters and their desires must be blueprint clear; we never have to infer motivations as we do with novels and films—in twenty-two minutes there's no time for guesswork. "In every sitcom

I've worked on, if we're having trouble clarifying characters' attitudes or sharpening opposing points of view—telling the audience what's at stake—we apply the Ralph Kramden test," says Matt Williams, the *Roseanne* and *Home Improvement* creator. "We go back through the scene to figure out where Ralph would say, 'Alice, you take that job and you're out of my life!' or, 'Alice, if your mother comes through that door and calls me fat one more time, I'm throwing her out the window!' *Knock, knock.* 'Hi, Mom.' "

Good character-driven sitcoms have at least one character, like Ralph, with an extreme point of view. Thus Lucy, who desperately wants to break into show business; Archie, who fears "coons," "spics," and "hebes"; and Hawkeye, a zealous pacifist surrounded by war. Bad shows have characters with quirks and traits; good shows have characters with a worldview.

"Great sitcoms are character-driven," says former Warner Brothers comedy executive Scott Kaufer, echoing many in Hollywood. "A mistake even experienced writer-producers make is to pitch occupations and locales—'How'd you like a comedy set in a firehouse?' You want people to pitch Archie Bunker and Mike Stivic."

What we treasure about a show is not jokes and plot points, but characters and relationships—people we'd like to be like, friendships we'd like to be in. I was always skeptical about *Bewitched* because when Dick Sargent replaced Dick York as Darrin, the characters pretended nothing had happened, while I felt as one might toward a new stepfather. (Only years later did I realize Samantha was much too smart and creative for *either* dimwit Darrin.)

People don't care about people who don't care, so even the most abrasive characters must hide a heart of gold. We needn't love them—we don't love George Jefferson or *Coach*'s Hayden Fox— but we must empathize. Miles Drentell of *thirtysomething,* perhaps television's most interesting character, couldn't have survived on a half-hour comedy: erratic and unfathomable, he would have made a sitcom seem . . . unsafe.

"A series is like a dinner guest," says Gary David Goldberg. "If you're scintillating but you open a wound, you won't get invited back. You *must* be nonthreatening. Early on, the audience didn't understand how Alex felt about Mallory when he teased her, and they weren't laughing. So we did a show in which Alex, instead of going to his Princeton interview, comforts her when she's been dumped by her boyfriend. We had to say, 'Hey, he really does love her.' "

The characters' love—or anger or ambition, their strong drives— must be expressed within a family or surrogate family, socialized lest it undermine the core group. (Even in Fox's dysfunctional-family sitcoms, the family goes everywhere together and its members always support one another in the end.) In the early, unsteady going of *Happy Days,* Arthur Fonzarelli was the audience favorite, but he was a loner, a mere sexy supporting hood with no real connection to Richie's family. "I knew that if I could get him [living over the Cunninghams'] garage," *Happy Days* creator Garry Marshall has said, "I could get him into the kitchen; he could become a member of the family." The Fonz moved in; the show went to number one.

This sort of development enacts the truth that the French express as *tout comprendre, c'est tout excuser*—if you really get to know a character, if you really understand someone like Louie De Palma, you will excuse him completely, as his fellow characters do. In good sitcoms the malcontent, brat, loner, lout, clodpoll, or witch creates disorder, then gets slowly drawn back, redomesticated, through the love of others and the private dawning of wisdom. Lucy, Ralph, Sam Malone, and Bart Simpson—the child characters, the raging ids— are shown the error of their disruptive ways, and we can identify with both the high jinks and the penitence.

The danger of this dynamic was remarked upon by Nabokov, who warned that easy psychological identification with fictional characters gives way to sentimentality and dulls your sense of the work as a whole. The mistake we sometimes make while watching a sitcom is to think that *because* we're watching a sitcom (which we know is meant to be nonthreatening), characters who feel emotionally minatory must really be hiding a heart of gold, so it's okay to identify with them. Sometimes they're not and it's not.

Bad sitcoms make their malcontents conform not through love, but through sermon and coercion; anyone with a variant idea is mercilessly mocked. Critic Mark Crispin Miller rightly pillories the jeering dynamic on *The Cosby Show,* citing an episode in which Cliff Huxtable ridicules some verses Denise has written for the school choir ("I walk alone . . . I walk alone"); Denise does a rewrite ("My mother and father are my best friends. . . . Their love is real, their love is real") and receives a big kiss. Cliff "strikes his children as a peach," Miller writes, "until they realize, years later and after lots of psychotherapy, what a subtle thug he really was."

"What Bill said was often mean and unacceptable on the page," says Matt Williams, who wrote for *Cosby.* "He would verbally abuse his kids, lie to them, hide things from them—but the audience knew he loved them." Did he really, or were we just hoping?

Do we so love the very idea of the sitcom family that we'll watch terrible shows *because* we know the characters right off the bat, *because* we've seen them a dozen times before on other shows? "There are a lot of cynical people [in Hollywood] manufacturing just the right dose of warmth," says Conan O'Brien, a writer for *The Simpsons.* "Watching it starts to make you feel like a lab ape. The networks want a mother and father who are good-looking and in their late thirties to appeal to baby boomers. They have some money because people like seeing nice possessions but not too much money because then people can't identify. Their cute teenage daughter is just starting to date, which appeals to teenage girls and guys. There's a bratty kid like Bart—kids love kids who can get away with stuff—and, look, there's a little black kid who hangs around, because old people and little black kids love little black kids. And they have a big, furry dog."

In the last decade alone that recipe reasonably describes *Who's the Boss, Growing Pains, Diff'rent Strokes, Gimme a Break!, Family Ties, Webster,* and *The Cosby Show.* It's fair to wonder who's running whose maze to get a food pellet.

Many such sitcoms end episodes with "the warm moment"—"the hug." Everyone embraces and we learn a lesson: Prejudice is bad;

sharing is good; slow and steady wins the race. Thus, in the Big Lie plot, the wiseacre invariably learns the biblical proverb that a stone will come back upon he who starts it rolling. This, like most such epiphanies, illuminates one of the core sitcom truths: "Don't rock the boat." The other core sitcom truth is "Just be yourself," which would seem to contradict "Don't rock the boat," except that you should be yourself only insofar as it doesn't rock the boat.

"Just be yourself" is also something of a sly disclaimer, because the networks are skittishly aware that millions tune in to *learn* who they are and how they should behave. "A lot of latchkey kids are watching alone," says Gary David Goldberg, "and, frighteningly, you are many people's closest friend. So you avoid certain ambiguities. I will not make a casual drug joke. I will not show teenagers drinking. I will show kids doing the chores and Dad cooking dinner without anyone remarking on it. Or when you start a scene, someone's reading. Or when someone goes out, you have someone say, 'Put your seat belt on.' "

"The sitcom has taken the place of church, of religious training," says Susan Borowitz. "If an episode is just a romp or a farce, the audience isn't as satisfied. Sitcoms work better if they're little sermons or parables." (In his novel *Generation X,* Douglas Coupland defines *tele-parablizing* as "morals used in everyday life that derive from TV sitcom plots: *That's just like the episode where Jan lost her glasses!*") In many families, watching sitcoms together is an almost sacred obligation: when the set goes on, the couch becomes a pew.

But sermons—the *deus ex telemachina* descent of poetic justice— mark a craven sitcom, a point made deftly on a *Simpsons* episode. In "Blood Feud," Bart donates lifesaving blood to Homer's boss, Mr. Burns, who presents the family with an ugly stone head.

MARGE: The moral of this story is, A good deed is its own reward.
BART: We got a reward; the head is cool.
MARGE: Well, then, I guess the moral is, No good deed goes unrewarded.

HOMER: Wait a minute, if I hadn't written that nasty letter, we wouldn't have gotten anything.

MARGE: Well, then, I guess the moral is, The squeaky wheel gets the grease.

LISA: Perhaps there is no moral to this story.

HOMER: Exactly. It's just a bunch of stuff that happened.

"A *lot* of people loved Homer's line," says *Simpsons* executive producer Mike Reiss. "They all got the joke."

The sermon gap between bad and good sitcoms is precisely the distinction between fables and fairy tales. "The question for the child is not 'Do I want to be good?' but 'Whom do I want to be like?' " Bruno Bettelheim writes. Fairy tales inspire the latter question, whereas "fables demand and threaten—they are moralistic—or they just entertain. The fable always explicitly states a moral truth; there is no hidden meaning, nothing is left to our imagination."

Fables—whether via Aesop or CBS—are hack work, no matter how sitcom producers gussy them up with highbrow claims. "There's a lot of underlying philosophy to the characters on *Gilligan's Island,*" its creator, Sherwood Schwartz, has said. "They're really a metaphor for the nations of the world, and their purpose was to show how nations have to get along together or cease to exist." So I guess Mr. Howell, overdressed and fussy, would be France; Gilligan, underfed and disaster-prone, would be Bangladesh. . . .

Compare *Gilligan's Island* with the famous "Chuckles Bites the Dust" episode of *The Mary Tyler Moore Show.* While leading a parade, WJM's kiddie-show host, Chuckles the Clown, is killed by a rogue elephant that tries to shell him out of his Peter Peanut costume. First Murray, then Lou, then Sue Ann relieve their astonished grief with wisecracks.

LOU: This could have happened to any of us, Ted.

MURRAY: Somewhere out there, there's an elephant with your name on it.

Mary is shocked and priggish: at the funeral she says, "A man has died. We came here to show respect—not to laugh." Many a sitcom would stop with that lesson. But when Reverend Burns gives his eulogy and mentions Billy Banana, Mary has to stifle a snicker. When he reminds the congregants how Chuckles's character Mr. Fee-Fi-Fo "would always pick himself up, dust himself off, and say: 'I hurt my foo-foo,' " she giggles. Everyone glares, and she pretends she's coughing. Then Reverend Burns mentions Chuckles's ditty, "A little song, a little dance, a little seltzer down your pants," and Mary can't restrain a loud cackle. The reverend asks her to stand and "laugh out loud. Don't you see, nothing could have made Chuckles happier? He lived to make people laugh. Tears were offensive to him, deeply offensive. He hated to see people cry. So go ahead, my dear—laugh for Chuckles." Mary bursts out crying.

First of all, "Chuckles" was hilarious. When Ted says, "If it were my funeral, this place would be packed," we laugh. Cut to Murray, and we chuckle, anticipating. "That's right, Ted," he says, "it's just a matter of giving the public what they want." Another laugh. This familiar byplay between antagonists, this three-laugh transaction, is like the chorus of a great popular song to which we can all sing along.

"Chuckles" also went against type. By this, her sixth season, we'd spent more than sixty hours with Mary and had come to understand her in a way possible only on a long-running sitcom, and we knew she'd be mortified to laugh at a funeral. "Chuckles" also risked making Mary unlikable when she primly reproved her friends. And the episode flaunts—indeed, comments on—*MTM*'s empathy-encouraging verisimilitude: its characters laugh when other characters say funny things, as they would in life, instead of saying "What?" or ignoring the line, as they would on *Full House*.

Furthermore, the lines aren't necessarily written to be funny on the page. "One of the definitions of a great sitcom is that you can't repeat the jokes out of context to a friend," says *MTM* writer Treva Silverman. "You have to explain, 'Murray is coming into the newsroom and Ted is reading his script and Mary has been feeling sad and she's wearing a red dress with green buttons.' " In great sitcoms, lines are funny *only* because a specific character is saying them.

Contrast that with these two- and three-beat gags:

> WOMAN: Is there something you don't like about my cooking?
> MAN: Yeah—eating it.

And

> MAN: You made sponge cake the other night and used a real sponge.
> WOMAN: But you ate all of it.
> MAN: Yeah—but it was the best thing you ever cooked.

The jokes come from *The Jeffersons* and *Good Times;* they could come from anywhere.

Finally, "Chuckles" offers no lesson, only the same implicitly socializing example found in fairy tales (e.g., we make up our own minds what it means that Little Red Riding Hood dallies on the way to her grandmother's house, enjoys a sexy interlude with the wolf, gets eaten up, and is rescued by the fatherly hunter). We are subtly encouraged to consider how these people we love deal with life's absurd affronts. We are permitted to discover, if we care to, that Mary's glossy perfection hides a deep fear of death. But because it's Chuckles who died, not, say, Rhoda (who just got canceled), we aren't threatened. Great sitcoms address our deepest dilemmas with immense tact.

—

Sitcom writers are fond of depressing themselves by reciting a catechism that goes something like this: " 'Chuckles'-is-great-it's-the-best-we-can-do-but-is-it-great-art?-I-think-not." They see themselves being well paid to crank out a commercial product that they believe—or profess to believe—is beneath their true talents. They bemoan the straitjacket buckles of their form—the need to keep things fundamentally light; the need to goose the studio audience with easy jokes; the up to twenty ads per half hour that deflate the gathering joy with pitches for marshmallows and incontinence underpants; the timid frettings of the networks; the actors' interference (according to writers' legend, *My Favorite Martian* star Roy Walston once vetoed his lines, explaining, "A Martian would never say that"); the Sisyphean demand for new episodes, many of which are written in a week and completely rewritten in three days; and the Tony Danza syndrome—likability, likability, likability.

"I used to have such grand designs," says Matt Williams. "I thought every half hour could be a one-act play revealing a deep truth about the human condition. The truth is, it's twenty-two minutes, you're constantly interrupted by commercials, the phone's going to ring, and the dog's going to pee on the carpet. The *most* you can do is entertain and scrape the surface, be *artful*. If you want to delve deep into the human condition, go write a novel, or a film script no one will make."

Williams is judging sitcoms by the old standards of great art. But his capitulation is too profound. Even if, for the sake of argument, we allow traditional standards to frame the debate, it seems clear that great sitcoms both instruct and entertain: Aristotle's two criteria for art. What they don't do is threaten our deepest beliefs; they confirm rather than confront. If the world were like sitcoms, sitcoms wouldn't be necessary. They exist as a response to pain, a palliative to ease and smooth our path. Our laughter is how we speak back to TV, how we thank it for helping us. Even if we sometimes feel abandoned by our TV families, our laughter reconnects us with the community, with the millions of people who think that Rob Petrie tripping over a hassock or Archie Bunker being kissed on the cheek by Sammy Davis Jr. is funny.

Sitcoms aren't great art because great art is, in some way, more than we can bear—it is awesome or terrible, it daunts and dares, it asks us to be more than we are. Great art is admirable, and it can be loved, but it can never be fully lovable. Good art, because it is human and frail, is lovable. Great character-driven sitcoms should he judged not by the standards of great art, but by the standards of fairy tales. These, our lovable modern fairy tales, are good art, because they provide life examples and seek to assuage our needs and fears. They ask us not to be more than we are, but simply to be ourselves.

The strength of our collective hunger to be ourselves yet feel approved of by others is astonishing and a little alarming. But good art that reaches thirty million people and makes them feel connected may have more to offer us now than great art that reaches three thousand people and makes them feel more or less alone. In our time the standards for art have changed, expanded. The future belongs to Bart Simpson.

(1993)

THE SHORT, HAPPY LIFE
OF RIVER PHOENIX

Heart Phoenix sat on the edge of the stage and beckoned everyone near. The 150 people in Paramount Studios' screening room gathered around like disciples. A short, tan woman with graying hair, Heart has a way of soothing fears. The mourners needed her now; her son River's memorial service had been wrenching. During their tributes, Christine Lahti, River's mother in *Running on Empty,* and Iris Burton, River's agent and "second mother," had broken down.

They and others had recalled Phoenix's mercurial abandon, his peculiar combination of heart-stopping innocence and ageless wisdom, his "vegan," or ultravegetarian, beliefs, and, always, the eggshell beauty of his acting. Seeking consolation, they had groped to trace in Phoenix's life a narrative arc, a theme, even a moral.

But River Phoenix had a stubborn case of the vagabond disease that afflicts celebrities: he affected others deeply yet narrowly before moving on. Iris Burton was not the only one present who had privately wondered, in the three weeks since Phoenix's death, whether she had really known him, whether he hadn't been acting a part around her.

Heart spoke, holding Rob Reiner's hand for support. Her hopes for her son had always been on a wholly different plane from most stage mothers'. "We believed we could use the mass media to help change the world," as Heart puts it now, "and that River would be our missionary." She tried to explain that calling to the mourners, saying that she'd sensed from the beginning, as her labor extended to three and a half days, that River didn't want to be in the world. She told how she had awoken two days after his death, understanding for the first time why dawn is called "mourning," and suddenly had a vision of how God had tried to convince River to be born one more time. River told God, "I'd rather stay up here with you." So they bargained, Heart said, smiling. God was persuasive, and River offered to go for five years, and then ten, and finally agreed to visit earth, but only for twenty-three years.

A beatific silence filled the room, vibrating like a sustained bass note. "I was shocked by how many strong, grown-up people River had gotten to in such a deep, emotional way," says director Alan Moyle. "We were all united," says actor and publicist Mickey Cottrell. "The room seemed almost hallucinatorily beautiful."

Heart then invited others to speak. After a few further testimonials, director John Boorman suddenly blurted out from the corner of the stage: "Is there anybody here who can tell us why River took all those drugs?"

The question quivered in the air. River's young sisters Liberty and Summer ran out of the room, and Heart looked astonished.

And then Samantha Mathis, Phoenix's girlfriend and the costar of his last completed movie, *The Thing Called Love,* spoke from the front row for the first time. "River was a sensitive," she said with great tenderness, using the word as a noun. "He had so much compassion for everyone and everything that he had a weight on his heart." She paused and added that Phoenix "was obsessive. When he wanted to eat artichokes he would eat ten at a time. He did everything to that degree."

Mathis's was a brave statement, as she had been heartsick with Phoenix for breaking his vows to stay drug-free. But her gloss on

Phoenix's life—that he was a Byronic hero, felled by outsize pain and hunger—joined a long line of unifying theories. For instance, that "this innocent little bird got his wings clipped in the most evil city in the world" (Iris Burton); that he was a moody, hard-partying hypocrite who got what he deserved (the *National Enquirer* and other tabloids); that an artist had taken the risks of Method acting too far (Peter Bogdanovich).

Each theory is alluring because it provides *an* answer to the riddle of human motivation, but finally unsatisfying because it seems not quite *the* answer. "John Boorman's question was a good one," Heart Phoenix says now. "It's what everyone was thinking. 'Why, when you're living this dream, when you can have any car, any house, any girl, you're so famous—why? Why?' The only understanding I can come to is that River knew the earth was dying and that he was ready to give his passing as a sign."

But River Phoenix's story is not just a passion play; it is also a drama of fierce internal conflict. It was Phoenix's loneliness and anguish, after all, that backlit the sadness in the characters he played. And it was that bewitching confusion that later led him to drugs.

"He's already being made into a martyr," says Phoenix's first and longtime love, actress Martha Plimpton. "He's become a metaphor for a fallen angel, a messiah. He wasn't. He was just a boy, a very good-hearted boy who was very fucked-up and had no idea how to implement his good intentions. I don't want to be comforted by his death. I think it's right that I'm angry about it, angry at the people who helped him stay sick, and angry at River."

—

"The main thing in film acting is something going on in the face," said Gus Van Sant, "and with the really good ones, it's pain." Van Sant was in the basement of his sprawling Tudor house in Portland, Oregon, staring at his darkroom wall. On it hung five photos of River Phoenix in *My Own Private Idaho*, Van Sant's film about Mike Waters (Phoenix) and Scott Favor (Keanu Reeves), two street hustlers who travel to Idaho and Italy looking for Mike's mother.

We've both just heard the coroner's report on Phoenix's bloodstream: cocaine and morphine (metabolized heroin), each in toxic doses, as well as traces of marijuana and Valium. "You don't read it as pain"—Van Sant drew on a Camel and moved closer, scrutinizing River's half-averted face—"but when you really look, it's pain."

Phoenix was never photographed grinning and very rarely smiling: he mistrusted cameras. And yet it was the camera that fixed Phoenix's image as a disillusioned innocent. Milton Nascimento, the Brazilian singer, once flipped on the TV in his New York hotel room and was transfixed by the last half of *The Mosquito Coast,* in which Phoenix weeps over his maniacal dying father. Nascimento wrote the ballad "River Phoenix (Letter to a Young Actor)" to celebrate that moment.

During *Idaho*'s filming in the fall of 1990, nine cast and crew members, including Phoenix and Keanu Reeves, slept on scattered futons in Van Sant's house. It was a college dorm, a tribe, a family. Van Sant showed me his garage, where a bona fide garage band of Phoenix and Reeves and other *Idaho* actors, as well as Flea, the Red Hot Chili Peppers' bass player, often jammed late at night.

They played the sweet, off-kilter lyrics Phoenix had written for himself and for his band, Aleka's Attic—"Run to the rescue with love / and peace will follow" or "Hey, lo, where did your halo go?" They played the Beatles and Led Zeppelin, balancing ashtrays on Van Sant's black BMW and drinking wine, smoking marijuana. Sometimes they ended up in tears with Phoenix as he talked about the vanishing rain forests.

Back up the passageway was a gray-carpeted landing where Phoenix played guitar after everyone else had turned in. He liked the alcove's particular echo and played there ecstatically, until his fingertips bled. Music was his true love, what he intended for himself after he'd quit acting.

Phoenix's musical knowledge was encyclopedic, but he had never seen a James Dean film, much less one with Orson Welles. When director Peter Bogdanovich called him about *The Thing Called Love,* he discovered that Phoenix hadn't heard of him or his movies. Says Van

Sant: "River was interested in movies only as they applied to his own character drawing."

Of his roles, the character Phoenix drew in *Idaho* resembled him most: "kind of isolated, a nerd, a misfit," as Phoenix's friend Bobby Bukowski puts it. Mike Waters, as written by Van Sant, is a narcoleptic street hustler who sleeps with men to get by. Phoenix completely reimagined a campfire scene with Keanu Reeves so that it becomes the movie's fulcrum: Mike haltingly admits his feelings for Scott and says, "I really want to kiss you, man." "The character I wrote was blasé and noncommittal," Van Sant says. "River made him gay and committal; he redeemed him with emotions."

Phoenix, who loved to catalyze and connect, found the low-affect Van Sant a challenge. "River was always doing things like saying, 'I just love you,' and lunging to hug me," says Van Sant. "I'd freeze, maybe because my father used to grab my knee in a certain way. River didn't like that, so he'd hug me again, and I'd freeze again, and he'd yell at me."

Hugging Phoenix could be complex. "When he was being aloof I'd impulsively try to trap him in an emotional gesture by hugging him, and he'd flip out of my arms," says Alan Moyle, the script doctor for *The Thing Called Love.* "Ten minutes later he'd sneak up and hug me from behind. He wanted it to be *his* spontaneity, and more creative— he'd sidewind you, but you would consider yourself hugged."

—

After talking with Van Sant, I went with Mike Parker to Portland's Vaseline Alley outside the city, a seedy gay nightclub where boys as young as twelve troll for forty-dollar dates from cruising johns. Parker, twenty-three, a friend of Van Sant's who is a former runaway, was Phoenix's main source for the character of Mike Waters: the two of them often came down here at night to watch pickups.

"River would do what I had told him was a date grabber," Parker said diffidently, "looking as young and innocent as possible, giving bursts of uncontrollable laughter, doing this—" He scuffed his feet boyishly. "All the marketing tricks."

Parker's quick, shy eye movements, his graceful hand gestures emerging from head-down repose, were *exactly* Phoenix's in *Idaho*. Parker said he felt Phoenix "extracting" those moves, "but River was really interested in the brotherhood of the kids out here, how we were looking for acceptance and some man to be close to, looking for family."

Phoenix was also curious about what Parker called "the glamour of men wanting to touch our bodies." While filming his previous movie, *Dogfight*, Phoenix had received oral sex from another male actor, saying he "needed to do it because he was going to play a gay hustler." He had other brief involvements with men over the years, and it was no big deal to friends who knew. Phoenix simply didn't censor his affections. "If he loved somebody, male or female," says one of Phoenix's longtime girlfriends, Suzanne Solgot, "he felt he should check it out."

"River dropped clues about his sexuality, but I never really followed them up," says Van Sant, who is gay. Phoenix asked ceaseless questions about Van Sant's relationship with his boyfriend: "What, exactly, do you do in bed? Which side do you sleep on? Do you ever tell him to shut up? If you're angry at him, do you still buy him an expensive birthday present?" Van Sant says, "I would laugh because these questions were so personal, and he'd say, 'What? What?' "

In late 1992, a gay filmmaker (not Van Sant) staying at the Château Marmont in Los Angeles heard a knock at midnight and discovered Phoenix outside, drunk and wanting to talk about his struggles with bisexuality. The filmmaker reassured him that it would all work out. Phoenix's friends say that this moment may have been acted, dramatized—he seemed at times to try on complicated emotions, applying the Method to his life. Phoenix realized that these virtual-reality scenes left a confusing trail and confessed in an interview that by his having "lied and changed stories and contradicted myself . . . you could read five different articles and say, 'This guy is schizophrenic.' "

A self-described chameleon, Phoenix almost recklessly "invited the demons of the role into himself," as Bobby Bukowski puts it.

Bukowski was the cinematographer on *Dogfight,* in which Phoenix played a marine. "After *Dogfight* I remember thinking he was being a real jarhead asshole—it took a month for him to become sweet again," Bukowski says. "And the street urchin character in *Idaho* stayed with him and played into the whole drug thing."

Mike Waters's outlaw glamour left its residue. *Idaho* marked the real beginning of the struggle in Phoenix's life between his "drug friends" and his "goon," or sober, friends; between his urge to party and his urge to withdraw; between his urge to help the addicted and his urge to help himself.

The struggle seemed almost to play out on his face. "His eyes made him the focus of energy in every scene, the centrifugal force so strong you didn't even try to duel him for control," says Dermot Mulroney, who later costarred with Phoenix in *Silent Tongue* and *The Thing Called Love.* "The off-center eye [Phoenix's lazy right eye] read as madness, and the other read pure sanity. In a close-up, from one side he was the guy next door, and from the other he was absolutely insane."

Phoenix had long been intrigued by the drug culture in Jacksonville Beach, near his home in Micanopy, Florida. On New Year's Day 1990, he watched a rough cut of Van Sant's previous movie, *Drugstore Cowboy,* and was fascinated by the mechanics of "spiking," or shooting up. He tried pharmaceutical morphine and heroin soon after, and that fall in Portland smoked heroin several times.

"River started with heroin out of malaise, and because it's a delicious drug, but then the reason changed," says Phoenix's friend Matt Ebert, a former addict and hustler who advised him on his *Idaho* role. "Heroin makes you reflective, you look inside—and then you face the consequences of looking into the chasm."

———

"Once when we were fifteen, River and I went out for a fancy dinner in Manhattan," says Martha Plimpton, "and I ordered soft-shell crabs. He left the restaurant and walked around on Park Avenue, crying. I went out and he said, 'I love you so much, why? . . .' He had such pain that I was eating an animal, that he hadn't impressed on me what was right." Her voice slows, becomes ragged. "I loved him for that, for his dramatic desire that we share every belief, that I be with him all the way."

Phoenix's friends often ended up being vegan like him. "He'd say about meat, 'That's not good for you, man, that'll kill you,' " says Peter Bogdanovich. "And he'd be smoking a cigarette, and I'd look at it and he'd say, 'I know, man, I know.' " Phoenix scorched through people's barriers very fast: he had a gift for making everyone feel like his closest friend. He was a celebrant, "the kind of guy," says his friend Wade Evans, "that if you walked outside and it was snowing, you knew that the first thing on his mind was making a snowball."

He was both reflectively and spontaneously generous, serving himself last at dinners; asking that his *Silent Tongue* costar, Sheila Tousey, be given his trailer because she spent so much more time in makeup; jumping to his feet when Kevin Kline beat him for best supporting actor at the 1989 Academy Awards. "I had to stop River from running to hug Kevin," his mother says. "It never crossed his mind that *he* hadn't won."

His public responses were often that unexpected. "He told me he didn't have a sense of humor until he was nine," says Gus Van Sant, "and that he never really got its logic, the surprise of the unexpected. You know: An elephant and a hippo go into a bar, something is introduced, punch line. And he'd be like, 'Yeah, so what happened then?' "

Phoenix was the champ of hanging out. Many of his friends were much older, and he would spend days or even weeks with them, writing poetry, drinking wine, making videos, wrestling, playing Frisbee (with considerably more enthusiasm than skill), cooking veggies (ditto), scarfing Japanese and Indian food. He couldn't sit still to be bored. "If the news was on when he came over to my house, he'd make a face at the TV and then leave," says Josh Greenbaum, the drummer in Aleka's Attic. Phoenix was always on the phone, making funny little jig movements with his hands and face, singing "Hey, Jude" when he was feeling heady. Jude was his middle name; the Beatles song had arrived in the world, like River, in 1970. When he was uncomfortable, Phoenix's feverish energy could seem like arrogance. He'd write a song, decide "it's brilliant, brilliant," and refuse to change a word. "He was always pushing how far he could go," says Van Sant, in a comment echoed by others. "He'd go, 'Can I say I feel like jerking off? Why can't I say that? Why? Why can't I say that?' If you said, 'Not so loud!' he'd think that was a funny reaction, like you were paranoid. He'd get into shouting matches with people, where they were both screaming 'You fucking moron!' but he'd end up liking them. He liked people who didn't let him get away with things."

—

Phoenix's skepticism of social conventions came from a childhood whose outline has become a singular fable of innocence. He was born in a log cabin in Madras, Oregon, to John and Arlyn (who later renamed herself Heart), itinerant fruit pickers who named him after the river of life in Hermann Hesse's novel *Siddhartha*. The family joined the Children of God sect, then moved to Venezuela as missionaries in 1975. River and his younger sister, Rain, sang spirituals on the street to raise money, while the family slept in a rat-infested hut on the beach.

They left the church and took a freighter back to Florida in 1977. Inspired by Joaquin, age three, who'd seen men kill fish against the hull during the voyage home, River and Rain, ages seven and five, convinced the rest of the family to adopt the vegan, Garden of Eden ideal of not using animals, even down to not eating milk or honey. In 1980 the family drove their Volkswagen bus to Los Angeles, depending on River in particular, but also Rain and Joaquin, known as Leaf, to make it big in entertainment.

The children sang on street corners and amazed casting directors, greeting them with kisses and an airy "Hi, we love you." They had no tarnish of greed or ambition; they shimmered in the sun. When Phoenix first saw a western upon returning from Venezuela, he was convinced that "companies paid people's families money to kill them. I just believed it."

At age eleven, Phoenix was on the TV show *Seven Brides for Seven Brothers;* at sixteen, he was acclaimed as both an actor and a teen hunk for his role in *Stand by Me.* In 1987 the Phoenixes returned to Gainesville, and River bought the family a spread in nearby Micanopy in 1989, as well as a ranch in Costa Rica.

In many respects Phoenix's was a magical childhood—no television, no formal schooling after fifth grade, and unstinting encouragement to care for others and to share his feelings. Consider how he lost his virginity: At age fifteen, on location for *Stand by Me* in Oregon, Phoenix was enamored of an eighteen-year-old family friend. They came to Heart and John and asked, "Can we have your good wishes?" River's parents, far from objecting, decorated a tent for the couple. "It was a beautiful experience," says Heart.

Phoenix's tutor, Dirk Drake, recalls some white-power skinheads taunting Phoenix at a party in 1988. "He smiled with an unbelievable innocence," Drake says, "and said, 'If you really want to kick my ass, go ahead, just explain to me why you're doing it.' The skinheads were dumbfounded. One guy stayed to say, 'Ah, you wouldn't be worth it.' And River said, 'We're all worth it, man, we're all worth millions of planets and stars and galaxies and universes.' "

Phoenix was always creating families as he traveled, making new "brothers" and "sisters" and, particularly, "fathers," like Harrison Ford on *The Mosquito Coast.* Kevan Michaels, who was "dad to buddy son" with the sixteen-year-old Phoenix on the set of *A Night in the Life of Jimmy Reardon,* remembers calling him a few years later on New Year's Day. "I can't understand why we're talking right now," Phoenix said, almost resentfully. "When you make a film you're a family, but when the film is over so is the family."

The outburst may have been provoked by some of Phoenix's own family difficulties. For his upbringing also contained a deep contradiction: He found himself part Atlas, shouldering the pain of the world, and part Antaeus, receiving strength only from contact with the unpolluted earth.

Says Martha Plimpton, who stayed with the Phoenixes after she and River met while filming *The Mosquito Coast* in Belize: "I love River's family; they brought him up to believe he was a pure soul who had a message to deliver to the world.

"But in moving around all the time, changing schools, keeping to themselves, and distrusting America," Plimpton continues, "they created this Utopian bubble so that River was never socialized—he was never prepared for dealing with crowds and with Hollywood, for the world in which he'd have to deliver that message. And furthermore, when you're fifteen, to have to think of yourself as a prophet is unfair."

"Our kids were so comfortable with everyone, so mature," Heart Phoenix responds. "But as River grew," she admits, "he did become more and more uncomfortable being the poster boy for all good things. He often said he wished he could just be anonymous. But he never was. When he wasn't a movie star, he was a missionary. There's a beauty in that—the man with the cause, the leader—but there's also a deep loneliness."

The family had had prophet problems before: they'd actually left the Children of God because its leader, David Brant Berg, began encouraging the women in his flock to seduce potential converts—a tactic known as "flirty fishing"—and proudly referred to them as hookers for Jesus. Berg also advocated incest and sex with toddlers, and mailed circulars with graphic pictures of molestation. The Phoenixes felt betrayed, and River rarely talked about the sect. "They're disgusting," he would say angrily. "They're ruining people's lives."

River also had problems with his father, John Phoenix, a bearded, poetic man who hated cities. Phoenix hugely admired John, wrote songs with him, and before his death was planning to direct a movie about John's abuse-punctuated boyhood, called *By Way of Fontana*, with Joaquin playing John. But John had troubles with alcohol. Indeed, drinking ran in John's family.

"River would drink with his dad, so they could relate," says Suzanne Solgot. "But he worried the disease was in his bloodline." Recalls Martha Plimpton: "We had five million talks about his compulsive personality and his guilt and fear over not being able to save his father.

"His parents saw him as their savior," Plimpton says, "and treated him as the father." Eventually, because the family was so generous about sheltering lost souls, up to a dozen people lived near or on the Micanopy property, in a motor home, two travel trailers, and in Phoenix's apartment above his recording studio; River supported them all.

Known to River's self-sufficient friends as "the Klingons" or "the tofu mafia," they worked as gardeners, security guards, secretaries, or simply grocery unloaders. Many of them were gentle spirits whom Phoenix loved being around. "But in River's mind he was their father," Bobby Bukowski says. "And he had some anger about that."

"River and his father were *always* having breakthrough conversations where River would tell his father his feelings about alcohol, about their roles," Plimpton says. "But the next day nothing would change. River would then say to me, 'Well, it's not *that* serious, it's not *that* bad.' "

Plimpton had begun hearing the same refrain from Phoenix about himself. "He really liked getting drunk and high," she says. "But he didn't have a gauge for when to stop. When we split up, a lot of it was that I had learned that screaming, fighting, and begging wasn't going to change him, that he had to change himself, and that he didn't want to yet."

———

Phoenix tried to keep things lighter with his next girlfriend, Suzanne Solgot. When he met her, at a party, he shyly introduced himself as "Rio," and when another woman there said she was sure he was River Phoenix, he denied it: "I'm not that guy, I'm nothing like him." "He was very private and mysterious," Solgot says. "We never talked much about our past or who we were, though I was always curious."

When they broke up last January, after three and a half years, it was for a familiar reason. "He didn't want me nagging him," Solgot says, "pointing out the contradiction between his public stands and what he was doing to his body."

Phoenix responded that his body was "a horse." But tormented by his public responsibility, he'd worry aloud, "What would those twelve-year-old girls with a picture of me over their bed think if they knew?" (He didn't even want his fans to know he smoked and warned interviewers on that point.) Then he'd get angry that he was "under the microscope" and couldn't just cut loose like a normal young man.

All along he was a shepherd to friends who were really cutting loose. He knew that almost everyone his age in the business had smoked, snorted, or shot up. That drugs, long a sign of rebellion against the mainstream, now *are* the mainstream. And that whereas it used to take years for people to kill their pain for good with alcohol, now they can do it instantly and without really trying.

"He had called me twice in the last couple of years to ask me to intervene with friends," says Bob Timmins, a drug counselor for Ringo Starr, Aerosmith, and the Red Hot Chili Peppers, among others. "And he had made it passionately clear that he was committed with his time and money to making sure these people didn't die. In one case he drove [a prominent musician] to a clinic in Arizona."

In June of 1991, Phoenix was horrified to hear that a famous young actor he'd worked with had shot so much heroin that his arm had abscessed, halting his film for three days. Phoenix confronted his friend and got him to admit "that it was true, that it had freaked him out, and that he hadn't done any smack since."

Still, by 1991 the evidence that Phoenix had his own problem was there to read. "You'd have to be really dumb or naive not to know he was high when he was," says Bobby Bukowski. "He was so clearly high, he was like an alien."

In December 1991, Dirk Drake, who tutored all the Phoenix children, had a screaming match with Phoenix at Flea's house in Los Angeles. Flea was away, and River was sharing space with several of Flea's friends, who would become known as River's drug friends.

One of them, in a drug-induced jealous rage, had chased Phoenix around the house with a butcher knife.

"I told him I was furious about the glamour those friends attached to skag [heroin]," Drake recalls. "Don't worry," Phoenix said, "I have the fear of God." Drake sarcastically told him to become a Baptist preacher. "No, no," Phoenix said—he'd meant his unique sense of religious election. "I want to live to see what the higher power's purpose is for me."

None of the people Phoenix tried to help offered help in return; indeed, in an excruciating irony, the Persian Brown heroin that helped kill Phoenix was provided by a friend he'd gotten into rehab. There are several reasons Phoenix wasn't flagged down: His drug use came in spurts, and he was often clean; even close friends saw him infrequently and had difficulty assessing the problem, particularly as he bounced back well the next day; he had a beguiling trick of preemptively telling friends "a really stupid rumor" about his exploits and assuring them "what those assholes are saying" wasn't true; and he had a magisterial authority that convinced even knowledgeable addicts that he was in control. "He fooled a lot of people, and he fooled himself," says Suzanne Solgot. "He was a great actor."

—

As he grew away from his family in the last three years of his life, Phoenix's missionary goals began to change. He never swerved from veganism, nonviolence, and universal love, and he still gave to Earth Save, Earth Trust, People for the Ethical Treatment of Animals, Greenpeace, and Farm Animals Institute, among others. But he'd started his own private projects: he was going to build a school in Costa Rica, and was larkishly happy working on a nationwide education project for middle and high schoolers.

"River realized that his family's ideas had been a little simplistic," says one close friend. "The fact that when he bought up rain forest in Costa Rica he was preventing Third World people from making a living there left him confused and unhappy."

Phoenix began to reexamine some of his core precepts. A director recalls, "He'd say to me, 'How about we do this movie where my brother and I and this gooner here'—some strange and interesting person River had taken under his wing for a few days—'travel across the country killing people—no, no, first we fuck them, and then we murder them.' He was kidding, but he was also wondering how to get people's attention and blow their minds."

Making movies had become more of a chore, and it's noteworthy that aside from James Wright, his seductively moody country singer in *The Thing Called Love,* Phoenix's last films don't amount to much. The brute capitalism of the business depressed him: while filming *Sneakers* in 1991, a movie he advised friends not to see, he grumpily told a friend, "I want to make $1 million on my next picture, $2 million on the one after that, and $3 million on the one after that." (He did, in fact, earn $1.5 million for *The Thing.*)

"He was very disappointed that his music never hit," says Dirk Drake. "In the late eighties he had always felt it was just a matter of days before the world would be healing itself with his beautiful music, before he was touching everyone the way the Beatles did."

Phoenix's sweet, breathless phone voice began to drag. "His language had become at times totally incoherent," says Martha Plimpton. "He'd often be high when he called, and I'd listen for twenty minutes to his jumbled, made-up words, his own logic, and not know what the fuck he was talking about. He'd say, 'You're just not listening carefully enough.' "

Phoenix's drug use wasn't ruining his acting, but one producer who weighed working with him in 1992 decided he was "largely unreliable." And there were two days filming *The Thing* in Nashville that fall when, director Peter Bogdanovich says, "the feeling was that he'd taken something. I wasn't sure he could drive the truck [as required for the scene]."

Phoenix was insulted and told Bogdanovich, "This is bullshit. I had half a beer and a cold pill." Some of the rumors about Phoenix's behavior on that set are attributable to his lazy eye: when he flutter-blinked to center his iris, he looked under the influence. That said, he sometimes was.

Flea, who was himself in recovery (and who was not a drug friend), spoke to Phoenix about his drug use that Christmas, and so did Bobby Bukowski. After Phoenix came over one morning, still blasted on heroin and cocaine, Bukowski waited until Phoenix had taken a nap and eaten one of the garlic-and-raw-veggies-and-serial-glasses-of-water meals he used to cleanse his system and then gently confronted him.

"I'd rather you just point a gun at your head and pull the trigger," Bukowski said. "I want to see you become an old man, so we can be old friends together."

Phoenix wept and wept. "That's the end of the drugs," he promised. "I don't want to go down to the place that's so dark it'll annihilate me."

For several months afterward Phoenix would sometimes call Bukowski for support when he felt the urge to get high. But in January Heart noticed that he'd become distant, almost surly. Phoenix had striven mightily to keep his drug use from her, and he largely succeeded. But this time she realized "a substance might be involved" and asked River. He denied it.

Heart and John repeatedly urged River to take a long vacation in Costa Rica, but he continued to shun the demands of solitude. Yet he was troubled by intimations of mortality. Early last year he had a recurrent daydream that spirits were coming for him, and he feared the fateful numerology of turning twenty-three on the twenty-third of August. When a friend saw him in a heroin stupor that spring and said, "River, you're going to kill yourself," Phoenix just looked at him, the friend says, "like 'Yeah, so?' "

Last fall Phoenix filmed *Dark Blood* in an area in Utah reputed to be a magnet for alien visitations, which fascinated him (his latest karmic catchphrase was "Thanks be to UFO Godmother"). He told friends he'd been levitated over his bed, and he would sometimes lie on his patio and shout to the heavens, "Take me, I'm ready! What else is out there?"

But Phoenix was clean and focused in Utah, as he had been that summer. He was in love with Samantha Mathis, whom he'd puppyishly pursued during *The Thing Called Love,* telling friends "his head was going to pop off if he didn't get to hold her hand." And he had finally started sifting through his anger, spelunking into his own fault lines. His friends agree that he was strong enough to reemerge; that he was not ineluctably lost, like Jim Morrison or John Belushi.

But back in Los Angeles for three days in late October, depressed by the pain of his role as a lonely desert dweller in *Dark Blood* and by continual on-set fighting, he began with drugs again. He'd always hated Los Angeles. Previously he'd been a public, celebratory user; now he used privately at the Hotel Nikko. Rain and Joaquin had flown out to Los Angeles that final day because Joaquin had an audition for the role of River's brother in *Safe Passage.* River was excited about the chance to play, at last, a normal young man, who heals his father's blindness. But Rain and Joaquin also sensed that River felt very alone.

In his last two movies Phoenix had darkened his hair to look older, and it's poignant that River, fed up with his pretty face, went unrecognized by Johnny Depp that night at Depp's club, the Viper Room. Phoenix looked thin and strung-out in black jeans and Converse sneakers; he looked, finally, anonymous. It was a terrible death, of course—the stricken 911 call from Joaquin; River's eight-minute seizure, his head jerking and his knuckles banging the sidewalk—yet it was a mistake of youth. It was easy to forget that he was only twenty-three.

———

A few nights after Phoenix died, his family and a few close friends like Bukowski and Solgot sat around the table in Micanopy, drinking Gentleman Jack whiskey, John's favorite brand, and remembering River. They got in an uproar of laughter, and a tumbler that came with the whiskey abruptly shattered. Later, when Solgot was at the sink, three more of the tumblers broke simultaneously in the dish rack. "River's a joker," she says.

In two separate memorial services, both held outside on still days, when everyone joined hands to think of Phoenix, the wind suddenly whipped up. He has often been in his friends' dreams, assuring them he is fine, though he seems quiet and sometimes melancholy. "I am still connected to his energy," Heart Phoenix says. "When the wind blows I see River, when the sun shines I see River, when I look in someone's eyes and make a connection I see River. To have death transformed into another way to look at life is his huge gift."

But for others the question of how to remember lingers. In London, Dermot Mulroney ran into one of River's drug friends, a screenwriter, and slammed him against a wall. "This is how I feel about River's death," Mulroney said. "How do you feel?"

Certain scenes of Phoenix's movies are freshly piercing: When Phoenix stops clowning and admits in *Little Nikita* that "whenever people tell me to be myself I don't know what to do . . . I don't know what myself is"; when he gleefully snorts cocaine in *Idaho;* when Keanu Reeves reflects on their three years hustling and says, "What I'm getting at, Mike, is that we're still alive." And in the just released *Silent Tongue,* the sequence when the spirit of Phoenix's dead Kiowa Indian wife goads him to commit suicide. In rehearsal, director Sam Shepard roped Phoenix and Sheila Tousey with twine to cement the inescapability of their joint doom, and they play the scene hauntingly; when Phoenix maneuvers the mouth of the rifle under his chin, it's almost impossible to watch. Our wince would not be what Phoenix desired as his legacy.

Nor would he have wanted the other extreme. When 250 people gathered for the family's memorial service under a huge live oak tree at the base of the Phoenix property, the tenor of many of the remarks from the Klingons was, as Suzanne Solgot puts it, "River's in heaven, blah blah blah, it was his time, blah blah blah." "You would have thought he was ninety and had died in his sleep," says Martha Plimpton. "The people who were saying this felt tremendous guilt that they had contributed to his death."

After hearing yet another speaker say, "River needed to go, and he's free now," Bradley Gregg, who'd played Phoenix's elder brother in *Stand by Me* and who became like an actual brother to him, leaped to his feet and shouted, "River didn't have to die to be free!" Not everyone heard, so he shouted again, "River didn't have to die to be free!" Gregg's wife, Dawn, added a clarion, "Wake up, wake up!" her tears soaking the baby she held in her arms.

(1994)

NOTES ON THE DEATH
OF THE CELEBRITY PROFILE

Exhibit A. A few years ago I had a brief and mutually unsatisfactory conversation with one Charlotte Parker, Arnold Schwarzenegger's PR flack at the time. I had just met Arnold while reporting a Planet Hollywood story for *Esquire* when Parker drew me aside: "We'd like to get Arnold on *Esquire*'s cover," she said. "He's been everywhere else."

"Oh?"

"How much time with him would you need?" Parker asked. "Half an hour? Forty-five minutes?"

"Well, *if* I were going to do it, I'd want to hang around over a few days," I said, rather stiffly.

"Oh, God," she said disgustedly, "this wouldn't be one of those profiles where you try to *figure him out,* would it?"

—

Exhibit B. *Us* magazine, December 1997.

Us: "What [do] you loathe about yourself?"

Richard Gere: [Laughs darkly] "You are someone I met ten minutes ago, and now you want to get into the deep, dark questions about my being?"

—

Exhibit C. In the October 1997 *Esquire,* Tom Junod wrote a cover story entitled "Kevin Spacey Has a Secret." Junod was sheepish about his hateful task—trying to out Spacey. So he began by quoting his own mother: "Well, *I* hear he's gay." Then Junod sought to confirm his "reporting," growing increasingly sour and antagonistic as he looked for someone, anyone, "to betray [Spacey], to divulge his one essential secret, to give him *up,* finally, once and for all." *Esquire*'s editors archly justified this ninja mission by asserting that "a celebrity has no secrets; he belongs to all of us, completely, not only his artistic output, but his every secretory, excretory, and ejaculatory effort as well."

Two months later, in the same magazine, Mike Sager wrote a cover story on Robert De Niro. De Niro is famously pen-shy—when sitting for a *GQ* cover story he left after one question—and he gave Sager just thirty minutes. De Niro's sole memorable remark was that celebrity journalists are "kind of pathetic." Sager filled the rest of his allotted five thousand words with man-on-the-street interviews, biographical rehash, professions of love for his son, Miles, and maunderings about how "in the end, we are all just people." "You want to know about De Niro?" a defeated Sager concluded, relinquishing any claim to insight, let alone ownership. "Go see his movies."

—

I've written celebrity profiles myself over the years. They've been no better than anyone else's, and as transactions they've made me increasingly gloomy. Even after reading my musings on Linda Fiorentino or Kristin Scott Thomas, friends ask, "So what's she really like?" They know I can't really capture in print someone I've met so briefly—especially an actress who doesn't usually wish to be captured.

But they also hope I might pass on some of the magic of direct contact, a whiff of the mystery. As director George Cukor (*Holiday,* *The Philadelphia Story*) once remarked, actors are alluring precisely insofar as they have a secret: "There's always *something* about them that you *don't* know that you'd *like* to know," Cukor said. "You feel very close to them, but there is the ultimate thing withheld from you—and you want to find out."

At its best, a celebrity profile articulates not the source of a star's secret, but the effect of it on the star, and on us. In his 1978 *New Yorker* profile of Johnny Carson, the hipster critic Kenneth Tynan observed that the *Tonight Show* host was at his best when a joke bombed, that he instantly sensed the failure "and react[ed] to it ('Did they close the hall? Did they have a drill?') before any critic could. . . ." Man's greatest fear is of humiliating public performance; Carson's glory was that he acted as our daily proxy in confronting, struggling with, and conquering that anxiety.

These days, what the writer wants to say, and the reader wants to learn, and the actor wants to reveal are wildly at odds. The compromise is heavily weighted toward the actor. "I was a starving actor for a few months," Tom Cruise recently told *Vanity Fair* writer Jennet Conant with what she described as "a blinding grin that eliminates the necessity of further explanation." Tom Cruise's secret, we suspect, is just how much self-doubt fuels that blinding grin; but Cruise wants—and gets—a puff piece content with the grin itself. (Some stars—a Keanu Reeves, say, or a Mariah Carey—just want to keep secret the fact that they have no secret.)

The last thing Cruise wants is a repeat of the *McCall's* situation: in a 1995 Nicole Kidman profile, the downmarket women's monthly suggested she and Cruise had married solely to "squelch the gay" rumors about Cruise and that in return the talent agency CAA secretly promised to make Kidman a star. *McCall's,* which had to publish a complete retraction, doesn't want a repeat, either—it needs to preserve access to the stars whose photos on the cover sell the magazine.

This unholy confluence of needs explains why celebrity profiles, by and large, suck. In 1996, *Entertainment Weekly* managing editor

James Seymore Jr. killed his magazine's lengthy actor profiles. Seymore says he felt they were all "just carefully crafted publicity devices—junk food" and notes with some satisfaction that readers haven't missed them. Similar restiveness has come to *Vanity Fair,* which had long treated celebrities like Nobel laureates and itself like the Swedish Academy. Its self-loathing writers have recently described themselves as passively transcribing while one star sits "dutifully pumping quarters into the publicity machine"; as "whores of the press [who] haul out our hoariest adjectives" for another phenom; and as "not proud of doing celebrity profiles." *VF* editor in chief Graydon Carter told *The Wall Street Journal,* "You can only have so many tough things in an issue, and I think it's foolish to waste it on an actor."

Most profiles nowadays are almost scripted by the PR agency. It's a return to the 1950s, when studio minions misinformed us that Bing Crosby was jolly and Rock Hudson was girl crazy. River Phoenix's handlers, for instance, forbade reporters from revealing merely that he smoked cigarettes (let alone snorted heroin). PR agencies recently rejected amiable writer Robert Sullivan as too tough for Winona Ryder, nixed each of *GQ*'s suggestions for a writer for a cover story on John Travolta, and muscled *Harper's Bazaar,* which wanted Julia Roberts for its June cover, into letting Roberts handpick her writer. Roberts chose director Billy Bob (*Sling Blade*) Thornton. Sample question: "What's your favorite southern food?"

The chosen scribe, miserable at having passed muster—am I really such a wuss?—then gets perhaps an hour with the actor. Or a bit more, if the magazine is important enough; all this is negotiated as laboriously as the Yalta Conference. Demi Moore, though granted *Vogue*'s cover, would talk to me only between takes of *The Juror,* and felt she'd sloughed enough material after about twenty minutes.

The musician profile doesn't suffer from flacks and peep-show availability. But there's an alterna-script just the same: Up-and-coming bands happily hale the writer onto the big bus to see how hard they work, how disaffected and paranoid they truly are—how authentic. A Gavin Rossdale emulates writer/directors like Quentin

Tarantino; both seek to lend street cred to their commercial narratives. And what rapper profile is complete without a tender scene of him playing with his kids?

—

When a new actor like Matt Damon pops up, he's on the cover of *Vanity Fair* and *Interview* and has become a character in our heads even before the (invariably lame) movie's out. There's a brief window when a Damon believes in each writer's goodwill—thereby conciliating it. Fiona Apple, at twenty, maintains sufficient ingenuousness to bring *Spin*'s writer home to meet her mom. But soon they'll become part of the machine. Every Damon profile will have the yada-yada about how Damon is/is not like his new character; breathy quotes from costars and directors about how he is "generous" and "truthful," "an old soul in a new body," plus Damon's trademark ruminations about how he feels ugly next to Matthew McConaughey. (These observations may all be true, but truth plastic-wrapped as formula swiftly becomes false.) Punning headlines will trace his arc: from WELCOME, MATT to (amid drug use, vanity projects, thuggish entourages, foredoomed marriages) DAMON'S DEMONS; finally, after rehab, Scientology, Montana, and a relationship with a sexy native healer, in the newfound-peace-while-playing-Dan Aykroyd-roles phase, BACK IN DAMON-D.

Long before then, Damon's minders will have taught him to control access, to fear spontaneity. He'll be on to the trick of the writer toting a prop (a rubber duck, an Uzi) to provoke a fresh response: as if! He'll be happy to be described as "contradictory" and "complex" because he played a serial killer but didn't dismember anyone in the writer's presence. And, to ensure no more than that level of analysis, he'll sit for a single bluff meal, or he'll briefly tolerate the writer's presence as he's coated in Prada and Tenax and then shot for the magazine.

These static rituals explain why so very, very many profiles begin with food or clothing anecdotes manipulated to make some symbolic point. Thus when *The New York Times* observes, "The miniature cheesecake sat in front of Stevie Nicks like a cruel temptation . . . ," it develops that the wee pastry must bear the weight of being an indication the onetime substance- and food-abusing "Ms. Nicks knows something about indulgence, and about paying the price for it." In *Time*, the fact that "Mary J. Blige is looking as fine as she wants to be"—that she has donned haute couture for a *Time* photo shoot, rather than her usual gangsta-girl threads—is tortured into demonstrating that Blige is newly mature and "ready to step out."

The photo shoot is replacing the interview as the moment of truth. The star brandishes the factitious secrets of her clothing and styling, and encourages us to fetishize them. And we do—such grotesqueries are the entire raison d'être of magazines like *In Style*. *Vanity Fair* proudly displayed a "Behind the Scenes" photo demonstrating that it required eleven people and a golden retriever to create the cover shot of Matt Damon larking in a bathtub. *People*'s one hard rule for profiles is that the star must agree to be photographed in his house: the appropriately thievish-sounding "home take." For as Demi Moore told me: "Nobody"—pause—"remembers"—pause—"the articles." Pause. "Everybody"—pause—"remembers"—pause—"the photographs."

Soon the only words left will be info-haikus, like this recent *People* snippet from *E.R.* actress Gloria Reuben: " 'Moments are cherished,' says the unattached Reuben, who learned to scuba-dive in the Cayman Islands over the summer. 'Everything means something else than before.' " *What does that mean?*

———

It was not ever so. In his classic sixties profiles, Gay Talese took for granted that he could report what Joe DiMaggio and Frank Sinatra were thinking because he came to enjoy "the confidence and trust of his subjects." Talese spent six weeks following the initially suspicious Sinatra on his boozy rounds from recording studio to bar to Vegas nightclub, and eventually, exhilaratingly, was able to demonstrate that when Sinatra had a simple cold, it caused "a kind of psychosomatic nasal drip within dozens of people who work for him, drink with him, love him, depend on him for their own welfare and stability."

Kenneth Tynan devoted twenty thousand words to his famous 1979 profile of former silent-film star Louise Brooks. But even more striking than the length he was afforded was Brooks's attitude: the seventy-one-year-old recluse admitted to feeling with Tynan "a sensation I have never experienced with any other man"—love. "Wouldn't it be wonderful," she wrote him, "if [you] told me what I have been running away from for seventy-one years? And more baffling still, what I was running to?"

The idea that a profile should reveal or change a life is long gone. What's left is the possibility of moments, as when *Life*'s Brad Darrach described Mel Gibson, preparing to play Hamlet on screen in 1991, secretly trying on the old bloodstained shirt Laurence Olivier had worn for the same role. "For a long moment he stared at himself in the mirror. A shiver ran through him; Olivier he wasn't. Hastily taking the shirt off, he put it back in the box."

Yet Gibson, the subject of largely favorable press, has suggested that prying journalists should be dosed with 1080, a pesticide that causes catastrophic brain hemorrhage. When writers come carrying roses, stars feel only the lurking thorns. Consider *Vanity Fair* profile writer Kevin Sessums. Sessums somehow manages to be at once vainglorious (taking credit for Julia Roberts's marriage) and offensive (quizzing Johnny Depp about why he sleeps only with white women; asking Meg Ryan how husband Dennis Quaid's cocaine use affected his erections). Sessums's stylings reached a peak when he held Andie MacDowell in his clammy clutch. Sessums described her "head of hair curlier than the consonants in Mississippi" (?); her voice as a "haunting strategem . . . filled with the lulling feminine grace of a coastal breeze sashaying right past South Carolina" (!); and asserted that her resilience comes from having had "to parent her divorced mother at the same time she was trying to cope with the dilemma of being a child herself." Everyone on the planet has to cope with "the dilemma of being a child."

Then Sessums "teased" MacDowell that having children had

given her not only the "depth" she claimed, but more "width" as well. She didn't get it. Sessums writes: " 'I was talking more about your birth canal,' I correct her. 'Ohh,' she moans [. . .] 'You're talking about my *vagina*?' " Yes, sirree.

Writers are briefly ushered into the world of limos and high cheekbones, then flung out, howling, like Satan into the pit. John Gregory Dunne, a novelist and screenwriter of middling talent, recently memorialized Jimmy Stewart for *The New York Times*. Though brief, his elegy reeked of bitter almonds. We learned that Stewart "was deaf as a post, and a little distant because of it" and that "he never wore his hairpiece when he was at a private social occasion." And, finally, that in their only real conversation Dunne asked Stewart, who'd been in the Air Force, about the differences between flying the B-17 and the B-24. Though Dunne "can't remember how [Stewart] came down" on the question, he suggested that Stewart engaged as he never would have with a question about acting: "I have always thought that most male American movie stars are slightly embarrassed by what they do, as if acting is an unmasculine profession."

The final thrust was that Dunne found this half-remembered exchange "a more enduring memory of Mr. Stewart than any of his pictures." Dunne, his face pressed to the bakery window, was eager to associate himself with the star yet evidently furious that the worst of Jimmy Stewart's pictures will outlast the best of his own books.

What dynamic best explains these fantasies and jilted furies? That of an aborted affair. Editors try to bamboozle the celeb by sending a writer of the opposite sex, hoping the sexual frisson will provoke indiscretions. It usually works the other way around. Thus, Cathy Horyn in *Vanity Fair* on Nicolas Cage: "Nick Cage is one dreamboat worth losing a little sleep over. He is somewhere between over-the-edge and out-of-sight, between the man you think you want and the one you shouldn't have." Or on Mel Gibson, whose voice is "so low and dusky you don't know whether to weep or cross your legs." Weep, I think. Three minutes into our conversation, Demi Moore languorously told me that during her last take sweat "was dripping down between my *breasts.*" Two minutes later we were dry-humping in her trailer. Then I wrote a superflattering profile. (Well, that—minus the dry humping—was Moore's expectation. A quickie, in short.)

As Mira Sorvino observed in an excellent profile last August by *GQ*'s Andrew Corsello, "with single male reporters . . . there's almost a script, you know, where I playact this sex-symbol persona." You'd think Corsello would have killed to go outside the script, as Sorvino invited him to do with her meta-textual commentary on Corsello's "writerly premise"—he cooked her a meal—and on the formalized role play. But Sorvino was so vocal, so eager to examine her characters' motivations and the right feminist line on horror films, that Corsello, finally, wanted her to "shut up." He remembered her most happily, in fact, when she was quiet, in repose under a big white blanket on her couch late at night: "It is the only time she will manage not to utterly demystify herself with overexplanation."

What does this couch moment evoke? The movies, of course. The camera pans over the star's brooding face, as shadows from the fire suggest passionate depths. She has a secret, and a kiss will unlock it. As readers we have only a momentary interest in Dennis Quaid's lazy ding-dong. We don't really want the celebrity's frailties revealed; we want their desires suggested. A good profile is like a good second date: it stocks up kindling for the imagination.

The best celebrity profile I've read recently was Chris Heath's take on Winona Ryder in *Us*. The article illuminated Ryder's fear that despite all her success, she was not glamorous. We learned that she had a dream where Julia Roberts told her she was only on the set to play "the family dog," and that Ryder and Gwyneth Paltrow acted out their own homemade Spice Girls video as Sporty and Baby Spice, with the camera watching blank eyed from the mantel.

Interesting, appealing, and ultimately mysterious. Even with the best will in the world, it's impossible to explain a star who wants to be Baby Spice.

(1998)

THE EIGHTEEN-YEAR ITCH

Hollywood is too small a town for two people to have lunch in by themselves. Around every A-list table for two hovers a host of shades, unseen mentors and advisers who whisper in ears, sift for conflicts of interest, register minute shifts in the balance of power, and—after raising an eyebrow at the price of sparkling water—make sure that their man doesn't get stuck with the check.

On February 5, Warren Beatty and Brad Grey had a three-hour lunch at Sushi Ko, a Japanese restaurant off Mulholland Drive. Present in spirit were at least three other well-known entertainment industry figures who have negotiated with each other over the years. Each man in the room, corporeally or not, was trying very hard to do the right thing. And, if the right thing couldn't be done, each was going to try doubly hard to insure that nobody thought the lunch was his idea.

Grey and Beatty were attempting to negotiate a reconciliation between Grey and Garry Shandling, who is one of Beatty's closest friends. Grey is the chairman of Brillstein-Grey Enterprises and is Hollywood's most powerful personal manager, with a stable of 130 producers, writers, and actors, including Brad Pitt and Nicolas Cage. Shandling is the star of and the creative force behind HBO's darkly brilliant sitcom *The Larry Sanders Show.* For eighteen years, Grey and Shandling, his close friend and signature client, were a classic odd couple emerging from the same limo at the Emmys: Grey slight and sleek, cagey, with a cocky bounce in his walk; Shandling stiff and embarrassed-looking, but quick with deadpan one-liners about his lame sex life, his dandelion-thistle coiffure, and his emotional isolation. ("My friends tell me that I have an intimacy issue—but I don't think they know me.")

The proximate reason for the lunch was that on January 15 Shandling had sued Grey for $100 million in California Superior Court. He alleged, among other things, that Grey had "double-dipped," taking fees from HBO both as Shandling's manager and as the executive producer of *The Larry Sanders Show;* made lucrative television deals by trading on his relationship with Shandling without cutting his client in; and inveigled writers from *Larry Sanders* to create other shows for Grey's television studio.

Beyond that, accounts of what happened at Sushi Ko—and what occasioned the lunch in the first place—are astonishingly various. Brad Grey says that the lunch was Beatty's idea and recalls the heart of the conversation as follows: "Warren said, 'This is simply a case of Garry feeling you didn't love him enough.' And I started, foolishly, to say, 'That's just not *true!*' And he said, 'No, no, no, no. It doesn't matter what you think. *He* thinks you didn't love him enough.' I said, 'I understand, but I don't love him enough to get this back on track. I just want it to be over.' "

But the lunch wasn't all soap-opera dialogue. To smooth things over, Grey says, Beatty suggested that Grey make a TV production deal with Shandling and take him back as a client. Beatty proposed that the adversaries meet with him and Michael Ovitz, the legendary dealmaker and a friend of Grey's, to discuss the matter without any lawyers. "Do you trust me? Do you trust me?" Grey says Beatty asked him. "I trust you as much as any actor I met half an hour ago," was Grey's joshing reply.

Warren Beatty's memory of the lunch is distinctly different. He agrees that he suggested a four-man meeting without lawyers and that the peace process foundered the next day when Shandling wanted his attorneys present. As for the rest of it, he told me incredulously, "I don't believe that Brad Grey said those things to you." He denied saying that Shandling was feeling unloved, denied outlining specific proposals for a rapprochement, and denied, in a particularly nettled tone, that the "Do you trust me?" exchange took place: "Brad was much more respectful than that."

Beatty also said that the instigator of the lunch was actually an old friend of his, the entertainment attorney Bert Fields—who also happens to be Brad Grey's lawyer. When I asked Fields about this, he reluctantly acknowledged that he might well have suggested the meeting. "As a matter of tact, as Warren's friend, I'd probably have formulated it to him as 'This is not good for either side.' But my own view is that the suit will be terrible for Shandling, when all the proof comes out."

The question of who proposed the lunch reveals the deeper issues in the legal dispute, which friends of the litigants compare to a bitter divorce, with both men seeking custody of their shared power and reputation. Both sides are afraid of appearing weak, so neither wants credit for having initiated the meeting or for having voiced a willingness to reconcile. Each man now claims that the other would never have broken through to success without his help. Shandling, in his suit, says that he was Grey's most important client, the bell cow that attracted comic talent to Grey and led an "inexperienced personal manager" into the world of television production. In his cross-complaint, Grey says that Brillstein-Grey's funding and production of *It's Garry Shandling's Show* on Showtime, from 1986 to 1990, "gave Shandling the public exposure and creative freedom he sought, and was a great career boost for Shandling." (In March Grey countersued Shandling for $10 million, claiming that the star's lazy and abusive behavior had cost Brillstein-Grey heavily in excess production costs.)

With the lawsuit pending until next year, each man has retained lawyers and public relations specialists to proclaim his version of the story and sneer at his opponent's. Shandling has encouraged friends to talk, but he declined to be interviewed. In a statement released through his publicist, he said, "Brad Grey betrayed my trust. His stories about me are false and he knows it, but he's telling them in hopes of discouraging me from pursuing my claim against him. Or he has me confused with Larry"—a reference to Shandling's high-strung alter ego, Larry Sanders. (A close friend of Grey's acknowledges that airing Shandling's idiosyncrasies is indeed Grey's media strategy.)

The breach has become a parable about the hazards of mixing business with friendship—an ordinary arrangement in Hollywood. Both men are engaged in a kind of brinkmanship that seeks to triumph by exposing frailties discovered and confided during a long intimacy. The intensity of the struggle, in which Grey and Shandling are speed-dialing to enlist allies, has alarmed their friends and caused people all over Hollywood to wonder how solid their own alliances are. "It's horrible that their relationship has come to this," one of the industry's most famous businessmen says. "They blew it. The combination of money, mistrust, divergent career paths, jealousy, and emotion—that's the recipe for a take-no-prisoners lawsuit, where both men will lose."

It is a measure of just how jumbled professional and personal loyalties have become in Hollywood that two observers familiar with the Sushi Ko lunch offer yet another interpretation of the peacemaking effort: they say that the meeting was Michael Ovitz's idea. One man spins a long, paranoid-sounding tale about Ovitz's alleged conflicts of interest when, years ago, he personally advised Brad Grey while his company, Creative Artists Agency, was representing Shandling. Ovitz, this person says, is on Shandling's deposition list and doesn't want that conflict to come out. The other observer makes the novel suggestion that Ovitz simply wanted to help.

"Trust no one" is the theme, as it happens, of *The Larry Sanders Show*. The series, now in its sixth and final season, is a formally innovative backstage look at a Letterman-style talk show, which reveals stars and their handlers engaging in a furious roundelay of fudging, arm-twisting, backstabbing, bald-faced lying, and every other conceivable species of bad faith. "If it is true that Garry believed everything Brad told him," says one television executive who knows both men well, and who believes in Grey's probity, "then he's an idiot, and he deserved to get taken."

—

Brad Grey said, "Okay, prepare yourself." He pulled out a photograph of himself with Garry Shandling, backstage after a stand-up comedy show in the early eighties. Shandling wore a brown leather jacket with a fuzzy black collar, a look that was mildly unfortunate, but Grey sported a white-mesh "Eddie Rabbitt" cap, hair that screamed REO Speedwagon, and forty extra pounds.

"Now, this is the one I've been thinking about," he said, sliding across the desk an eight-by-ten from 1984: Shandling, his arm around Grey, was slim and handsome in a well-cut jacket. He looked like a star. But Grey was still pudgy and unfocused—someone's awkward kid brother. "And," he said, pausing as he overlaid that photograph with a small shot of the forty-eight-year-old Shandling in a recent issue of *Entertainment Weekly*. Grey, who is forty, pivoted in his chair in the middle of his large, surpassingly clean office on Wilshire Boulevard and carefully propped his black shoes on a sofa. He waited as I noticed that Shandling looked wan, worn out.

With just a few images, Grey had introduced the idea that he and Shandling had switched roles over the years—that the acolyte had become the mentor. Having asked to see the photographs, I now pushed Grey to interpret them. He said, "Well, I was overweight and very unattractive, just a kid. He has a sparkle in his eye, and you can see that he's in charge—I've since thought he hired me because he knew he'd be in control. But I think *I* have the sparkle now, and he looks like a troubled soul."

Grey told me a story that introduced the idea of envy. Last fall, shortly before he dropped Shandling as a client—and while Shandling's lawyer was inspecting Brillstein-Grey's files—Grey says, Shandling showed up at the house that Grey was building in Pacific Palisades. Shandling told the construction foreman that he was a friend, and just sat for a while, gazing at the Prairie-style shingled mansion. Shandling's home, in Brentwood, is legendary in Hollywood as a source of expense and dissatisfaction to him, and Grey says that it was "unsettling" to hear about Shandling eyeing his house. "I guess he might have been jealous of me, of my . . . happiness. He's alone in a house that he hates, pretending to be happy, with no love in his life." Through his lawyer, Shandling says that Grey had invited him to drop by and that he later told Grey the house was "beautiful."

Peter Tolan, a longtime *Sanders* writer, scoffs at Grey's characterization of the dispute as a latter-day version of *A Star Is Born*. He defends Shandling against the charge of lifestyle envy in a somewhat backhanded fashion: "He wouldn't have given a shit whether Brad Grey was successful or not. Garry is marvelously self-absorbed—that's why his work is so good."

In the beginning, Shandling and Grey seemed buoyed and absorbed by each other's promise. They were introduced by Grey's first client, Bob Saget, in 1979, at the Westwood Comedy Store. Shandling, a former writer for *Sanford and Son,* signed with Grey, and he introduced him to other promising young comedians, including Dennis Miller and Dana Carvey. In 1983, Grey met his future partner, Bernie Brillstein, after a Shandling gig in San Francisco. Brillstein, the manager of such clients as Jim Henson and Lorne Michaels, liked Grey but didn't take to Shandling. "I thought Garry was a road-company David Brenner," says Brillstein, who is now sixty-six and a genial white-bearded presence. "But Brad said, 'No, you'll see—he's a genius.' "

In 1985, Grey joined the Brillstein Company and quickly underwent an astonishing transformation. "Brad was a roly-poly guy who was quietly studying Bernie, never saying a word," says a close friend of Grey's. "Then suddenly he was running eight miles a day, losing weight, cutting his hair, and changing overnight into Bernie's partner, into a mogul—into Brad Grey." Grey then switched his attentions to the agent Michael Ovitz. "You cannot be trained for our business—you have to observe and learn," Ovitz says. "Brad is a great sponge."

Brillstein says, "If Brad is fifty percent himself, he's thirty-five percent me and fifteen percent Ovitz. From me I think he learned an instinct for talent and honesty. From Ovitz he learned the ability to spin the press and the illusion of power, which is more important than power itself."

For decades in Hollywood, agents and personal managers generally had a low profile. Like Woody Allen's Broadway Danny Rose, they tended to be servile schleppers in bad suits, handlers whose role was to schmooze and to soothe show business egos. But in the 1980s, as Michael Ovitz became known as the most powerful man in Hollywood, these backstage figures started becoming stars in their own right, even more important in the industry food chain than their clients.

Brad Grey's route to stardom was his realization that by packaging the talent his company represented, he could create his own television studio. Today he has eight shows on the air, including the hits *Just Shoot Me* and *Politically Incorrect.* And he has grown rich from a 1994 joint venture with Capital Cities/ABC, which invested more than $100 million to create Brillstein-Grey Communications, and from a $90 million deal with Universal Studios, in 1997. Last year Grey bought out his old mentor, Brillstein. Along the way, Grey has befriended industry leaders such as David Geffen and Edgar Bronfman Jr., and last summer he received the ultimate sanction: he was invited to the investor Herbert Allen's annual conclave of media titans in Sun Valley, Idaho.

By controlling both the talent and the production company that employs the talent, Grey has become what Lew Wasserman, the chairman of MCA, was prevented from becoming in 1962, after an antitrust investigation forced him to divest MCA's talent agency and stick to making television shows. Unlike agents, personal managers are not prohibited from producing entertainment. But by doing all this on a relatively large scale, Grey has essentially become the whole food chain, leaving himself open to new kinds of conflicts of interest.

Meanwhile, Garry Shandling's fortunes were soaring, too: in the late eighties he served as a frequent guest host for Johnny Carson and created two groundbreaking television shows, in which he starred—*It's Garry Shandling's Show* and *The Larry Sanders Show,* which started airing in 1992. *Sanders,* which Brillstein-Grey produces and co-owns, brought Shandling near universal critical praise, with the *Times* certifying it as "the smartest and funniest series on television." Movie stars like Alec Baldwin and Robin Williams vied to go on the show and seem smarter by satirizing themselves.

But after Grey's $100 million deal with ABC—a large investment for a relatively unproved producer, whose only long-lasting shows were the two with Shandling—Shandling was said to be irritated. He felt that Grey was putting his company's interest over his client's. One well-known agent recalls hearing Shandling ask plaintively, "Why does Brad have more money than me?"

By Grey's accounting—which Shandling's lawyers certainly question—Shandling has made $16 million from the *Sanders* show, while Brillstein-Grey, after paying for production cost overruns, has netted only a million or two. "That's a lot of money for a guy in cable," Grey says of Shandling's profits.

Eventually it became Shandling's belief, and the linchpin of his claim for $100 million, that in both the ABC and the Universal deals Grey got rich by selling Shandling out. Shandling's suit claims that the transactions, particularly the ABC deal, were predicated upon Grey's promise to his new partners that he could deliver Shandling and Shandling's ideas—a promise made without Shandling's knowledge or his financial participation.

Both Ron Meyer, the president and COO of Universal Studios, and Ted Harbert, then the president of ABC Entertainment, deny that Shandling figured in their calculations. Yet one important television executive subscribes to Shandling's underlying concern. "Ideally, if you're Brad Grey and you're being paid fifteen percent of your client's money to do what's best for him," the executive says, "you look at Garry Shandling and say, 'I can turn this guy into a television factory.' Or you do what Brad did, thinking of Brad, and you build your own television business off of Garry's back, off his cachet."

Self-interest cut the other way in 1993, when Shandling had Grey negotiate with the networks for him to host a real late-night talk show. Shandling confided to several friends that he had no intention of taking such a job, and kept negotiations going merely to generate publicity for himself and for *Sanders*. But he never told his manager, and Grey discovered only much later that he'd been on a fool's errand.

In recent years, Shandling, who, like many stars, had a knack for calling with a crisis whenever his manager was on his way out the door, had noticed that Grey didn't seem as devoted. "Garry was in love with Brad," one person who knows both men well told me, "but he wanted him all to himself." Shandling, many of his former writers and producers agree, requires absolute fealty. "He had to humiliate everyone," says one writer. "He'd say, 'Come to my house Sunday at nine A.M. to work on the script.' And you'd go, and he'd say, 'Can you come back in an hour?' And then, an hour later, 'Oh, I'm so embarrassed, I forgot something I have to do—could you just wait half an hour?' If you were still there after all that, he knew you were weak enough to work with." The writer adds, "I used to think of his corporation, How's My Hair, as the company that loves misery." (The widely remarked-upon similarities between Shandling and his character, Larry Sanders, a neurotic perfectionist who can express himself only through wincing jokes, has led Dana Carvey to routinely call Shandling "Ga-Larry.")

Grey seems to be at pains to view Shandling's complaints about his waning attentiveness as a personal issue rather than as a business matter. "I would explain to him that our success together proved that this *worked,* but that I was much more interested now in going home to see my kids than in hanging out endlessly at his house to talk about the script the writers hadn't delivered. I had heard it for so long." One writer sums it up more succinctly: "Brad got rich, and he didn't need the aggravation."

—

Grey dates the problems in the relationship to December 1996, when Shandling vanished while shooting the last episode of the *Sanders* season. "Garry finished one take, and suddenly he got beet red in the face, walked off the set, took his jacket off, and kept going out the door, into his car. It was like Scorsese's Copa scene in *Good-Fellas*—one fluid shot."

Shandling didn't return for the final day of shooting, and the episode was edited around him. "He told me he just burned out—he snapped," Peter Tolan, who wrote the episode, says. Shandling, according to colleagues, often felt that he was single-handedly keeping the ship afloat, a sentiment that the show's actors fervently share. But eight writers and producers who have worked on *Sanders* told me that Shandling, who tended to be chronically dissatisfied and withdrawn, was the show's chief production problem.

For his part, Shandling felt that the writing staff never helped him enough. And he began to think of Grey in the same light, complaining that Grey wasn't earning the $50,000 executive producer's fee he received for each episode. Many *Sanders* staff members say that Grey's involvement after the first two seasons, when Brillstein-Grey regularly booked its own clients on the fledgling show, was minimal. "Brad Grey was a mandarin, a collector of information and a creator of nothing," says one former *Sanders* producer. "He would have kept his height to himself if he could."

Shandling, after walking off the set, spent three weeks in Hawaii and Fiji. Grey says, "He had told me that last day on the set, 'I'm dying here, I'm dying.' I thought it was just an expression. He just had to get through four more monologue jokes and one more day's shooting. But he later told me he truly meant it—that he thought he was going to die, and I should have known that. And he said that John Ziffren"—the show's producer—"whom he'd also told that to, should have sent him home, and because he hadn't, he could never trust John again as a human being." Ziffren had produced the show for five years in harmony with Shandling, but he quit because of the incident. Sounding extremely pained, Ziffren told me, "I did everything I could *not* to disappoint Garry, and I'm very sorry I did, like everyone else."

Grey's bottom-line approach may have been what a good businessman does, but, as Shandling evidently felt, it was not the way a friend—or a careful nurturer of clients—behaves. Handling talent means handling the difficulties, and providing constant support and reassurance. The successful handler makes sure that Marlon Brando gets his hamburgers in Tahiti; assures Roseanne that her grabbing her crotch while singing the national anthem was a bold creative choice; helps Martin Lawrence explain that it was "exhaustion" that made him wander naked into traffic while carrying a gun. But Brad Grey felt he had grown beyond that role.

In Fiji, Shandling stayed, as he often did, with his friend Gavin de Becker, a personal security consultant and the author of the bestselling book *The Gift of Fear.* De Becker disputes the apparently indisputable premise that Shandling walked off the show. "Garry Shandling is the producer and star of that show," de Becker told me. "So there is no 'supposed to' about coming to work the next day. He has no time sheets." Jeffrey Tambor, who plays Sanders's sidekick Hank, agrees: "Hey, man, it's Garry's ball game."

When de Becker was asked about Grey's assertion that Shandling had some sort of crisis, he laughed. "You can say that de Becker laughed on hearing that characterization," he said. "He wasn't being wheeled around like Hannibal Lecter. While he was here, he swam like an athlete, he snorkeled, he laughed, and he edited two episodes of the show." The idea that Shandling was unstrung, de Becker says, "is fully malodorous bullshit."

The next time Grey saw his client was in February, when the two had an emotional meeting in Grey's office. Grey recalls, "Garry said, 'You don't care about me, about who I am.' Finally I said, 'I don't want this energy in my life. We should end this.' He got tears in his eyes. 'You don't want to work through this?' he said. And I said, 'I have a *wife* to work through this stuff with. I don't want to go into couples therapy with you.' " Though the two patched it up, "it was never the same," Grey says.

Through his attorney, Jonathan Schiller, Shandling denies that Grey sought to end their alliance. He says that the meeting was difficult only because Shandling demanded an explanation of accounting discrepancies suggesting that Grey had been secretly taking commissions on Shandling's *Sanders* fees. (Grey denies taking any such commissions.)

A few months later, Shandling hired an outside lawyer, Barry Hirsch, to look into all his contractual dealings with Grey. Shandling later alleged that the clearest proof that Grey was bilking him was that Grey always discouraged him from hiring a lawyer, saying, "Don't you trust me?" Grey says with a faint smile, "If I told Garry Shandling not to get a lawyer, the very first thing he would do is get a lawyer."

———

Hollywood is honeycombed with divided and overlapping loyalties. "Unless you're Colonel Parker and you only represent one client, Elvis Presley," Ron Meyer, of Universal, says, "there's always the potential for conflict."

"I don't think that anybody knows where the line on conflict is anymore," says Jon Vitti, a former *Sanders* writer, who is mentioned in Shandling's lawsuit as one of the writers Brillstein-Grey "diverted" to write a pilot. Vitti says that the charge is "true, to a degree, but whether it's a legally meaningful degree I don't know." The contract he signed with Brillstein-Grey when he was hired at *Sanders* stipulated that he write a pilot for the company. The conflict, in other words, was built in. Grey argues that *Sanders* had so few episodes (about fifteen a year, compared with the usual twenty-two) that he had to make overall deals with some top writers so that he could pay the going rate of $1.5 million a year.

Shandling was not pleased that several *Sanders* writers went on to create successful TV series for Brillstein-Grey. "I always assumed that Garry was getting a cut from Brad's other shows because he'd trained the writers in his comedy college here," says Rip Torn, who plays Larry Sanders's fierce producer, Artie. "He should have been Brad's president of development." The bloodiest battle of all occurred when Paul Simms, the valued head writer of *Sanders,* quit and created the NBC show *NewsRadio* for Brillstein-Grey. Shandling threatened to sue, but he backed down when Simms stood firm. "I said to Brad, 'Fine, I'd rather spend the next three years in court than spend another day working at the *Sanders* show,' " Simms told me.

The moment Grey began producing TV shows as well as managing talent, he entered a world of clashing responsibilities. "At ABC," Ted Harbert says, "we knew that Brad was often in a tough position, representing the interests of the joint venture, his TV company, and his client at the same time. But there's no hiding here—the conflicts are all out in the open."

For instance, Grey arranged for his television studio to pay Shandling $2 million to consult on pilot scripts from 1994 to 1997, in part because, he says, Shandling needed money after sinking nearly $7 million into his house and later settling a palimony claim and a sexual discrimination suit with an ex-girlfriend and former *Sanders* cast member, Linda Doucett. (Shandling's lawyer denies that his client was having financial problems and says that Grey misrepresented the terms of the deal.) Grey took a 10 percent commission on the deals: deals that he'd made with his own production company, using ABC's money—a curious arrangement. Grey defends the commission and adds more generally, "Partnerships in Hollywood bleed all the time. It's a business of relationships, and this happens every week all over town."

Some of the disputes could probably have been avoided if Shandling had had his own TV production company; his writers could then have been launching new shows that enriched Shandling instead of just Brillstein-Grey. Grey says that he suggested this to Shandling last spring, offering him $20 million over four years to create two prime-time shows a year. But according to Shandling's attorney, all Grey offered was another consulting deal. In August Shandling said that he was "uncomfortable" with $1.2 million in commissions that Grey had taken on Shandling's consulting fees from ABC and on roughly $12 million that HBO had paid Shandling in "exclusivity fees," to supplement his various creative fees connected with the *Sanders* show. This issue became the tipping point in the two men's relationship.

"I thought the commission was completely appropriate," Grey says, "but I said fine. I didn't want him to be unhappy." Grey agreed to write Shandling a check for $1.2 million, and Shandling joined Grey and his family in Hawaii for two days. "I said to Brad, 'I think you're making a really big mistake,' " a powerful friend of Grey's says. " 'It'll be thrown back in your face in a lawsuit, and it'll look like you're admitting guilt.' This decision wasn't coming from a good business place—it was coming from a personal place of wanting to make Garry feel better."

And, normally, making a client feel better would have been good business sense for a personal manager. But the personal and the business strands of Grey and Shandling's eighteen-year relationship had begun to unravel. "It felt good to Garry to get that kind of money returned," Gavin de Becker says, "but it didn't feel good overall. Garry began immediately to ask more questions. You hire a lawyer, the lawyer has trouble getting documents from your manager, then the manager returns $1.2 million right after you ask for it? That doesn't smell right."

At the first read-through for the new *Sanders* season, in October, Grey says, Shandling cut him dead. "I got in my car, and I knew that was it," he says. "I sent a letter resigning as Garry's manager. It felt really sad, because even though I knew it was best for him and for me, it felt disloyal, and I pride myself on my loyalty."

As Grey shapes the narrative, the next thing he knew was that Shandling's lawyer told his lawyer that he was going to be sued. Grey says that Shandling's agent later suggested that his client might drop the suit for $10 million. (Schiller denies this.) But Grey didn't pursue settlement talks. For some weeks, in fact, Grey's own lawyer, Bert Fields, had been urging Grey to sue Shandling for libel. A January draft of the potential libel suit shows that Grey worried that Shandling had begun "a campaign of malicious falsehood and character assassination" against him with the media and with Brillstein-Grey clients. The draft alleges that Shandling was saying he had fired Grey for fraud, and declares that those calumnies would ruin Grey's reputation and cost Brillstein-Grey in excess of "the sum of $25 million." In the margin alongside a passage describing Shandling's alleged abuse of *Sanders* personnel, Grey had scrawled, and then crossed out, "In addition to pattern and history with ex-friends, accountants, part actors, architects, agents, fiancées, decorators, producers, directors, etc. Now it's me, which leaves him to live his life alone, angry and bitter."

But Shandling filed first, on January 15. Fields says that Grey had already decided, as a matter of strategy, "to let Garry be the one to explode this thing." Many in Hollywood had been unaware of the strains—"When I read about the lawsuit," says *Sanders* actor Rip Torn, "I thought it must be a publicity stunt for the new season"—and Grey braced himself for a pillorying. "I was concerned for my business after what I read in the newspapers," he says, "but, honestly, I got very emotional when I saw the response, with Bill Maher, Lorne Michaels, Dana Carvey, and so on calling out of friendship." The fact that Grey, feeling betrayed by his friend, was still happy to mix business and pleasure says a lot about relationships being the best currency in Hollywood. "Brad Pitt came over to my house to bring me a Tiffany lamp," he recalls, smiling, "and he said, 'We're going to hang out.' I'm much older than Brad, but he gave me a talk about life. He said, 'Listen, people are going to disappoint you.' And that's right."

Grey's friends are urging him to settle and move on. One writer who had a contractual dispute with Shandling says, "You don't play chicken with a guy who's strapping his foot to the gas pedal." Grey says, "I would probably advise someone in my position to settle. On a business level, I can make that case all day long. But I guess I'm still too emotionally engaged."

Shandling's friends say that he seems revitalized by the struggle and that this final season of *Larry Sanders* is the best yet. The hour-long farewell show, airing May 31, features an extraordinary roster of talent, mustered without Brillstein-Grey's help, including Warren Beatty, Sean Penn, Tim Allen, Jim Carrey, Jerry Seinfeld, Ellen De-Generes, David Duchovny, and Greg Kinnear. "Garry's much more creatively fertile," Peter Tolan says. "Go figure—maybe he feels he's taken control of his life."

"This has been a lesson for me," Grey told me at the end of a three-and-a-half-hour conversation. "But I'm not sure I know what it is yet. I guess my mistake with Garry was that I actually thought he was my friend and that he was happy for me as I was growing. But as his manager I should have known what was going on with his feelings." He drank some Evian and said intently, "I was blind to it because he was part of my world. Maybe, as I spent more time with my kids, maybe, as Warren said, he felt I didn't love him enough."

David Geffen, who has seen an enormous wash of ambition and vexation throughout his long career in entertainment, and who has himself been sued by a client, draws a much simpler moral: "Never invite your artists to your house if it's bigger than theirs."

(1998)

COPY CATS: HOLLYWOOD
STOLE MY STORY!

This summer, Americans spent 575 million hours in darkened cinemas and saw, at most, two new things: the harrowing D Day sequence in *Saving Private Ryan* and the hair-gel joke in *There's Something About Mary.* Yet as popcorn movies have become a tagteam-written jumble of curvy scientists, ninja studs, morphing cyborgs, and basement-loving psychos, one obscure writer after another has come forward to advance the claim that a studio stole his brainchild. Hollywood movies may never have seemed more derivative, but the copyright suits they inspire display an ingenuity and a nuanced concern for story development worthy of the young Orson Welles.

Our sympathies in these cases tend to go to the little guy—to plaintiffs like Mark Dunn, a soft-spoken clerk at the New York Public Library, who is suing Paramount Studios, the producer Scott Rudin, and the screenwriter Andrew Niccol for $300 million. Dunn alleges that his play *Frank's Life,* about the unwitting subject of a TV series, was secretly used as a blueprint by the creators of *The Truman Show* after they had rejected it as a potential movie. Dunn has earned less than $25,000 from his many years of writing for what he calls the "Off-Off-Broadway ghetto"; *The Truman Show* has grossed $125 million to date.

Dunn's suit lists 149 purported similarities between *Frank's Life* and *The Truman Show*. That seems an overwhelming number, and Dunn's lawyer, Carl Person, says that the two works' resemblances make the suit "the best copyright case I've ever had." This is not saying much, however, for Person hasn't yet won any of the five movie copyright cases he's filed. He probably won't win this one, either—and maybe he shouldn't.

Paramount will undoubtedly argue that Andrew Niccol came up with the idea for *The Truman Show* independently (Niccol's former manager says that he has the writer's copyrighted treatment, written in 1991, a year before *Frank's Life* was staged) and that Person's client is either deluded or a stickup artist, or both. In June, Lynn Pleshette, Niccol's agent, patiently explained to the *New York Post*, "Every time a big movie comes out, a moron tries to sue." Though plaintiffs like Dunn radiate aggrieved sincerity, Paul Rudnick, the writer of *Sister Act*—which also fought off a Carl Person lawsuit—notes dryly that "the prospect of eight figures inspires a lot of sincerity." Furthermore, as any cost-conscious producer will tell you, it's usually much less expensive for a studio to buy a property than to steal it.

But the reason that Dunn and Person will probably lose their suit has less to do with the perceived integrity of the plaintiffs and the ostensible skullduggery of the defendants than with the fact that most copyright plaintiffs overestimate how much protection they have under the law. Even more important, they misunderstand how the Hollywood blockbuster gets created. Studios generally don't *want* to make something so original that they'd have to steal it from an unsung genius; they want to recast familiar stories and have them endlessly rewritten until every star feels his part is juicy enough. Movies are often sold to the studios in the first place as the genetically predictable offspring of two prior hits ("It's *Working Girl* meets *Marathon Man*!"). Many studios believe that if something is totally new—*Koyaanisqatsi*, say—we won't want to see it.

In copyright law, it's the details that matter. The idea of Tom Cruise playing an idealistic recent Harvard Law School graduate who gets pulled into a sinister case that's way over his head sounds copyrightable—and ridiculously commercial—but it describes equally well two very different films that came out only months apart: *The Firm* and *A Few Good Men*. That example explains why, under federal law, ideas—and most characters—can't be copyrighted.

Sixty-eight years ago, in the landmark case *Nichols v. Universal Pictures Corporation*, Judge Learned Hand determined that the author of *Abie's Irish Rose*, a generic play about Irish-Jewish intermarriage, had no claim against *The Cohens and the Kellys*, a generic movie about Irish-Jewish intermarriage. Calling the Irish father in the play "a mere symbol for religious fanaticism and patriarchal pride, scarcely a character at all," and the Irish father in the movie "only a grotesque hobbledehoy, used for low comedy of the most conventional sort," Hand testily declared that neither story deserved legal protection. "The less developed the characters," he wrote, "the less they can be copyrighted; that is the penalty an author must bear for marking them too indistinctly." Thus, you couldn't copyright a wrinkly but adorable creature, or the idea of his being hunted by narrow-minded humans—which explains why the producers of *E.T.* were able to fend off three copyright claims from people with prior scripts about wrinkly but adorable creatures, etc.

In theory, you can't copyright mere ideas because the government wishes to encourage free expression—to prevent pioneering writers such as Washington Irving and Nathaniel Hawthorne from locking up all the good American stories. In practice, the law insures that studios aren't stymied by the success of *Die Hard* but can illuminate vast new regions of the human soul in *Die Hard* on a bus (*Speed*), *Die Hard* on a plane (*Air Force One*), *Die Hard* on a mountain (*Cliffhanger*), *Die Hard* on a boat (*Under Siege*), and *Die Hard* on a bigger, slower boat (*Speed 2*).

You don't even have to go as far as to change a milieu from Vietnam to an L.A. office building (as *Die Hard* itself did with the *Rambo* story) to be deemed a "creator" in the eyes of the law. Small changes suffice. Indeed, one could argue that the very definition of creativity in Hollywood is the subtle but legally distinguishing tweak. In 1994, Curt Wilson and his partner, Donna Douglas, sued Walt Disney Pictures because *Sister Act* resembled a script they had earlier submitted to the studio: both stories were about a woman hiding from the Mob by disguising herself as a nun, though Disney's movie was much more playful. To the plaintiffs' amazement— they'd spurned a million-dollar settlement offer—the jury found for the defense. "They would have had to copy our stuff *verbatim* for us to prevail," Wilson says disgustedly.

Most copyright lawyers believe that if Shakespeare were alive today and had preserved his copyright on *Romeo and Juliet,* he would find it difficult to win a case against *West Side Story.* Leonard Bernstein and Stephen Sondheim would testify that they'd vaguely heard of Mr. Shakespeare and his Italy-based twist on the star-crossed-lovers scenario, but they'd certainly never read it. The defense would parade experts to testify that Mr. Shakespeare's melodrama was utterly different, since it contained few, if any, Puerto Rican seamstresses and ballet-dancing street gangs. And they would also make the legally weighty argument that because Mr. Shakespeare had himself, as usual, stolen his plot—in this case from Arthur Brooke's tedious epic poem *The Tragicall Historye of Romeus and Juliet*—he had no basis for a lawsuit. The legal term for his predicament is "unclean hands," an evocative but uncopyrightable metaphor that was borrowed, one likes to imagine, from Shakespeare's own Lady Macbeth.

—

The copyright plaintiffs' legal steeplechase begins with an attempt to show that the studio had the opportunity to borrow from their work. This is the one hurdle plaintiffs can usually clear. If they have written a play or a book, then someone connected with the movie could easily have read it. "Or they submit the script to CAA, looking for an agent," Creative Artists Agency executive Robert Bookman says wearily. "The agent never sees it, the reader is the lowest person on the totem pole, it's a pass, the agent looks at the last page of the coverage, sees 'pass,' and his assistant writes a nice note. Then these plaintiffs say, 'We sent it to CAA. *That's* how Michael Crichton' "—a CAA client—" 'got the script.' "

But after proving "access," the plaintiffs must demonstrate that the two works are "substantially similar." This entails stacking up "articulable similarities between the plot, themes, dialogue, mood, setting, pace, characters, and sequence" of the two works. In addition to this "objective" test, the court also applies the "subjective" test: whether a layman would perceive a substantial similarity in the works' "total concept and feel."

Mark Dunn's list of 149 similarities between his play *Frank's Life* and *The Truman Show* includes the pervasive ("Hidden cameras placed all over the sprawling set and unknown to Frank/Truman"; "Frank/Truman were having what appears to the TV audience to be a normal sex life with the actor wives, raising various unspoken moral issues"), the picayune ("A specific volcanic island, within a group of such islands or archipelago, in the southern Pacific Ocean, with double-sounding name—Pago Pago/Fiji—is used as remote place . . . to escape from the effects of the Show"), and the perplexing ("The genre of Frank/Truman is a comedy, but with a uniqueness which is difficult to otherwise categorize").

The courts have held, however, that such lists are "inherently subjective and unreliable," particularly where "the list emphasizes random similarities scattered throughout the works." Louis Petrich, a copyright-defense lawyer, says, "You can tell that the plaintiffs are stretching if their lists abstract or trivialize. In the first case, they say, 'When the boy falls into the pit, that's like our scene of the man being chased by the bull, because in both there's "jeopardy." ' And in the second case, they say, 'Each story has a red Chevy.' Sure, but what does the Chevy have to do with the story?"

The highest hurdle that plaintiffs face is the fact that most scripts contain a lot of boilerplate that has no particular "author"; it consists of segments that are known legally as *scenes à faire*. As the court defined them in *Alexander* v. *Haley,* a 1978 copyright case against *Roots, scenes à faire* are "incidents, characters, or settings which are as a practical matter indispensable, or at least standard, in the treatment of a given topic." Thus the court suggested that when one is writing about slavery, one would almost perforce include, among other things, "attempted escapes, flights through the woods pursued by baying dogs, the sorrowful or happy singing of slaves." Another court held that a realistic portrait of cops in the South Bronx would necessarily contain "drunks, prostitutes, vermin, and derelict cars."

The notion of *scenes à faire* is capacious enough to include the manner in which a reasonable person might develop an idea even if another reasonable person had earlier developed the same idea in the same way. For instance, if dinosaurs were reanimated, they'd obviously have to be kept far away from the nearest nursery school. So a writer who claimed that he had banished his velociraptors to a remote island before Michael Crichton did the same in *Jurassic Park* got nowhere in court: the judge ruled that "placing dinosaurs on a prehistoric island far from the mainland amounts to no more than a *scene à faire* in a dinosaur adventure story."

The well-known Hollywood lawyer Bert Fields, who is defending Fox Searchlight Pictures in a copyright suit against *The Full Monty,* breezily explains the film's similarities to a play called *Ladies Night* by offering a similar argument. "Once you've got the idea of male strippers," he says, "it's all *scenes à faire:* the inevitable scene when they first put on a G-string, the inevitable scene when someone's naked body is shown as rather unattractive. You've got to have a problem for each of the six guys, so one guy having impotence just goes with the territory."

A further obstacle for plaintiffs is that courts have tended to rule that "copying deleted or so disguised as to be unrecognizable" is not, legally, copying, and therefore that early drafts of a movie's screenplay—even drafts that show evidence of copying—are not legally relevant. Martin Garbus, a copyright lawyer and First Amendment expert who has often sued the studios, says ruefully that people in Hollywood "know to change a description of Lincoln just enough—to put 'black hat' at the end of the sentence and 'legs like a grasshopper' at the beginning, and then take two other sentences from somewhere else. These are very sophisticated people."

Plaintiffs have an especially hard time when there's no paper trail. While aspiring screenwriters dream of a chance collision with a moviemaker (a screenplay was recently handed to Emma Thompson as she was being slid into an MRI tube), nothing could be worse from a plaintiff's point of view. If a producer is stuck on a ski lift with a writer who regales her with his nifty twist on the asteroid-hurtling-toward-earth plot, and she steals it, that's just too bad for him. He can try suing on the ground that there was a tacit mutual assumption that promising material would be paid for—the theory of "implied contract." But unless the writer is already known as a high-concept guy, someone whose very laundry list or drunken e-mails might contain the germ of a billion-dollar idea, this imaginative legal strategy rarely works. Bert Fields says, "If I'm talking to Tom Clancy, there is probably an implied contract. If I'm talking to my dentist"—who had pitched Fields an idea the day before—"probably not."

After contemplating all these barriers, many potential plaintiffs decide not to sue, simply because they lack the necessary funds. Martin Garbus told me, "The people who file these suits can't afford the $250,000 to $500,000 to mount a fight against the studios and their big insurance companies. The studios' theory is that if you spend the money and fight, you'll wear your opponents down and discourage others from suing. It's a successful tactic."

Not always. In 1980, the prolific fantasy writer Harlan Ellison won $337,000 from ABC and Paramount, which had shanghaied his idea for a TV series about a robot cop. He then spent $7,000 of his booty to rent a billboard across the street from Paramount Pictures, which read, "Writers, don't let them steal from you! Keep their hands out of your pockets!" "I did it to piss the shit out of them," Ellison says, "and to send the message that writers can't be ripped off."

The studios aren't as invulnerable as they appear. Bert Fields, who has represented them in dozens of copyright cases, told me, "People have learned that the studios often settle if it's cheaper than the cost of litigation"—and that cost shoots up $650 an hour when Fields gets involved. "Studios will throw out $5,000 if it's a weak case and $200,000 to $300,000 for a substantial case. Sometimes much more." Last year, Barbara Chase-Riboud sued Steven Spielberg for "brazenly stealing" from her novel *Echo of Lions* to create his film *Amistad.* Then she suddenly dropped her suit and declared, "*Amistad* is a splendid piece of work, and I applaud Mr. Spielberg for having the courage to make it." One can't help but hear in such public reversals the *ka-ching!* of the cash register in the background.

Yet many plaintiffs, it seems, don't want hush money as much as they want recognition. Last January, after a jury rejected the writer Stephen Kessler's plagiarism claim against Michael Crichton for *Twister,* there was a curious moment when Kessler tried to shake Crichton's hand (Crichton refused). The copyright-defense lawyer Louis Petrich says, "The plaintiffs don't see themselves as calling the defendants thieves and jeopardizing their careers. They think that now they're in show business, one of the big guys." Certainly Mark Dunn is an unabashed fan of his opponents' work. Dunn owns an early-draft *Truman* screenplay but says, "I feel guilty even looking at it," because it was smuggled to him without the producers' knowledge. This is a touching amount of reverence for a script that Dunn believes is premised on his own play. "Hollywood inspires yearning and delusion," Paul Rudnick observes, "and this sort of litigation is really a kind of affection and fanship—a foothold."

—

The giddiest aspect of copyright suits is how often the studios try to prove that their story was so derivative that they couldn't have stolen it from any one source. Thus, while some reviewers acclaimed *The Truman Show* as a bold departure, Paramount may well point out at the trial that it wasn't. At least seven previous works featured unwitting subjects on camera, including the sixties TV show *The Prisoner,* three *Twilight Zone* episodes, and a short Paul Bartel film,

Secret Cinema. When millions of Americans are watching television, it will inevitably occur to more than one of those watchers that television may be also watching them. Ideas occur unpredictably, in odd, fractal clusters. A butterfly flaps its wings over China, and suddenly everyone decides that the next big thing is a mad bomber, an erupting volcano, or a nostalgic look at disco.

You might think that mankind's collective imagination could churn up dozens of fictional ways to track a tornado, but there seems to be only one. When Stephen Kessler sued Michael Crichton for *Twister,* he was upset because his script about tornado chasers, *Catch the Wind,* had placed a data-collection device called Toto II in the whirlwind's path, just like *Twister*'s data-collecting Dorothy. Not such a coincidence, the defense pointed out: years earlier two other writers had written a script called *Twister* involving a device called Toto, and all the Oz puns had originated with a device used by real tornado chasers that is called, um, Toto.

In the *Sister Act* trial, the producer, Scott Rudin, testified that the credited writer Paul Rudnick's idea was not really novel, and Rudnick acknowledges that "the idea of a nun, or someone in disguise, has been used many, many times before." He continues, "Plus, after my script had been rewritten by half of Southern California, I'd used a pseudonym on the film, so being sued for authorship under those circumstances was sort of hilarious." Still, Rudnick stresses the gulf between an idea and its expression: "Yes, they also had a nun," he says. "But a nun is not a story or a character. A nun is a noun."

And once you have a nun, certain scenes and associations necessarily follow. The *Sister Act* plaintiffs highlighted the fact that both their screenplay and the movie likened nuns to penguins and contained the phrase "God works in mysterious ways." Those aren't *scenes à faire,* exactly, but any screenwriter who didn't include them in a nun comedy would be criminally incompetent. What these suits' lists of similarities reveal is that the human brain is hardwired to write scenes that hurry toward predictable surprise.

Two characters who can't stand each other invariably wind up handcuffed together in a rolling boxcar or a shuffling chain gang. An innocent schnook arriving at an airport must within ten seconds pick up the identical-but-drug-filled suitcase. After the tomboyish girl next door dresses up for the prom, the boy can only look flustered and say, "Why, Miranda, you're, you're . . . beautiful!" Snooty matrons gigglingly confide, as soon as they are within earshot of loud funk music, that all they really want to do is "boogie down" or "knock boots." When hard-bitten military men see an alien spacecraft, they ease off their glasses to peer more closely—and to allow us to register the childlike wonder in their eyes. And heroes who have only moments in which to defuse a ticking bomb rip off the casing to discover the statutory red wire and blue wire—another explosive device crafted, apparently, by the Acme Company for Wile E. Coyote.

Underlying such scenarios, by Hollywood legend, are a mere seven basic stories. Or maybe eight. (Or, as the Supreme Court of California once determined in an excess of hairsplitting, thirty-six.) One legendary core story is "the buddy movie"; another is "ordinary man in extraordinary circumstances"; a third is "boy meets girl, girl hates boy, boy woos girl." But no one can quite agree on what, precisely, the others are (is Eddie Murphy's *Coming to America* "fish out of water" or "lord in disguise"?) or on who thought up the list in the first place (Aristotle? Simpson and Bruckheimer?).

In truth, no one in Hollywood seems to care enough to nail those answers down, since all that matters is what type of story the last hit was. "It's an industry that tries so hard to copy success," Martin Garbus says. "You know there are a lot of people out there writing *Wag the Dog II,* and when *Wag the Dog II* comes out everyone's going to sue, saying, 'Hey! That was my idea!' " Perhaps, but not anymore. As long ago as 1945, a federal judge admonished that most copyright suits were premised "partly upon a wholly erroneous understanding of the extent of copyright protection; and partly upon that obsessive conviction, so common among authors and composers, that all similarities between their works and any others which appear later must inevitably be ascribed to plagiarism."

But while the studios may win the copyright battle, they aren't exonerated from the charge of laziness in the first degree. The courts seem to have the same feeling upon viewing the plots and characters in evidence that we have upon trailing out of the Cineplex: Haven't we seen this before? One court wrote, with an Olympian weariness that is otherwise found only among film critics, "The common use of such stock . . . merely reminds us that in Hollywood, as in the life of men generally, there is only rarely anything new under the sun." Which is a steal from Ecclesiastes—but tweaked just enough to be original.

(1998)

LAUGH RIOT

In a large white office at Walt Disney Studios in Burbank, an office that falls under the bashful gaze of the seven dwarfs who adorn the pediment of corporate headquarters across the way, four men are brooding about art, commerce, and the fate of their television show. It is a late afternoon in mid-July, and the show's creator, Aaron Sorkin, sits at his desk smoking a Merit and sneaking glances at the computer screen, where the script of his second episode awaits him.

ABC, the network that will air their situation comedy, wants it to be filmed in front of a live audience and have a laugh track. To Sorkin and the others in this room, a laugh track represents all that is truckling and mediocre about television and would destroy their show. "It feels like I've put on an Armani tuxedo, tied my tie, snapped on my cuff links," Sorkin told me, "and the last thing I do before I leave the house is spray Cheez Whiz all over myself."

The show, *Sports Night,* which debuts on ABC this Tuesday night, September 22, at 9:30 P.M., is about six smart producers and anchors of a late-night sports-highlight show that resembles ESPN's *Sports Center.* Some of the best sitcoms have been about the world of television—*The Mary Tyler Moore Show, The Dick Van Dyke Show, The Larry Sanders Show*—but Sorkin intends an unusual mixture of comedy and drama, with runs of banter that are funny but not jokey intercut with serious, and even solemn, moments. In the first episode, Casey, one of the anchors, is getting a divorce and contemplating quitting the broadcast because sports has become a greedy and violent business; in a later episode, a female character named Dana, the producer of *Sports Night,* reveals finely nuanced crises of conscience about how to broker, publicize, and conduct an interview with a star football player who just exposed himself in the locker room to the show's young female reporter. It's because of this mixture that the network has been so insistent on the reassuring overlay of "audience response" sound.

"The show starts off confusing viewers," Jamie Tarses, the president of ABC Entertainment, explained to me. Though she acquired the show and has championed it at the network, she's worried about it. "People will wonder, 'Am I supposed to think this is funny, or serious?' So we're nervous about it. People need the comforting aural cue of laughter. It's conditioning."

Sorkin, writer of the screenplays for *A Few Good Men* and *The American President,* had not planned his first foray into television to be a traditional sitcom, but something moodier and more realistic. "In film," Sorkin had told me, "my critics will tell you that nobody hugs the middle of the road tighter than I do, and I do feel comfortable there—you don't watch *A Few Good Men* and go, 'Wow, this is different!' But while in any other art form mixing comedy and drama is three thousand years old, in the half-hour TV show it's unheard of." Though Sorkin merely wants to create a well-crafted amalgam of comedy and menschy melodrama—*The American President* on the small screen—the half-hour form is so hidebound that what he proposes is akin to adding contraception to Catholic dogma.

The men gathered in Sorkin's office are by turns defiant and fretful. "The problem with the laugh track is that it makes all television the same," Thomas Schlamme, the show's director, says. Schlamme developed the unorthodox camera style of *Larry Sanders* and directed last year's live episode of *E.R.* With his baseball cap, and his glasses dangling on a lanyard, the director is the picture of L.A. cool, but he's also the group's bomb thrower. "*Suddenly Susan* and *Seinfeld* have the same laugh track, though there's not a fucking laugh in *Suddenly Susan* and there's a thousand in *Seinfeld.*"

"I'd like to see Jamie and say we don't want the audience," says Tony Krantz, the co-chairman of Imagine Television, which is producing *Sports Night.*

"With all respect," says Rob Scheidlinger, an executive producer on the show, "it's too easy for them to say no to you." Krantz needs to maintain smooth relations with ABC's executives if he wants to sell them other shows in the future, and he is by nature a mediator. "There's only one man who has the leverage with ABC," Scheidlinger continues, "and that's Aaron."

Sorkin looks uneasy, and lights up another cigarette. A handsome, high-cheekboned thirty-seven-year-old with a mop of dirty-blond hair and rimless glasses, Sorkin is wearing one of his fourteen white Gap Oxford shirts, paired with a narrow tie. This is a look meant to evoke the old-photo insouciance of his idol, the playwright and Algonquin wit George S. Kaufman. "I'd like to say, 'Jamie, you have two choices,' " Sorkin says finally. " 'Put the show on or don't. But if you do, do it our way.' "

"How far are we willing to go on this?" Schlamme asks.

"We're not willing to cancel the show," Krantz says quickly.

"Aren't we?" Scheidlinger asks.

"Well, I think we are," Sorkin says. "I think we have to do this show for thirteen episodes, and then be canceled, if that's what's necessary." There is a silence, and then Sorkin launches into one of his articulate tirades.

"ABC says they want the audience because it opens up the actors' performances, makes them brighter, but they actually just want the two hundred people there on Thursday night so they can tell if it's good—otherwise *they have no idea.* If I'm a creative person, I'm going to write or direct or act, I'm not going to go work as an ABC exec. They do not understand that it's about taking risks, and about taste." Sorkin doesn't necessarily believe this, but it sounds impressive and he's rolling. "And furthermore, the idea that two hundred people from Canoga Park who've just passed through a metal detector are determining what's funny in television is truly scary."

"I just don't get it!" Scheidlinger bursts out. A short, balding man who was formerly Sorkin's agent, he often sits through these meetings in a brown study, and then startles everyone by finishing someone else's half-articulated idea with an apt, gnomic phrase such as "causeless anthropomorphism."

"It's fear," Krantz says coolly—the chief resident diagnosing a puzzling fever for the interns. "Fear is the reason TV is the way it is. It's about the bottom falling out in the ratings, about worrying about looking stupid—it's about playing it safe, about not getting fired for not taking a risk. Do you give in to the fear, and give the audience the past, or a repurposed past, which they're familiar with?"

"What will happen with this audience is that ABC will have control," Schlamme says, his face growing red, "because they can see the effect of what we do on the audience. And they get to keep saying, 'More Jeremy falling' "—a reference to the show's brainy but sometimes bumbling associate producer character—"And 'Make Jeremy bigger, more laughs. More, more, more!' That's not the show I signed on to do." He looks intently at Sorkin.

Sorkin says, "So this, right here, is the struggle for the soul of *Sports Night*." He picks up the phone and calls Tarses's office to make an appointment for the next day. But he's feeling queasy. He fears that Tarses—who regularly pokes fun at the formality of his manners, and who has suffered through a number of his tantrums—doesn't like him. "I'm not good at confrontation," he tells me afterward. "I either blow up or I cave. And threatening to quit seems like an awfully big bat to use on people you're supposed to be collaborating with."

———

There are three rules for creating a hit network television show. Unfortunately, no one knows what they are. Don Ohlmeyer, the president of NBC, West Coast, likes to tell the story of how he watched twenty minutes of the pilot for *E.R.*, then turned to the network's entertainment president, Warren Littlefield, and said, "Either the audience is never leaving, or they're never coming back."

"I didn't know," Ohlmeyer told me blithely when I visited him in his office not long ago. With his yellow cashmere sweaters and loafers worn without socks, his cigarettes two-fingered from an elegant box, the silver-haired Ohlmeyer embodies the Bel Air style, a kind of weary sapience. After thirty-one years in the industry, he concludes, "Hey, if you bat a hundred in television, you're in the Hall of Fame. For a show to be a breakout hit, there has to be some magic that happens with the audience. Nobody knows what that is. *Nobody fucking knows.* But everybody's chasing that magic."

The chase has become exceptionally desperate of late. Twenty years ago, NBC's head programmer, Paul Klein, believed that the only way viewers would not watch a network show was if you startled them somehow. His "least objectionable programming theory" was predicated on the belief that on any given Thursday viewers tuned in at eight P.M. for *CHiPS* and kept watching whatever NBC happened to show until bedtime. The trick was not to disturb their reverie: "Thought, that's tune-out, education, tune-out," Klein wrote. "Melodrama's good, you know, a little tear here and there, a little morality tale. That's good. Positive. That's least objectionable."

At that time, though, NBC, ABC, and CBS attracted 91 percent of the prime-time viewers. Today, with the roaring growth of cable and of the newer networks—Fox, Warner Bros. (the WB), and United Paramount Networks (UPN)—the big three are drawing only 47 percent.

"Historically the business was about 'flow,' " Don Ohlmeyer says, referring to the belief that viewers would seamlessly flow from one show to a similar one in the next time period. It doesn't work that way anymore: he cites network research showing that less than 50 percent of the people who watch *Friends* Thursdays on NBC at eight P.M. are still watching NBC when *E.R.* appears at ten P.M. "Today it's about appointments," Ohlmeyer goes on, meaning that

remote-clicking viewers will only schedule time to watch their favorite shows. All twenty-two prime-time hours have to be appointments, and each half hour has to be an appointment. There is no 'the
audience' anymore.'"

Steven Bochco, who created *Hill Street Blues* and *NYPD Blue,*
says, "I liken the networks to a guy who, as he loses more and more
hair, invents a more and more elaborate comb-over in denial. 'We're
stemming the tide.' 'No one else can do what we can do.' 'We still
reach more people than anyone else.' Yap, yap, yap, yap, yap. In
fact, as any idiot can tell, we're getting our brains beaten out.'"

The traditional broadcasters worry that if they don't figure out
some way of recapturing the audience from such edgier pleasures as
South Park, they'll become known as the county fair of the information age—as the antiquated place you visit twice a year to catch the
Academy Awards and the Super Bowl. Recently, the networks have
begun to ask themselves a novel question: What if we take a stab at
the fresh, the daring, the alternative? Not long ago, NBC's Entertainment president Warren Littlefield gave all his executives granite
stones engraved with a single word: *Risk.*

Two years ago, the imperative to take risks led ABC to hire Jamie
Tarses, then thirty-two, away from NBC, making her the first
woman to head a network entertainment division. The largely male
Hollywood establishment still sifts compulsively through the minutiae of her behavior (which is by turns playful and brusque) looking
for signs of hauteur or simmering sexual tension—motivations it
would never impute to a male executive.

Tarses, for her part, upheld the network's new credo last fall
when Sorkin was pitching *Sports Night* to her. "The greatest thing
about you is that you don't know the rules—we don't want you to
follow the TV handbook," she told him. "TV is about the writer, and
we're executives. Our job is to let you succeed or fail wildly."

—

Traditionally, ABC had done neither. For most of the past decade, it
has been the family network, known for shows like *Growing Pains*

and *Full House*. But last year it fell to third place in ratings among eighteen-to-forty-nine-year-old viewers—for the first time, it lagged behind even the upstart Fox—so throwing away the TV handbook started to sound smart. ABC Entertainment chairman Stu Bloomberg, a shy man with a soul spot and a dot of a beard, told me that the ABC of the future will be defined by distinctive shows like *Sports Night,* and by the network's ubiquitous, bright-yellow we-love-TV ad campaign. "Hopefully, this fall our programming has caught up to the campaign," Bloomberg said. It's a curious idea—trying to program to match the standard of your ads, rather than vice-versa. It's an even more curious one, given that the thrust of TBWA Chiat/Day's campaign is to provoke a blanket nostalgia for the pre-cable world of indiscriminate viewing ("TV, so good, they named a frozen meal after it").

Sports Night, as it happens, came straight out of cable's sensibility. Five years ago, Sorkin was living at the Four Seasons hotel in Beverly Hills, rewriting *The American President* through the night. "I kept the television on for company," Sorkin says, "and it was tuned to ESPN's *Sports Center.* There was this rotating group of anchors that I liked: they knew a lot and didn't suffer foolishness. And I thought, If I worked there, I'd meet my girlfriend and my best friend. I wanted to be part of that family." The subject of sports isn't particularly suited to a TV series, but likable characters who like sports are. "Creating a friendly environment that people want to be part of is TV," Sorkin says. Specifically, it is a TV sitcom: hour-long television shows usually take you on some sort of journey (*The Love Boat*), while half-hour ones encourage you to be happy where you are, with your family (*Roseanne*) or your workplace family (*Cheers*).

Television encourages brief, fierce loyalties. This is why, as the medium has matured, the sitcom has become its most popular form: there are now more than sixty sitcoms in production.

Indeed, in the half century since the first sitcom, *The Goldbergs,* aired in 1949, even middling situation comedy—*Family Ties* or *Married . . . with Children*—has become a mainstay of the entertainment economy, earning hundreds of millions of dollars for the network and similar amounts for its creators when sold into syndication. These shows are mass culture at its most potent and pervasive, and, often, at its schlockiest. But once in a while a show arrives that actually deserves its gigantic audience and helps imprint a cultural moment, be it the seventies political rants of *All in the Family* or the nineties narcissism of *Seinfeld.* Those few we call classics.

Hoping to create such a classic, Aaron Sorkin took his idea to Tony Krantz's Imagine Television, which is half owned by the Walt Disney Company and which serves as a bridge between the "talent" and the networks. Brian Grazer, who is best known for producing such films as *Apollo 13* and *Liar, Liar,* and who is Krantz's cochairman, often seems restless with his role as intermediary, and with television, of which he says "most everything fails and at best it's mediocre." When I had breakfast with Grazer and Krantz last June at the Polo Lounge, Grazer was jittery, his hair sticking up like Alfalfa's. "You're meeting with Jamie?" he asked distractedly. "She'll probably show up topless." Minutes later he blurted out, "Aaron's very intense. He has a brittle quality—at the table read, he scared me! He's like an assault weapon!" He glanced at Krantz, who was radiating his usual brown-eyed, Yogi Bear calm. "Maybe I should backtrack on that," Grazer said.

Krantz said smoothly, "I think what Brian is referencing is that Aaron was totally focused, totally on his game."

When I spoke to Krantz later, he was candid about why he took the show to ABC: Disney owns not only the network (whose license fee of $800,000 per episode of *Sports Night* is much higher than the industry average of $500,000) and Touchstone Television, which is co-producing the show, but also ESPN. So opportunities for cross-promotion abound.

"I'm dreaming aloud here," Krantz said, "but if we prove ourselves, there may be opportunities to promote the show with *ESPN* magazine, at the theme parks, on *Monday Night Football.*"

When I brought up the idea of synergy to Brian Grazer, he mumbled non sequiturs and then laughed uneasily. "I'm just camouflaging what seems so crass—obviously, when it comes to time slots or staying on the air, Disney is going to choose their children over other children," he said.

Krantz's first order of business, though, was to introduce Sorkin to the rarefied ways of sitcom development. "Tony would get out a pen and a legal pad," Sorkin recalls, "and say, 'Okay, tell me about the characters. There'd be a producer, right, a girl? And a boss who's a Lou Grant type? And some interns?' He doesn't do that anymore." Sorkin hates to be prodded, and he inveighs against television's schematizing tendency, in which "characters are defined by career goals and libidos—this is the one who works too hard, this is the horny one, this is the gay guy." Yet he also wanted the show to click. By the time he'd finished conceiving his characters, they included a producer who was a girl, a boss who was a Lou Grant type, and an internlike assistant producer, Jeremy.

More ambitiously, Sorkin planned to challenge many of the rules of sitcom scene writing, rules that even the best sitcoms often follow. The rules run more or less as follows: Shows have an "A" and a subsidiary "B" story (and sometimes a "C" story as well), which are "broken" across three acts or a "teaser" and two acts; scenes should have three laughs to a page; no character can leave a room without saying something funny; and a scene should end with a zinger that sends everyone into the commercial laughing. (For example, two characters ask the boss for a raise, the boss instead yells and storms out, one character says brightly, "Well, that went well.") This is the "button," or "blow," to the scene. Sitcom characters also behave in predictably eccentric ways: they move to new towns and only then decide if they're going to stay; sit around three sides of a dinner table (leaving one side for the camera); are always best friends with the people across the hall; spend every night with their friends in strangely uncrowded bars having strangely audible conversations; refer to sex with bizarre euphemisms ("She really rotated my tires!"); speak expositorily on the phone ("I know you're my mother, and you just want to remind me that my brother, Jonathan, is allergic to cats . . ."); run amok with new responsibilities until they're "drunk with power"; get embroiled in weird misunderstandings and rather than just explaining the confusion, instead break into someone's apartment to replace the message they'd left on the answering machine; never do any actual work; often learn lessons that require a group hug; and never watch TV themselves. (In its first few episodes, *Sports Night* presents characters who continually question their own right to assert power, spend much of the time passionately and intelligently pursuing their jobs, and also watch a fair amount of TV.)

Last Christmas, when Sorkin delivered his rule-bending pilot script about Casey's divorce and gloom, ABC professed delight. Tarses said at the outset, "I'm as excited about *Sports Night* as I've ever been about a show."

The network authorized the making of a twenty-one-minute-and-forty-five-second pilot; production expenses—including the building of the elaborate set—eventually mounted up to more than $1.9 million. With real money now at stake, the network's summons to break the rules and go for "wild success or wild failure" was superseded: a wild failure could cost ABC more than $10 million. So it began to nudge Sorkin toward the rhythms and protocols of television—and toward the eighteen-to-thirty-four-year-old demographic that is the advertisers' favored target.

The importance of the eighteen-to-thirty-four market explains why last year Fox could charge advertisers $200,000 for a thirty-second spot on *King of the Hill,* while CBS, the number one network for people aged fifty and older, could charge only $110,000 for the same ad on its show in the same time slot, *Touched by an Angel*—even though *Touched* had five million more viewers each week. "As the years go by," *King of the Hill* co-creator Greg Daniels says cheerfully, "their audience is dying and ours is getting jobs and spending money."

It also explains the repetitiousness of what we see. "Because everyone is sharing that demo," says Dean Valentine, the president and CEO of UPN, "way too many shows are *Friends* clones about affluent twenty-seven-year-old yuppies who wear black knit shirts, work in a magazine office, and just want to get laid."

Tarses felt that Sorkin's story needed a few tweaks. One of her trademark "notes" on stories is "Could we make the woman's role stronger?" and she suggested that he beef up the part of Dana, the show's producer; he says her "very, very good notes" inspired him to write a crucial scene in which Dana asserts herself. Tarses and her ABC colleagues also wanted Sorkin to take up the hints of a romantic interest between Dana and Casey, the just divorced anchor: like most network executives, she likes story lines about smoldering lust.

ABC wanted James Burrows, a veteran of *Cheers,* to direct the pilot, but Sorkin decided on Tommy Schlamme, in part because of his association with *The Larry Sanders Show.* Schlamme told Sorkin that the time had come to take the half hour, visually, where Steven Bochco had taken the hour with *Hill Street Blues.* In the traditional "four camera" sitcom, filmed before an audience, the cameras are out in front of the stage and the actors face forward from the living room, as if they were in a play. Schlamme wanted to film without an audience, using a "single camera" style in which the cameras can go deep into the set, getting better "angles" and also better "eyes," or close-ups. The single-camera style feels more like a movie. And it usually doesn't have a laugh track.

By television standards, the sitcom laugh track has deep roots. In 1949, the West Coast producers of *The Hank McCune Show,* a series about an inept TV show host, added the first laugh track because they wanted to replicate the feel of shows produced with live audiences in New York City—they wanted *Hank McCune* to feel like television. But laugh tracks quickly became a bass line underneath jokes, and they reached their peculiar apogee in the 1960s, when shows such as *The Munsters* featured metronomic guffaws every six seconds. (After the quiz show scandals of the 1950s, CBS, in a strange attempt to regain the audience's trust, put a disclaimer on its sitcoms declaring that the laughter we were about to hear wasn't real.) In the 1970s, shows such as *All in the Family* tried to distinguish themselves as more "real" by being "taped before a live studio audience." Then, in the 1980s, a number of shows—*The Days and Nights of Molly Dodd, Hooperman,* and *United States,* among others—tried to distinguish themselves as completely real by dispensing with the laughter and the audience altogether. Most were bombs; not one was a hit. Shows without laughs can sound dry and feel weirdly unsettling, though the audience often isn't sure why.

Today, when even game shows are "sweetened" with sounds ranging from the "low, warm chuckle" to the "innuendo laugh," the necessity of the laugh track has become an article of faith among network programmers. Sorkin recalls Stu Bloomberg telling him that *The Wonder Years* was the only one-camera show that ever worked. "I said, 'Stu, you have to allow for the fact that those shows didn't fail because they were single-camera, they failed because they were lousy.' "

The pilot for *Sports Night* was made in April, with a laugh track: the producers buckled simply to get the pilot on the air, and they planned to raise the issue with ABC again. In an unusual compromise, the show was filmed with an audience on one night, but there were also several days of shooting without an audience. Though the episode was unevenly paced and contained some uncertain acting moments, it was a promising piece of work, and in May, ABC announced that *Sports Night* would be on its fall schedule—in a favored time slot, between the network stalwarts *Spin City* and *NYPD Blue*.

By now a pattern had emerged, one familiar to countless previous television writers: The more promising Sorkin's work was, the more the network had at stake; and the more it had at stake, the more inclined it was to favor time-tested formulas over the innovations of a television neophyte like Sorkin. ABC wanted the show to be funnier and the characters to be more clearly sitcom types. To that end, they prevailed upon Sorkin to hire Tim Doyle, previously the head writer for the ABC shows *Ellen* and *Grace Under Fire,* and his two writing partners, all of whom were under contract to Disney. (Two other Disney writers were also pushed Sorkin's way.) "There's a lot of money involved here, and a lot of ambivalence about what Aaron has done, so Disney is looking to cover its ass in every conceivable way," Doyle explains. "They wanted me to be there in case everything turned to shit."

The day before a big laugh-track meeting in June, ABC, as if to ensure Sorkin's compliance, presented him with its audience-research findings. A survey of 288 viewers who had watched the *Sports Night* pilot found that it tested strongly, at a rating of 160 (100 is average), and skewed toward eighteen- to forty-nine-year-olds and, heavily, toward males. But follow-ups with four focus groups in Chicago and Atlanta revealed that viewers would not seek out the show because of the depressing story line, and that Casey was perceived as "whiny and weak." (Touchstone Television's own testing, Rob Scheidlinger says, showed that women found Casey "mopey and morose.") The research department concluded that "viewers need more depth and frequency to the comedy (one-liners were effective to a point) and only want drama used every so often as a tool to give the characters more dimension."

Many classic sitcoms—including *The Dick Van Dyke Show, M*A*S*H, Taxi,* and *Seinfeld*—tested poorly or had a chilly initial response from viewers. Testing rewards the nice, the familiar, not the fresh or ironical. Nonetheless, after staring at ABC's data, Sorkin had a difficult few days. "Everything untraditional was seen as fatally bad," he told me, with his usual passionate hyperbole, "and the gist of the research seemed to be that I should consider myself extremely lucky that ABC had ordered thirteen episodes, and that any further departures from the norm would end my participation on the show."

The other networks were following Sorkin's laugh-track battle with a more than sporting interest. However much the other networks like to see risky ideas succeed (enabling them to follow suit), they prefer to see them fail, because that vindicates the status quo. Don Ohlmeyer, at NBC, told me with a big grin, "I'd love for the show's creators to prevail on the laugh track—it would improve the chances for our show in that slot. Nobody's coming home from work saying, 'Gee, I can't wait to see that new show without the laugh track'— that's just creative caca. So what makes Aaron think he's so right?"

Sorkin and the other producers had naively thought that they'd win because they believed the show was clearly better without laughs. Then came the big June laugh-track summit in Stu Bloomberg's corner office, where it became apparent that the network's position was unyielding. Both Lloyd Braun, the chairman of Disney's Buena Vista Television, and Tony Krantz delivered impassioned speeches suggesting that the network would remain in third place unless it took chances like not having this laugh track, unless—in that fitting phrase—ABC "got out of the box."

"You delivered a pilot with a laugh track, and we bought it," Bloomberg observed. "Now you're trying to pull the rug out."

Tarses brought up *M*A*S*H*, a show whose sensibility Sorkin had said he'd like to emulate, and pointed out that it had a laugh track. Sorkin groused, "Yeah, but Larry Gelbart"—the show's cocreator—"didn't like it very much."

"The show ran for eleven years," Tarses said reasonably. "Who gives a fuck whether he liked it or not?"

An hour after the meeting ended, Sorkin called Bloomberg and Tarses, and apologized: "Is there anything I can do to disabuse you of the notion that I think you're jerks?" They laughed. But the mutual unease remained. Tarses told me, "Everything we say to Aaron has the unspoken sentence in front of it: 'You're extraordinarily good at what you do—we're in awe of your ability.' And then we say, 'But here's what you must do, or here's why what you did sucks.' Our criticism is really just suggestions, and a desire to collaborate. I feel bad because Aaron does view it very personally as criticism, and so he causes himself far more pain."

———

It was a morning in mid-July, and a group of the *Sports Night* producers were sitting in Aaron Sorkin's office scarfing Doritos and peanut M&M's and talking about the prospects for their show. Slouched on chairs and couches were Sorkin, Schlamme, Scheidlinger, and Tim Doyle. Doyle, a hulking man with a salt-and-pepper beard, was dressed in the TV writer's uniform: jeans and an unbuttoned flannel shirt over a T-shirt. This was also the classic male adolescent uniform in 1978, when many current TV writers were watching a lot of TV, which may not be a coincidence.

The topic of the moment was what kind of language you could get away with on television. Everyone was wondering if a piece of innuendo from another writer's script, in which Jeremy refers to someone's takeout Peking duck by saying, "I never eat anything with a face on it," would slip by the network's Standards and Practices department. (Sorkin would say later: "It doesn't matter—it's a bad joke and not the kind of thing we're going to do.") The networks are trying to appeal to the young and hip with controversial words and scenarios while trying not to alienate Middle America or their affiliate owners, many of whom are conservative and religious. Sorkin gets weekly memos from the network's Standards and Practices department telling him, for instance, that the "use of 'hell' and 'damn' is excessive and must be reduced by ½."

"You can now say 'penis,' " Doyle informed the intensely curious men. "You can say, 'Put your penis in your pants.' You can't say, 'Suck my penis.' "

"What about 'playing with his penis'?" Schlamme asked.

"Maybe."

"What did you get away with on *Ellen* that surprised you?" Sorkin asked.

" 'Asshole.' "

Sorkin was outraged. "You got 'asshole,' and we didn't get 'son of a bitch'?"

"I got a couple of 'dyke's, too," Doyle says. "But I still have the Standards and Practices memo saying that Ellen couldn't kiss her girlfriend—that gays should 'express their affection in other ways.' "

Sorkin was even more upset about ABC's proposed ad campaign for the show. The network memo had suggested "testimonial tease spots (male/female POV)"—men declaring that they like the show's sports angle, and women saying they like its relationships. This struck everyone as formulaic. "Doing these ads is hard," Sorkin said, at his usual rat-a-tat-tat pace. "It's the Sunday crossword." He makes a characteristic "um ah ah" sound as his tongue catches up to his spinning brain, like a car double-clutching on a curve. "But you get a feeling from ABC that 'every executive producer says his show is different, and eighty-five percent of our shows fail, so why should we devote all this energy to you when you probably won't be around?' "

Sorkin had proposed a spot in which actors playing ABC admen sit around trying to come up with a campaign for the show. Tarses quickly rejected his idea, but Sorkin and Doyle now traded cheesy lines that the actors might say: "Could we have a sassy black neighbor?" "We have a campaign for a show we're not going to air that you could use." "We've had a lot of success with funny aliens." "We have a relationship with Fran Drescher—you could use her."

"What you'll be appalled by," Doyle said, "is that they'll do a twin shot of Michael J. Fox falling off the bed and getting his head stuck in the toilet"—on *Spin City*—"and Jeremy falling off the chair, and they'll say, 'Two, two, two times the fun, Tuesdays on ABC.' They'll sell the least desirable aspect of the show."

"Because it's easiest to sell," Sorkin said. "What kind of veto power do I have over these ads?"

"You have as much power as you assume," Doyle said serenely, "but it's ABC's show, and they can do what they want."

"You mean it's their air," Sorkin said. "It's not their show."

Doyle cocked his head and smiled slowly. "You don't have any real power, but you have leverage—they can't do the show without you."

This sort of griping is endemic to television writers, yet Sorkin seems to require an enemy even more than most. His friend Warren Beatty, who has high praise for his abilities, says, "I'd like to see Aaron become the head of a network"—he laughs—"so that his vestigial patricidal instincts are quelled. It's nice to put the problem off on someone, but he needs to learn that the creator is his own enemy, that the enemy is fatigue and stupor and cliché." Today Sorkin felt that the enemy was the rule book: "I'm trying to discourage the writers from their sitcom instincts," he told me, after the others had left, "from having all the characters hang out at the local bar. Every writer's script has a 'My God, you're the greatest' tear-welling-up moment about another character and we've got to pull them all out."

Later that morning, the group returned. One of the writers, Paul

Redford, came into Sorkin's office to ask for help with the C story in his script. "You don't have to talk about A story and B story and C story," Sorkin says, blowing cigarette smoke and starting to speechify. "That's a language imposed on us by network people, like 'back story' instead of 'exposition.' It's bullshit. We need to be a bit more magical."

Doyle sang out, "Maybe we can call them 1 story, 2 story, and 3 story."

Afterward, Redford said quietly, "Everyone always says they're going to blow away the rules, but it's a pretty rigid format." Indeed, Sorkin's own *Sports Night* scripts have classic A and B stories. What makes them distinctive is that he doesn't bait for laughs by doing setup lines and jokes as much as by stringing garlands of dialogue in which a phrase wends sinuously throughout. One character in these scenes is typically passionate about his or her agenda, the other is inattentive or just barely hanging in there. In the second episode, entitled "The Apology," the show's senior associate producer, Natalie, huddles with Casey:

NATALIE: I may have certain feelings for Jeremy.
CASEY: Ah.
NATALIE: I think it's possible that I have feelings.
CASEY: Okay.
NATALIE: I think these feelings could interfere with my judgment as far as his work is concerned.
CASEY: I admire your professionalism.
NATALIE: These feelings have been growing inside me, like a rush or a surge of—
CASEY: That's probably a little more than I need to know about the—
NATALIE: Fine.

Often Sorkin's scripts pivot on a scrap of dialogue in a way that suddenly introduces a confrontation, a *cri de coeur.* In this same episode, the other anchor, Dan, is in trouble with the network because *Esquire* has written about his membership in an organization that supports legalizing marijuana. Forced to render some sort of apology on the air, Dan unexpectedly apologizes to his younger brother, Sam. He explains to the viewers that Sam died eleven years ago in a car crash, high on the marijuana he'd seen his brother so often smoke. Haltingly, Dan says, "I'm sorry, Sam. You deserved better in my hands."

ABC had just told Sorkin that it loved the script, and he was now, briefly, jaunty. "It's unusual for half-hour television," he said. "Ordinarily a show about drugs is a 'very special' *Home Improvement*, in which the parents find a roach clip in Timmy's bedroom and give him a talking-to. Still, ABC's response was so amazed. I feel like a guy who goes to a desert island full of natives and pulls out a cigarette lighter and flicks it, and they think I'm a god!"

———

The night before Sorkin was supposed to have his final laugh-track showdown with Jamie Tarses, the producers and stars of ABC's shows had the promotional duty of mingling with ABC executives and television critics from around the country at a cocktail party in the Horseshoe Garden of the Ritz-Carlton in Pasadena. It was a Thursday in mid-July, and a swing band played "Me and Julio Down by the Schoolyard" as half-sozzled critics sought out the Olsen twins beneath clusters of yellow "ABC" balloons. Meanwhile, the producers of *Sports Night* began a series of skirmishes with the network's executives.

Sorkin and Schlamme cornered Carolyn Ginsburg Carlson, ABC's senior vice president of comedy programming, near a bed of ice stacked with glistening shrimp to ask again why she favors a laugh track. Carlson, a petite woman in an elegant white suit, glanced nervously up at the two men standing before her with their arms folded. "For me, the real issue isn't the laugh track but the audience—that's what we want," she said. "The night when we were shooting the pilot with an audience was the first time I saw the actors smile. It makes the actors more *generous*."

Sorkin muttered, "If they argue for an audience, they get a laugh track, too, without having to argue for it, which sounds so silly."

"I'd rather give up the eye candy," Carlson went on, referring to Schlamme's panning and Steadicam shots, "and focus on the relationships."

"I'm not arguing because I want my visual stamp on the show," Schlamme said with a forced smile, "but because this guy"—he tossed a thumb toward Sorkin, who had gone off to brace Stu Bloomberg on the same topic—"wants this show to feel real."

"I believe you can have proscenium shows that feel real," Carlson said, using shorthand for the way four-camera shows resemble a stage play.

"Really?" Schlamme said. "Which ones?"

"Well, you're probably going to laugh at me," she said, uncertainly, "but *Friends*—I believe in those characters. And *Spin City*—that's a world I believe in." Schlamme looked at her, politely incredulous. "Maybe we can try it your way," Carlson finally said. "But we'd only be doing it because we respect you and want you to be happy."

As the party was winding down at ten-thirty P.M., Sorkin took Jamie Tarses aside for an intense conversation in a corner of the hotel's huge green lawn. Afterward, he didn't speak until he and his wife, Julia, were in their black Range Rover driving home. "I got hosed, I got hosed," he said at last as the car crept down the 110 freeway. "You married a half-man, a fraction of a man. We'll film the show without an audience on Wednesdays and Fridays, and also tape it in front of an audience Thursday nights. There will be a laugh track."

"What happened?" Julia asked.

He sighed. "We talked about our relationship, and why it wasn't better, given that we have a similar sensibility and we're working toward the same end. She confided—maybe she says this to all the executive producers—that of all the new shows, *Sports Night* was the one she cared about. But she said that because our show is difficult, it needs a laugh track and an audience, so people will watch it and like it." Julia rubbed his arm gently. "And, in truth," he said after a wrenching pause, "there was part of me that agrees with her. So I told Jamie she'd won, for two reasons. Number one, she's the boss, and number two, I have to believe, based on her success at NBC, that she's got stuff in her head about how to make this work that's more credible than what I've got in my head."

"So it's not your show anymore," Julia said sadly.

"No . . . it's still my show," Sorkin said, slowly, as if he were trying to persuade himself that there was honor in retreat. "I decided to give in so we could win the next battles—about promotion, and about keeping us on the air when we're in ninety-eighth place."

Next morning the *Sports Night* office was downcast. "Aaron's inexperience in television hurt him," Tim Doyle told me. "He had all the leverage, because they couldn't do the show without him. You have to spend that capital, because no one gives you credit down the line. If the show fails, they still blame you."

Scheidlinger and Schlamme sat with Sorkin in his office and did a bleak postmortem. "I couldn't sleep, because I was thinking, What a waste!" Scheidlinger said. "The half hour is sick, they're trying to invite in new talent, to revitalize it, and then they hobble you."

"Jamie's idea is that talent, if allowed to run with abandon, will self-destruct and not be successful," Schlamme said. "But it's two different definitions of success. Ours is, 'We did the show we wanted, artistically.' Hers is, 'We put one hundred episodes on the air and made a lot of money.' "

Sorkin said, in a low voice, almost to himself, "I hope Jamie will respect that I've given in and feel she owes us one."

"Never happen," Schlamme said, looking flushed and wounded. "Last night three people said to me, 'You know, Jamie thinks of *Sports Night* as her baby.' And I was thinking, Oh, no—don't say that. She's a bad mommy."

———

It was five P.M. on a Thursday in August: time for the show's weekly audience taping on Disney's Stage Six. Two hundred people were in the stands, and they were watching the pilot episode on the monitors overhead. This is meant to introduce them to the show; it is also meant to rev them up for hilarity. The audience composition roughly mirrors the show's target audience: it is all white, mostly male, and fairly young.

Josh Malina, who plays Jeremy, the klutzy assistant producer, stands offstage near the crafts table, which is heaped with fruit and pastries. "Laugh, monkeys, laugh," he murmured, touching the pancake makeup on his nose; he could tell from the crowd's gleeful chortles that this was the point in the pilot tape at which Jeremy falls off a chair. Like all the actors, he'd prefer not to have to project his lines to the stands in the middle of two days of pitching them more intimately toward the camera. "I don't know why they come," he said. "All they'll see is an inscrutable play."

After the pilot concluded, the warm-up comic introduced the cast members, and then Tommy Schlamme ordered the actors to their places. The set is huge, complex, and unusually authentic feeling. It has numerous corridors and six different three-sided rooms, including a studio packed with fifty television monitors, which run video feed of sports footage. "And . . . action!" Schlamme said, facing the newsroom, where the first of the episode's fifteen scenes is set: Casey and Isaac, the Lou Grant–like boss played by former *Benson* star Robert Guillaume, are watching a football game, trying to predict what play the Seminoles coach Bobby Bowden will call. Schlamme kept his eyes on a quartet of monitors that showed the feed from cameras A, B, C, and X—and below, the feed when the fifth, handheld Steadicam was used for tracking shots. Schlamme asked for a second take. The audience laughed harder than it had before. On the third take, though, the laughs were desultory. This pattern is predictable: according to John Amodeo, the show's line producer, "the second take always has a bigger laugh—everyone gets it, even the stupid ones. By the third, they're bored with it, the fourth has no laugh at all. So the laugh-track guy's job isn't to make the show funny, it's to do a smooth fade of the audience level, reproducing the natural attack and decay of laughter and applause."

Curiously, none of the people in the stands were looking at the stage in front of them: they're all watching the monitors overhead—

watching television. After scene A is finished, Tony Krantz said to the actors, "Smokin'."

Sorkin and Scheidlinger sat in black director's chairs at the front of the stage, their backs to the action, listening on headphones and watching another quintet of monitors. ABC's Carolyn Ginsburg Carlson and her deputy hovered nearby, and they occasionally whispered to Sorkin: Carlson often wanted the actors to smile more. Peter Krause, the lithe actor who plays Casey, came over to Sorkin to ask for guidance after having given a smirky spin to a line about how his wife used to do up his tuxedo studs. Sorkin doesn't mention smiling: indeed, he'd earlier told Krause, "You were mind-fucked and bitch-slapped with all those notes from the network during the pilot. We'll shield you from notes like 'Smile more.' This is not a high school play." Instead, Sorkin, a former actor, did the line for Krause—"I used to have a wife for that"—giving it a small, bewildered shrug. "Make it real, a little hurt," Sorkin says. As Krause walked back, Sorkin raised his voice and added, "Don't make a meal of it": he hates any wallowing in emotion, mugging. In the next take Krause repeated his sitcom smirk and Sorkin grimaced.

—

Laugh-track battles and their equivalent are fought every day in television studios across Hollywood, and the compromises reached explain why we see what we see. "Programmed dissent" is the network jargon for its contradictory desire: enough edge for the young (the producers winning a point); enough hugs for the rest of us (the network winning a point). "Take a risk" often means "update by 10 percent or so." This January Fox will air another Imagine Television show, *The PJs*, as a midseason replacement. It's a very funny stop-motion foam-puppet show set in a housing project, with Eddie Murphy providing the voice of the project superintendent. In the original four-minute demo tape gunshots fly around, there's a realistic backdrop of filth and gloom, even a character named Crackhead. In the pilot episode of *The PJs*, Crackhead has become Smokey and is ostensibly in recovery. The sets are brighter, and the feel of the show is much cheerier. "Who wants to be in a world of squalor?" asks Peter Roth, the president of Fox TV. "Now the emphasis of the show is on family, relationships, friends. Nobody can afford to disinvite any audience on network television today."

Television is a singular medium because its visionaries routinely look backward. Susanne Daniels, the executive vice president of entertainment at the WB, told me, "We spend a lot of time talking about what's next, and very often it's about what used to be on, isn't now, and should be. One of the reasons we bought *Buffy the Vampire Slayer* was that we had been talking about *Kolchak: The Night Stalker* and how it was scary and funny at the same time, and we wanted to recapture that."

Peter Roth says he regularly pages through television books and circles shows that could be updated. "I circled *Kolchak,*" Roth says proudly, "and then had lunch with Chris Carter, and out of that conversation came *The X-Files*. Television is a derivative medium, and every top ten show has been seen before—the trick is to repackage it and contemporize it to make a modern hit. *E.R.* derived from *Marcus Welby; Ally McBeal* is *The Mary Tyler Moore Show; Seinfeld* is *The Honeymooners; Mad About You* is *I Love Lucy.*" And *Fantasy Island* and *The Love Boat* have returned to the networks twenty years later with even their titles comfortably intact. As the comedian and television host Fred Allen used to say, "Imitation is the sincerest form of television."

Felicity is a beautifully written college drama that arrives on the WB this fall with enormous positive buzz. But J. J. Abrams, *Felicity*'s co-creator, recently discovered television's conservative impulse when he planned a story line about an interracial relationship between a black student and a white proctor. Television content has broadened significantly since the early 1970s, when a CBS researcher told Alan Burns, *The Mary Tyler Moore Show* co-creator, that there were four types of people viewers wouldn't accept as a lead: divorced people, Jews, New Yorkers, and men with mustaches. But interracial relationships are still anathema; the networks believe them even more controversial than gay relationships. So the WB's

Susanne Daniels told Abrams, "Hold off. Do it in the second sea-son—if it's a hit, you can get away with it then." You can get away with a lot on a hit; the network executives' congenital anxiety then plays to the show's advantage, because they become afraid to tamper with a winning formula. Abrams had always enjoyed his dealings with the WB, but now he exploded, suggesting that by not fighting stereotypes, the network was condoning racism. Daniels felt equally outraged and remembers thinking, How dare you; this isn't about civil rights! This is just a television show—it's a business.

—

By the third week of August, with only a month remaining before the show aired, everyone's baseline nervousness had risen: ABC had done "awareness" and "intent to view" tracking all summer to de-termine how many people noticed its ad campaigns and how many planned to watch its shows. *Sports Night* fared poorly on the "awareness" and extremely well on "intent to view"—meaning that few knew about the show, but those who did planned to check it out.

"I would hope that we're going to be patient, if it doesn't come out of the box," Stu Bloomberg told me later that week. When I pointed out that as the network's entertainment chairman the decision was pretty much his, he scowled. "I *want* to be patient," he said. "But you don't want to give *NYPD Blue* a terrible lead-in. You can never look at a show in a vacuum, or else your affiliates will be on you."

I spoke with Jamie Tarses that same day. "So much of what hap-pens to *Sports Night* has to do with *Spin City* and how well it does against NBC's *Just Shoot Me,* which had a hell of a summer," she told me. "That's what September twenty-first brings—an inability to control anything in your life. And the stakes are so high! Half a share point means a difference of millions of dollars. It's so easy to fail, and if you fail one too many times, your reputation is at stake. So decisions get made from fear. Fear from agents, fear from pro-ducers, fear from us. It's hard to fight it. There are too many shows that I developed this year that I'm quite enamored of—and the odds are that many of them will fail." Curled up on her office couch, she smiled gamely. "You have to say to yourself, All the kids are a little bit sick, so you can't be surprised when some of them die."

The sick-ward anxiety was apparent at a Tuesday afternoon "network run-through"—a dress rehearsal of sorts. The show's writers and producers and the top ABC executives have come to the set in Burbank to shuffle around the stage in a herd, following the actors as they play each scene; it was the last chance for the network to weigh in before filming began on Wednesday. In this, the third episode, Casey expresses growing interest in Dana, and Jeremy gets ill after he sees a mother deer shot while he's producing a hunting show. In the last act, Jeremy delivers an impassioned three-page speech against hunting, which ends with his comparing hunting in Indian culture to what they had just done: "It wasn't food and it wasn't shelter and it sure wasn't sports. It was just *mean*."

William H. Macy, the actor, who is the husband of Felicity Huffman—Dana on the show—marveled to his wife, "That's a great speech Josh has. I'm a hunter, and I think it's all liberal horseshit, but it's a great speech."

Huffman, a delightful comic actress, said, "Hey, Stu Bloomberg was laughing earlier." She caught herself: "Isn't it terrible how we rate the scripts on whether the network guys laughed?"

After the run-through, the producers met with ABC's executives in the greenroom on the second floor. ABC's executives sat on one side of the oblong wooden table, with Disney and Imagine executives and *Sports Night* producers ranged around them. Tarses gave the networks' notes: The Jeremy story didn't land with them emotionally, and perhaps the script's three bits of bantery business should be cut to two. Both of these were useful observations, whose gist was that Sorkin left the Jeremy story alone too long in the middle of the show. Sorkin agreed and later he wrote a new scene to fill the gap. The network also wanted the performances to be brighter—a standard Tuesday note. Then Tarses referred to how Jeremy's oration was followed by another from Isaac, the boss. "You're asking a lot of your audience to sit through two long speeches," she said.

Sorkin, who had been monosyllabic, now snapped, "I often ask a lot of my audience."

"That's all we have," Tarses said quietly.

In the silence, Sorkin took a deep breath. "I hate to bring up an unpleasant subject again," he said, "but the laughs aren't working for us." Surprisingly, Sorkin had come to believe that the performances in front of the audience were brighter; he also told me that he found that "there are moments in the show where I now get nervous that there aren't laughs." But he and his colleagues still found the laughter on the rough cut of "The Apology" infuriating, and they had decided to plead one last time to shoot the show their way. Sorkin said the episode sounded like an *I Love Lucy* parody, and added, challengingly, "You may not even want to air it, because it's so bad."

The long-suffering Stu Bloomberg looked upset and said that his team couldn't respond to what they hadn't seen. "Why don't you watch it now?" Sorkin said. So ABC's four executives trooped into a production room while the producers and Tony Krantz huddled in Sorkin's office, and a fraught air settled over the entire suite. "We're holding their feet to the fire," Sorkin said grimly.

Upstairs, Jamie Tarses was in a gloomy daze. "I'd pretty much stopped speaking since they'd said we were going to hate the show," she told me later. "I was traumatized, because this show means so much to me. And we were watching, and midway through the second scene somebody stopped the tape because we were all laughing, and we looked at each other: 'Am I crazy? Isn't this wonderful?' And by the end"—when Dan apologizes to his dead brother, Sam— "I was crying, which is phenomenal. We laughed, we cried, we got everything out of that half hour we could have ever wanted to."

The ABC team walked into Sorkin's office with expressionless faces. "Then," Tarses says, "we had to say, 'I'm really sorry, but we *loved* the show.' " They hadn't found the laugh track jarring, because they laughed exactly when the audience did.

"In my mind," Stu Bloomberg told me, "that strange moment laid the laugh-track question to rest forever."

The episode even had Sorkin's version of the sitcom hug: before upbraiding Dan for his initial posturing about marijuana, Isaac says, "You know that I love you, don't you, Danny?"

Tim Doyle, not unkindly, maintained that the show had joined the sitcom fold. "*Sports Night* has become a surrogate family—Isaac the dad, Dan and Casey the brothers, Dana the sister—and now it sends the same message as *Caroline in the City* and *Suddenly Susan*. Single people living in the city can find all the emotional support they want at work. Because of that sentimental message, *Sports Night* has a chance as popular entertainment."

And so ABC finally became convinced that Sorkin knows what he's doing in television. Three weeks later Thomas Schlamme would say: "The marriage has begun to work—since that day they've never once said, 'Could you make it funnier?' " At the end of August, with ABC's blessing, Sorkin released the five Disney sitcom writers, including Tim Doyle.

—

Later that Tuesday night, over martinis and crab cakes at the Ivy restaurant, Sorkin and Schlamme talked about the long day. They were sitting outside, at the best table in Los Angeles's renowned power spot—and earlier Garry Shandling had stopped by, with the NBC sports reporter Jim Gray, to wish Sorkin well. But now the restaurant had emptied, and only the waiters and valet parkers still stood at their posts. Sorkin said to Schlamme, "You showed me today how the button on a scene works and the complete difference in sensibility when you're writing for a laugh track." The scene in question was a trademark Sorkin run in which the staff debates who wrote the poem that begins "I must go down to the seas again." The names Wordsworth, Byron, and Thoreau are tossed out; Casey insists it's Whitman. Isaac says, "It's not Walt Whitman," and Casey replies, "I'm sayin' I think it's *Slim* Whitman." Dan then tells Dana, with becoming sweetness, "We don't really know who wrote the poem."

Now Sorkin said, "I love Garry Trudeau because *Doonesbury* always has another panel after the joke, and that's the way I like to write. That *is* my writing. But you showed me how we have to cut Dan's line, because people are laughing over it. That single cut makes it a different show."

"They're laughing at the rhythm," Schlamme said. "Half of them don't even know who Slim Whitman is." He picked at a crab cake. "One kind of show honors the joke, one honors the reality. Once you start asking why all these people still live in the same apartment in *Friends,* then TV falls apart."

Sorkin couldn't help revisiting his struggle with the network—the irony of the executives telling him that he's succeeded in spite of himself—one last time, like the dog returning hopefully to his breakfast bowl. "I can't believe ABC loved what they saw—your direction was too good," he said in friendly accusation.

Schlamme shrugged: "Or your writing."

"Boy, they were really enjoying the fact that it was a checkmate," Sorkin said. He lifted his martini glass and drank, then set it down and subsided into an uncharacteristic silence, looking both pleased and somehow bemused. Today ABC had welcomed Aaron Sorkin into the sodality of television, a club whose sole membership criterion is that you must no longer trust your instincts about what the audience wants.

(1998)

THE TWO-BILLION-DOLLAR MAN

It is pitch dark when Ron Bass rises each day, four A.M. at the latest. Dressed unvaryingly in a flannel shirt, corduroys, and Weejuns, he pads through the halls of his home in Brentwood as his wife and two daughters are sleeping upstairs. In his office, he walks to a pine lectern near the window and places a sheaf of yellow foolscap on it, beside which he props "the Book," a fat vinyl binder that holds the DNA for his current screenplay.

Clipped inside the Book are two pencil cases: one filled with newly sharpened No. 2 Sundance pencils, made by Blackfoot Indians, and one to receive those that grow dull during the morning's work. Bass selects a fresh pencil and flips through the binder's thousand pages of "blocking," suggestions made by the six writers who work for him—his "Team"—about incidents or "beats" for each of the script's sixty-odd scenes. Bass mulls over the blocking for his next scene and paces, muttering his characters' lines aloud. If it is a sad scene—a mother with cancer saying good-bye to her children; a man rising at an AA meeting to testify about his love for his alcoholic wife—Bass's murmurings grow husky, and he may pause to weep.

Bass has brown eyes and brown hair and a shaggy graying beard, and with his nervous, bowl-you-over manner he often quivers like a spaniel that has just scented a squirrel. And now he's off! Perhaps today he is dashing through a closing scene in *Mozart and the Whale,* a script that he recently sold to Dreamworks SKG for more than $2 million. It's about a man and a woman who have Asperger's syndrome (a kind of autism) and their crabwise approach to intimacy. Bass has constructed a metaphor to suggest that we are all emotional amputees until love completes us. Let's take a peek:

The bride and groom turn to each other. And the depth of the look. The comfortableness of their silence. Stirs many hearts. The bride draws a breath . . .

ISABELLE: Donald. I have one leg. And so do you. But if we can hold on to each other . . .

And her smile splits the world. All the brighter for its softness.

ISABELLE: . . . I'll teach you to dance.

Somehow, that takes the groom's breath away. He sways a little, lost in the moment. And in her eyes. Bronwin's mother is moved to clap softly, and others pick it up, and little Gracie puts two fingers in her mouth and sends a piercing WHISTLE, which makes everyone LAUGH.
And the tension is gone. But not the magic.

Someday that magic will beam down from two thousand movie screens. But it all begins with the script. At the age of fifty-seven, Bass is the most prolific and commercially successful screenwriter in the world. When *Daily Variety* recently saluted him as its first "billion-dollar screenwriter," his agents at Creative Artists Agency checked the tally and discovered that his movies had actually earned well over $2 billion in theaters alone. Callie Khouri, who wrote *Thelma and Louise*, says, "Ron is to screenwriting what Michael Crichton is to novels—he has the gift for telling big stories to a mass audience in a way they seem to love. And he just doesn't stop." Bass has five television movies to his credit, as well as sixteen feature films that he wrote or co-wrote, including such hits as *Rain Man, Sleeping with the Enemy, Waiting to Exhale, Dangerous Minds, My Best Friend's Wedding, Stepmom,* and *Entrapment. Snow Falling on Cedars* opened at Christmas, and *Passion of Mind,* starring Demi Moore, is due out in May.

Most A-list screenwriters are delighted if they can complete two screenplays a year; Bass typically writes seven. Writers have traditionally been the hapless serfs of Hollywood—"schmucks with Underwoods," as mogul Jack Warner put it. But Bass has cracked the code: he routinely gets a producer's credit for his work, and more of his movies are made every two years than many highly paid screenwriters can claim in a lifetime.

To keep his assembly line humming, Bass works an average of fourteen hours a day, seven days a week. Michael Ovitz, his former agent, told me, "Creativity is usually part discipline and part undiscipline. Ron is all discipline. He basically took the creative process and channeled an intensity into it that is mind-boggling." Al Franken, the writer and actor, stayed in Bass's house a few years ago while the two men were writing *When a Man Loves a Woman,* which starred Andy Garcia and Meg Ryan as a couple confronting the wife's alcoholism. "At three A.M. there'd be this knock on my door," Franken recalls, "and I'd go, 'Ah, fuck.' But I'd get up immediately, because he's such a taskmaster. If I went to the bathroom, he'd say, 'Think while you're in there, and have a good line when you get back.' " To his many collaborators, Bass is Sergeant Screenplay: *On the double, go, go, go! You weasel, you call yourself a writer? Drop and give me twenty pages!*

Four or five projects constantly demand Bass's attention, particularly now that he is in the middle of a three-year deal with Sony, which pays him upward of $10 million a year to write only for that studio and to consult on its troubled scripts. John Calley, the chairman of Sony Pictures Entertainment, told me, "Ron is a combination artist and air-traffic controller, saying, 'I can get you into Kennedy, but only between nine-fifteen and nine-eighteen.' "

When Bass and I met at his Cape Cod–style house, it was at mutually inconvenient times—Sunday morning at seven-thirty was a regular compromise. We would sit in the living room in armchairs slipcovered in pale brown linen as the first light spilled through the bay window, and Bass would watch as I sleepily picked at a catered platter of bagels and fruit. Like a boa constrictor, he eats infrequently, usually only at dinnertime. Fear and desire, he says, are all the fuel he needs.

Fear is a big engine for Bass. Although he has homes in Brentwood, in the Napa Valley, and on Central Park West; although he buys his suits at Wilkes Bashford in San Francisco and regularly flies first class to Paris, he worries that it could all vanish at any moment. With unexpected shyness, he told me, "I always feel that someday they're going to find out that I'm just a little kid in an adult suit, and they're going to put me in my room."

So Bass is obsessive about maintaining control, and he is careful never to disappoint. "I began with certain business ideas from my experience as an entertainment lawyer," he said, referring to his previous career of seventeen years. "The powerlessness of the screenwriter is what makes him unhappy, and that powerlessness comes from the fact that he is always waiting for everybody else. But the only person who *doesn't* have to wait is the writer—you can always write. My technique for success was I'd spend six hours a day writing and eight hours preparing the next story, or two stories. People who finish a script and have this huge sense of giving birth and say, 'I'll go to Hawaii'—it's amazing how many people do that.

"I had a ritual," he continued, "where I would write 'Fade to black. Roll in credits' and close that notebook and immediately pick up the notebook for the next movie, write 'Interior. Raymond's Room. Night' or whatever, and make myself start writing the first scene. It all continues: comedy, drama, buddy film, caper—it's all one story, really, the story of who we are and how we relate and how we get it wrong."

Bass's Team helps him sidestep many of the screenwriter's other occupational hazards. Like all writers, he always hated getting notes from studio "D girls," or development underlings, who had taken Robert McKee's famous "Story" class on the basics of screenwriting and would simply repeat its jargon: "Could we make the protagonist more proactive?" "We need the inciting incident higher in the arc."

Bass recalls, "They'd hit you with this eight-page memo and see what happened. It's called 'throwing the meat under the door.' "

Five years ago, feeling the need for more control, and wanting to be even more productive, Bass hired a woman named Jane Rusconi as a sort of in-house D girl. The other five members of the Team were brought in one by one as Bass's workload increased. Three of them are upbeat young women—they're called "the Ronettes" by some of Bass's friends—who had worked in the entertainment and publishing industries. One is highly efficient, one is shy and graceful, and one is the class clown. (Another Team member, the youngest, was killed last fall in an accident.) The other two members are Bass's younger sister, Diane, a psychiatric social worker who advises him on family dynamics and autism, and David Field, a soulful man who was once an executive at United Artists.

In their enthusiasm for Bass and his Stakhanovite regimen, the Team is like one of those scruffy gangs in the movies that battle impossible odds: they are the Magnificent Six, the Dirty Half-Dozen, the Bass News Bears. The younger women work seven days a week, from their homes, and are on call should Bass phone them early on a Sunday morning to brainstorm ideas for his current script. Their most basic work is research: get me the perfect wedding poem; get me the names of all the machinery in play during a bypass operation; get me trivia about the 1927 New York Yankees.

Then comes a two- or three-day outlining marathon in Bass's living room, with the Team poised on armchairs, eating catered sandwiches, as Bass paces hungrily, saying, "The first scene is this, the second . . . ," performing dialogue in a white heat, speaking as the characters, dealing with the Team's objections as if in a dream, unable to remember later who said what.

The next day, Bass and the Team page-budget each of the script's sixty-odd scenes, debating whether a given scene requires three and a half pages or can be dispatched in three. Then everyone goes home and sends Bass a series of faxes on the blocking for each scene, containing ideas, pratfalls, bits of business, "beats," or "turns." He expects specifics: "If someone says, 'Then this gay guy comes out and makes this really swishy, biting comment'—that's assigning me to do all the work. I mean, any idea what that comment might be?" After he completes a scene and his personal assistant types it, she faxes it to everyone, and they call or fax Bass—and one another—with their responses.

"My guess is that if I wrote six scripts a year before, with the Team I write seven," Bass says. "At two million dollars, that extra script brings in more money than my payroll costs, so it all makes economic sense. But the huge advantage is in the quality." As a rule, if three Team members don't understand a line or a character's motivation, it gets fixed. Bass says, "Even an awful, inarticulate suggestion will make me think, Gee, I didn't realize George sounds antiabortion, or, She really *should* have known he was fooling around, and I'm going to change scenes fourteen to eighteen to have her be aware of that, as a secret. Every scene, every word, is more polished now."

Bass's setup is not just a writers' workshop but an independent production house, named Predawn Productions, with Bass himself as the product. The presence of the Team allows him to assign novels to be "covered" as possible stories for adaptation, allows him to hop from one fully prepared project to another, to sail in and give notes on other Sony projects—even as he receives fewer outside notes himself. Before, he proposed; now, he can dispose.

—

Because of his productivity and his clout, Bass provokes enormous envy in the screenwriting community. Bass's friend Jerry Zucker, who co-produced *My Best Friend's Wedding,* says, "You're on this pump cart, and you see someone zooming by on the next track with a locomotive, and you're bound to be bitter." There is a widespread assumption in Hollywood that Bass's Team writes some of his scripts for him outright, with Bass simply signing his name and collecting the fee. "Everyone knows that Ron has these development mice write his movies for him," one prominent screenwriter told me. Babaloo Mandel, who, with his partner, Lowell Ganz, has written numerous hit comedies, including *City Slickers* and *A League of Their Own,* describes his vision of the Bass system: "Picture a lot of Asians wearing coveralls tied to typewriters, and Bass shouting, 'Where's that scene!' or pointing to the different scripts: 'No! No! Yes! Yes! Brilliant! Now, on to the phony Louis Vuitton bags!' "

Bass is frustrated by these perceptions. "*I don't cheat,*" he says fiercely. "As much as I adore the girls, they can't do what I do. If they could write a script that would sell for two million dollars, I don't think they'd be working for me." After talking extensively with Bass and with the members of his Team, and reading many of his scripts and drafts, I am satisfied that the rumor is false. The Team suggests reams of jokes and plot points and "temp" dialogue that he may sometimes incorporate, but Bass does the actual writing alone, in longhand, with his special pencils.

The legend of Bass's script factory will be hard to eradicate, though, because his system both challenges and reinforces certain core screenwriting myths. First, writers are supposed to be solitary and weak. At Columbia, during the thirties, the studio's founder, Harry Cohn, would invite a new writer to lunch in the executive dining room and seat him, with elaborate ceremony, in a special chair—which promptly collapsed as everyone roared with laughter. "It's a *Story of O* scenario," says Stephen Schiff, who wrote the screenplay for *The Deep End of the Ocean* and for the recent *Lolita.* "The writer is the most wooed person in Hollywood—then, as soon as the story is extracted from him, he's lashed to a post and beaten senseless." So when producers see Bass arrive for meetings with a woman who carries a laptop to take notes, they feel obscurely threatened. A writer with six assistants seems as strange as a hermit with six butlers.

The idea of a "screenplay factory," however, is not entirely new. In the thirties and forties, Ben Hecht, who used an Oscar as a doorstop, had a stable of junior writers who turned his treatments into scripts, and in the fifties the Oscar-winner Philip Yordan hired at least five surrogate writers. The practice continues today. Lowell Ganz, of Ganz and Mandel, says, "We don't farm stuff out—if it's going to be crap, we'd like it to be our crap—but people say everyone does it."

Dennis Klein, a screenwriter who did aboveboard script doctoring on *Cocoon* and *Look Who's Talking,* says he has worked as an unofficial ghostwriter—that is, secretly contracted himself to the screenwriter—at least a dozen times, including a stint on a film that is one of the top ten moneymakers of all time. "I come in when the writer of record is burned out, blocked, or confused," Klein told me. "But the writer can't tell that to the studio—for the same reason that if you're wandering around lost in the desert, you don't tie a piece of fried chicken to your head." It is fitting that a writing community that is often burned out, blocked, or confused should project its shame about ghostwriting onto Ron Bass, who is never burned out, blocked, or confused.

But the chief reason the factory rumor will endure is that no one who matters really cares who writes Bass's scripts, as long as they're good. The movie industry is a business of results. "I suppose rough carpentry is being done by Ron's colleagues, that he then rewrites," Sony's John Calley says. "The astonishing amount of output suggests that he can't do it all himself. He's responsible for quality control and management, and that's what we're buying. If a director is really his cameraman and his editor, if they're the only reason he's great—well, who cares? As long as the movies work out."

———

Why do Ron Bass scripts command $2 million? Because they work. After at least five other writers had tackled the story, it was Bass's draft of *Stepmom* that introduced the crucial third-act conflict — a battle between the cancer-ridden mother and the father's fiancée over how the daughter should deal with her churlish ex-boyfriend. Bass's draft persuaded Julia Roberts and Susan Sarandon to commit to the film, making it a "go." Similarly, John Calley told me, "When Steven Spielberg expressed interest in *Memoirs of a Geisha,* our ability to make Ron available basically locked Steven in, because there was a very short list of writers he would work with. Getting *Memoirs* with Spielberg—that alone practically justifies the money we're paying Ron."

Bass's name is bankable: it reassures actors and directors and makes him their "comfort guy." He has an intuitive sense for what a mass audience will want to see. The playwright Moss Hart called this kind of gift "the Woolworth's touch." Like the Midas touch, it can be a mixed blessing. "The studios that hire Ron Bass hire him to deliver hundred-million-dollar movies," says Bass's attorney, Alan Wertheimer. "That's where the bar is set." Bass lives and dies by the box office numbers on opening Friday. "If *Entrapment* does only two million and it cost seventy," he says, "you want to jump off a bridge." (The movie actually did quite well.)

Bass is that key figure in any successful creative system: the 80 percent man. By applying a *Mir* cosmonaut's ingenuity, a televangelist's empathy for his audience's dreams, and a coal miner's capacity for backbreaking labor, Bass can take a film 80 percent of the way to excellence. But unless someone, usually the director or the actors, is inspired to add the final 20 percent, the film will probably become one of those airplane movies you half watch without renting the headset. (Often, that "addition" is actually a subtraction, a roughing up of Bass's crisp geometries.) In *My Best Friend's Wedding* many of the funniest lines and scenes—that crucial 20 percent—were the work of the director, P. J. Hogan, and Rupert Everett, who played Julia Roberts's gay friend George. Bass objected to Hogan's insertion of a sing-along scene, in which the characters suddenly start crooning "I Say a Little Prayer" and waving giant lobster-claw oven mitts in a crowded restaurant. He worried that it would stop the movie and break the "reality cover"; instead, it was the film's goofy highlight.

Bass is known for his way with structure. "Some writers can give you dialogue," Michael Ovitz told me. "Some can give you characters, some can give you structure, and very few can give you all three. Ron can give you structure." Bass's dialogue is skillful enough, actually, but a viable structure is what galvanizes producers and directors and propels a movie into production. The repartee, the characters' back stories, even the vision, can always be fixed later by other writers.

He can "crack" almost any story into the conventional, Aristotelian three acts, with a constant ratcheting up of the action and the stakes, so that expectations are raised (first act), confounded (second act), and then resolved in a mildly surprising way (third act). Arcs are completed, journeys are rewarded, and there is almost never an unjustified moment, a scene that unfolds for its own sake.

Bass's stories are linear, and what's at stake is explicit. In the first three minutes of *My Best Friend's Wedding,* the Julia Roberts character talks about her best friend, Michael: "We've seen each other through everything—losing jobs, losing parents, losing lovers. We've traveled all over. Best times of my life." Then she gets on the phone with Michael, who tells her he's about to be married and says, "I'm scared. I need you. If you can't come and hold my hand, I'll never get through this." Cut to Roberts heading to the airport, frantically explaining, "I've got exactly four days to break up a wedding, steal the bride's fella—and I haven't one clue how to do it." What follows is a tour de force of plotting, as Bass toys with our expectations of whether Roberts will get the guy.

Studio executives love Bass because his scripts speak directly to them. In *Mozart and the Whale,* Bass's stage directions help readers visualize "Donald trying to make the bed. Whatever he pulls, nothing stays even. Trust me. It's funny." Bass uses rhetorical snippets and quirky punctuation in his asides ("Oh." Or "A beat." Or "I'll. Just. Bet"), both to slow the pace of the dialogue and to suggest a scene's desired impact. "Ron is very skillful at showing you what you're going to be seeing *and* feeling," says Gareth Wigan, the co-vice chairman of Columbia TriStar Motion Picture Group. "Movie scripts are usually likened to blueprints, but most people need a model to imagine a house. Ron's scripts provide both the blueprint and the model."

Bass, however, values his architectonic skills less than his ability to go "soft," to give a film "heart." There is a screenwriter's term called "petting the dog": to show that a character is a good fellow, you have him pet a dog. Bass's characters live at the petting zoo. His scripts are necklaces of pearly moments: fathomless whispers, last breaths being taken, kisses that last a lifetime, soft-spoken insights, heroic speeches, dizzying smiles, manly handclasps, and hugs of warm and enfolding sisterhood. "Ron has a high-concept commercial gift for involving you in a communal moviegoing experience," says Hannah Shakespeare, a member of his Team. Less optimistically, Kenneth Turan, the film critic of the *Los Angeles Times,* once wrote that Bass "seems to have never met a tear he didn't like." Bass was stung by the line, but he refuses to repent. "If I cry writing a scene, you're going to cry," he says. "My cry meter is acute."

Bass's style owes a debt to Spielberg, and one of his crucial lessons in audience gratification came from the master himself, on the 1988 film *Rain Man.* Bass had written Dustin Hoffman's character, Raymond, as a sweet retarded man, ignoring Hoffman's suggestion that he be autistic. Spielberg—who at that point was planning to direct the film—sat Bass down and, as Bass recalls, gently said, "Dustin was right and you were wrong. Want to know why?"

"Sure," Bass said.

"This is a love story between two brothers. What's the most important thing in any love story? It's the obstacle—what is it that keeps these two people who are supposed to be in love from being in love until the end?"

"Right . . . ," Bass said cautiously.

"If the guy is retarded and runs around holding somebody's hand, what's the obstacle? Just that Tom Cruise is a hard case? You know

Tom's going to soften, and you can see the end of the movie coming at you down Fifth Avenue. But if the guy's an autistic, an incredible pain in the ass, he hates people—you've got a difficult love story."

"Yeah, right!" Bass thought for a minute. "But maybe it's too much of an obstacle—maybe the audience won't love this guy."

"Ah, it's all in the casting," Spielberg said. "Dustin can play it completely legit, totally autistic. He doesn't have to cheat, and the more obnoxious he is, the more you're going to love him. We solved it in the casting."

In a Bass script, even more than in a Spielberg movie, the love is always on the page. "I'm not much of a less-is-more guy," Bass says. "All the adulation that's paid to minimalism is frequently because people are embarrassed by big emotion. It's a conceit in art: show it, don't say it. It's *so* much more exquisite if you don't quite *do* it. But there are moments that need to be as big and juicy and on the nose as they can be."

Bass reveals his characters' inner lives in what amounts to a group-therapy dynamic—his movies are full of the lingo of self-help. His characters always gain the insight and muster the courage to voice the passionate avowals and confessions we wish our friends and lovers would make to us. These final-act turns revolve upon what Bass calls "a self-esteem point" and a "point-of-view point." A self-esteem point occurs when someone takes responsibility for himself, discovers the self-loathing that has been making a relationship dysfunctional. "In *My Best Friend's Wedding,* when Julia Roberts has to get on her knees and say to Dermot Mulroney, 'I'm pond scum,' that's the most important scene in the movie, because she genuinely seeks forgiveness and wants to change," Bass says.

A point-of-view point occurs when a character can step out of himself, gaze into another person's eyes, and know how that person feels. In Bass's original draft of *Snow Falling on Cedars,* his adaptation of David Guterson's novel about a murder trial in the Pacific Northwest, Carl and Kabuo, who have been fighting over the rights to seven acres of land, come to a rapprochement by discussing their separate experiences in the Second World War:

> KABUO: I killed men who looked just like you, pig-fed German bastards. And their blood don't wash off so easy. . . . So don't talk to me about Japs, you big Nazi son of a bitch.

> Carl laughs. And Kabuo chuckles, right along with him. Having kept his poker face the longer.

> CARL: I am a bastard. I'm a big Hun Nazi son of a bitch. And I still got your bamboo fishing rod.

> . . . The hands grip. And they hold. And the length of this clasp, and the straightness of their gaze, and the silence of the moment. Wash years away.

None of this made it into the finished film, but it is a style of jocular poignancy that we recognize from AT&T commercials and "Up Close and Personal" sports profiles and after-school specials and Norman Rockwell oils: love alone is never enough, but love and understanding, dished up with a sprinkling of humor, win every time. It is this message that makes a Bass script so familiar, so cheering, so like a cup of cocoa.

In his rejected draft of *The Bridges of Madison County,* Bass notably departed from Robert James Waller's novel. He had the adulterous lovers, played by Meryl Streep and Clint Eastwood, reunite after her husband's death. "I wrote a really lovely scene where her husband is dying, about how much she really did love him, and he sort of knew there'd been this affair, and he was grateful to her for sticking by him," Bass says. "Then, two or three years later, she gets off a train in Kerala, India, a rickety little depot, and there her lover is." He struggles to get his voice under control: "I'm crying even as I'm telling it to you. They are both many years older, they walk slowly together and lift their hands to just touch each other, and you fade out." His eyes are red. "It's very on the nose, my style. But why not? Why should we make a story that says that love can't be, that dreams can't come true, and that loyalty and integrity, which she had, can't be rewarded?"

—

"I love the fact that I'm scared every morning," Bass said one day last year. He was sitting beneath an awning twined with red bougainvillea close by his pool, which is encircled by four groups of cast-iron tables and chairs. Some mornings, he works here, shifting from table to table to track the light, like the shadow of a sundial. "Fear is the most valuable ally I've got. It stands between me and going downhill."

He lowered his voice. "It began with being bedridden as a kid. Not being normal has no upside to a kid—it means *inferior.*" Bass grew up in Los Angeles near Third and Fairfax, a half block from the Writers Guild; he was an invalid from age three to age seven, and he remained in bed much of the time until he was eleven. His high fevers, nausea, respiratory problems, and stomach pains were never satisfactorily diagnosed, but doctors at the Mayo Clinic said that he was the youngest ulcer victim they had ever seen.

"I know there was a lot of pain, but I've forgotten it, mostly," Bass said. "And I actually remember the time in bed fondly." Because he was rarely able to sleep at night, he'd put his ear to the radio or read instead, tearing through Dostoyevsky and Faulkner at an age when most children are tackling *The Chronicles of Narnia.* "What I remember is the comfort and security of being alone with my imagination, and how it raced from these books, which had me in awe—I knew I could never write something as great as *The Idiot.*"

A close friend of Bass's told me, "I think his Rosebud is the time in bed. He was so precocious that he was treated as a genius by his parents, but he needed to be loved. So I think he just shut down, psychosomatically, just said no. And now he's surrounded himself with this Team, so he can get the same attention. Just as in his movies he's accused of being manipulative, of wanting that love. It eases the sadness in him."

Bass's writing career started early, and then stopped dead. As a freshman at UCLA, he showed his novel *Voleur* to his English teacher, whom he adored. "She said, 'Oh, Ronnie, you have such talent,' " Bass recalls. "But she also said it wouldn't get published— I wasn't really good, in other words, just the best in freshman English. So I went home and burned the novel in a metal bowl. It was very dramatic and self-pitying." Then Bass took the advice of his father—who quit college during the Depression and became an automobile-seat-cover entrepreneur—and turned decidedly practical.

After graduating from Harvard Law School, Bass made the choice to go into entertainment law, "so I could be close to the people I wasn't good enough to be one of," and soon emerged as a brilliant, relentless negotiator at a leading Los Angeles firm. But his marriage, to Gail Weinstein, was falling apart, and by 1976 it was over. Bass says, "When Gail left, I thought I was never going to love again, that my life was broken. I had spent a lot of my childhood alone, and I didn't want to be alone."

Then things began to change. Bass went into therapy, four times a week, and fell in love with Christine Steinmann, who would become his second wife. He turned to *Voleur* again, and it was published by Jove, in 1978, as *The Perfect Thief*. He followed that up with two spy novels, having discovered that genre fiction sold better. His third book was optioned by a well-known producer, Jonathan Sanger, and Bass asked to write the screenplay. *Code Name: Emerald,* which starred Ed Harris and Max von Sydow, went straight to video. "It was about a German American under cover in Paris on D Day, but really it was about *people,*" Bass says. "They, of course, made it a World War Two movie. I heard it was rewritten by seven other writers. Seven. How can you be a lawyer for seventeen years in the movie business and see a thousand writers get screwed, and then you're *shocked* when it happens to you?"

In 1984, after writing screenplays at night for two years, Bass finally quit his day job when Fox signed him to write two scripts at $125,000 each. They were never produced, but soon afterward Bass's *Black Widow,* about a female serial killer, came out, and then *Gardens of Stone,* concerning life in the home guard during the Vietnam War. Suddenly he was a middle-aged golden boy who had ideas for everyone in town. Early on, he set up a meeting with Gary Lucchesi, an executive at TriStar.

"So tell me your pitch," Lucchesi said.

"I've got seventeen pitches," Bass replied.

"Um, well, tell me your favorite."

"They're all my favorites!"

Bass developed an innovative system whereby he would make "blind" deals with studios to write a screenplay, about a subject to be mutually agreed on, in a narrow time slot as much as two years in the future. He would promise, "I'll turn it in next July 20," and it would arrive to the day.

He became known as someone who loved collaboration, particularly with those above him on the food chain. "Ron's available to a good idea," Andy Garcia told me. "He embraces the actors, he's in the trenches with you." Contrarily, and particularly to those below him on the food chain, he developed a reputation as an enormous pain in the neck. One of his former agents calls him "this anal guy who goes off, becomes a wild diva in lawyer's clothing: 'I just got notes from So-and-so,' he'd say, 'and I can't *believe . . .*' " Another agent shudders as he recalls Bass berating him so fiercely over the car phone about a botched screen credit that "I had to pull over because I thought I was going to throw up."

The producer Jerry Bruckheimer, who worked with Bass on *Dangerous Minds* and *Swing Vote,* a television movie starring Andy Garcia, says, "Ron is very argumentative on every single point, fighting tooth and nail and explaining why a change in the first act will destroy two beats in the third act. He'll say, 'I'll do it, but it'll ruin the movie.' The same emotion he puts into pulling heartstrings he uses to become the litigator for these strong women he's written, to defend their place in these women's weepies. He can reduce studio executives to tears." One way or another, Bass leaves people crying.

—

Most afternoons, Bass can be found by the pool in front of Jane Rusconi's ranch house, in Sullivan Canyon. Rusconi has three dogs and boards five horses, and in this setting Bass seems almost outdoorsy—he carries a walking stick as he paces around, writing. Rusconi, a thirtyish woman in the Meryl Streep mold, remains first among equals on the Team; she and Bass often write TV movie scripts together, and he has his own phone line at her house.

One recent afternoon at Rusconi's house, she came out with a plate of chocolate-chip cookies for Bass. He grinned, then declined: "As you know, I'm on a diet."

"You need them," she said. He took a cookie. Sometimes she can even convince him to have a bit of lunch. They have an appealing friendship: when she drives them back from meetings, he will nod off in the middle of a sentence, one of his notorious sleep-deprived blackouts. Rusconi will nudge him: "You were asleep."

"I was not!"

"You were snoring."

After Rusconi herded the dogs indoors, Bass and I started talking about how his colleagues view his system. I mentioned that among other screenwriters there is a feeling that he and his Team fit in too neatly at Sony and that by becoming what Bass himself proudly calls "a quasi–studio executive and loyalist," he has deserted his peers.

I read Bass an observation made by Robin Swicord, the screenwriter of *Little Women:* "Ron has applied the model of the law office to the for-hire writer at a time when everything in the film business has become corporatized. Ron's model is high-volume—he can turn out many more screenplays than most of us can. He can fit the bill in terms of what the market is asking for. The studios aren't looking for a vision—they're looking for product."

There was a pause. "Oh, that's a shame," Bass said softly. "It's sad when people who you like and respect don't respect you. 'Product,' like we're stamping out sausage? It really does hurt my feelings, because when somebody says your work is just product, that means *you're* just product." He looked crushed.

I no longer had the heart to ask him for his reaction to a similar remark made by a member of his Team, who told me, unprompted, "I keep thinking that Ron's three-act structure is like sausage casing, and our job is to push the grist of the research through it, to find ideas, beats, spices to put in there."

Bass recovered countenance, but for the next few days he kept making pointed references to "product" and to being "on the nose," muttering, "Well, *Robin* might not think much of this idea I had, but . . ." Being liked is important to Bass, and he reveals this every time he tips a bellboy $20. When he wrote *Failure to Communicate* with Rusconi, in 1994, John Calley hated their take on a James Bond–like action adventure, and killed the project. "I was in a funk for months," Bass said. Over Calley's protests, he returned the studio's money, as he has done several times when he feels he has failed. He told me, "If Amy Pascal"—a Columbia executive—"doesn't like it, or Julia Roberts doesn't like it, even if strangers don't like it, boy, do I feel like a dog. I can't work harder than I do, and I can't write better than I write, so when they say, 'This is bad,' I just die. Because it means: 'You have an ugly baby.' "

Bass is passionate about his work, but he's most passionate about making it work. The screenwriter Joe Eszterhas has written that Bass is too complaisant, too eager to go along with what the studio wants: "How can you believe in any of your ideas if you are pitching eight of them?"

Bass sees this issue quite differently, believing that a writer who insists on telling a particular story at a particular time isn't a writer at all. "He's really a philosopher," Bass says. "The whole 'I don't want to be a whore, I want to be true to my own vision' yada yada—that's bullshit. That's the debate I went through when I was a beginner, and it made me very ineffective. We're in a collaborative medium, and the screenwriter's job is to find the change that everyone can agree on. You want your original vision? Go home and write down your thoughts and publish them as a novel, or just look at the pages on weekends and feel good about yourself."

Bass has even learned to welcome the public's "notes." "I started out, like every other writer, hating previews," he said. " 'You're going to let three hundred clowns in a mall in Woodland Hills tell us what to do?' Boy, was I wrong. You can preview a movie in ten places and the scores will be the same. And, by definition, *they're not wrong.* You sit with the director and people who are saying, 'Well, they're dolts, and isn't the film for us?' And the answer is no, the audience aren't dolts, and no, we didn't make the film for us—that's not what somebody spent eighty million dollars on."

At previews, viewers rate a picture as excellent, very good, good, fair, and poor, and the combined percentage of excellents and very goods, known as "the top two boxes," is tallied on a hundred-point scale. The resulting number carries considerable weight. Bass says, "If you have a forty-six-second walk-up where someone's getting out of a cab and ringing a doorbell, the director will have all these reasons why these beauty shots are artistic. If the picture is scoring in the eighties, then the scene is giving the picture 'air,' or room to breathe. But if the movie is in the sixties—and if it is, I'm scared—the scene is what we call 'shoe leather,' and it's got to go."

Preview audiences for *My Best Friend's Wedding* felt that Julia Roberts's character hadn't atoned for trying to steal Cameron Diaz's fiancé. "Previously, when Julia went to find Cameron in the bathroom, she made up some story about having kissed him—she was lying," Jerry Zucker, the film's co-producer, says. "We reshot it so she says to Cameron, 'He doesn't love me, he loves you.' She has tears in her eyes, it's hard for her—the audience buys it."

The test audience also hated that Julia Roberts ended up at the wedding in the arms of a brand-new love interest—people wanted to see more of Rupert Everett as her gay friend George. "Ron did a great repair job," John Calley says. (Bass rewrote the ending so that Everett arrives as a surprise and Roberts dances with him.) "The audience told us that the relationship between Rupert and Julia was what mattered. They told us not to worry about setting her up, because they weren't worried." Clearly, Julia Roberts—Julia Roberts, after all—was eventually going to be able to find love with a heterosexual man.

In Hollywood, the audience ends up as the ultimate studio boss. Bass argues that "it's not that there's good stuff, which never sells any tickets because it's so good, and then there's commercial stuff, which panders to everybody's lowbrow taste, and that's where you make money. Usually, something is successful because people like the thing that is good about it. Of course, *Gods and Monsters* will never sell as many tickets as *Armageddon*. Those are different markets. Within each market, though, everybody wants quality."

But quality in the blockbuster market, where Bass usually works, is often gauged by a film's profits. In that market, idiosyncrasy of vision is not encouraged. The very qualities that help Bass to get his movies made—his reputation for providing a structure that others can play around with, his eagerness to please—often conspire to defeat his ultimate hopes. In *Stepmom,* for instance, Bass's themes were interpreted very broadly by the director, Christopher Columbus. Bass admits that "some of my humor is cheesy and cornball, reaching out to be popular," and that "the ending is a ten-handkerchief affair, though I think it earned that." ("Okay," he adds, "it's not Shakespeare," and, "Okay, so don't give us an Academy Award.") But he still believes that some of his self-esteem-affirming vision shines through.

John Calley waves away the very idea that a screenwriter could impress his voice and vision upon the public. "Good scripts resemble one another, and not even the Writers Guild can distinguish one style from another," he says, drinking beef tea in his huge office and gazing out benignly at his private sun porch. "Everybody is rewritten by everybody so it flows and is intelligent. It's just not a literary medium—it's a suggestion of a visual medium, and as such wildly inadequate." Studio executives approach mainstream movies as they would a stew, with a battery of cooks constantly tasting from the pot as the refrigerator is emptied of leftovers. After the *Stepmom* pre-view, Calley told Bass, "Great film. We didn't even need the cancer."

—

"The Ron Bass story is wonderfully instructive," says screenwriter Dennis Klein, "because it reveals the thudding dead-endedness of the job of screenwriter—a eunuch who delivers Cokes and pizza to the lush villa of the actual moviemakers, whose orgy he glimpses through billowing curtains."

It turns out that even Ron Bass, the two-billion-dollar man, has to suffer the routine indignities of the screenwriter. Last spring, Bass finished up *The System* as a buddy film for Will Smith, but Smith told him the characters seemed too smart, and the project was put on hold. Bass then turned to *Bad Boys 2,* a sequel to the Martin Lawrence cop caper, and suddenly, he told me worriedly, "here's Martin in the hospital with his accident, or illness, or whatever we're calling it." (The erratic star had gone into a three-day coma after jogging while wearing heavy clothing.) *Passion of Mind,* from a Bass idea dear to his heart, was supposed to open last fall, but its release kept being delayed. "Paramount Classics is waiting for Demi Moore to be able to publicize the movie," Bass said gloomily. "She's the star, so we sit around waiting and coaxing."

He was eager to tackle a new draft of *Memoirs of a Geisha* for Steven Spielberg, but first the director had to make *Minority Report* with Tom Cruise, and that couldn't start until the actor had finished *Mission: Impossible 2,* which had run well over schedule in Aus-tralia. In the meantime, Billy Bob Thornton seemed likely to sign on as the director of *The Shipping News,* another Bass adaptation. Bass knew that Thornton did a lot of his own writing and might just toss Bass's draft, of which he was extremely proud. "Will I get to meet the great man?" Bass wondered. "I may be hanging with Billy Bob, or I may be fired and just see him at the premiere."

"Couldn't you just call him and ask about his plans?" I asked.

"Call him?" Bass said incredulously. "Oh, sure! I'd hear from the studio so fast—'You did what!' "

Then there was *Snow Falling on Cedars.* Bass's adaptation of David Guterson's novel attracted Scott Hicks, who directed *Shine.* Bass, in his role as producer, approved of Hicks's hiring, because the director said he loved the script—which departed significantly from the book. "To draw viewers into an adaptation, where you have only three percent as much time as a novel," Bass says, "you need to make the characters sparklier, more accessible—anything that helps the audience connect. David Guterson didn't like that at all. He saw the characters as more somber and internal, and he persuaded Scott."

Hicks took over the writing—he and Bass ended up sharing credit—and stripped out fifty pages of Bass's draft, including all the voice-over and most of the witty banter. Then he filmed a gorgeous but inert movie built around confusing multiple flashbacks and images of foggy fog and snowy snow and glittering salmon flopping on boat decks. "The film is so lyrical and challenging that people are going to say, 'That's really groundbreaking for you, Ron!' " Bass says, laughing ruefully.

Even the Team, the facilitators of Bass's polished and accessible style, sometimes strikes him as a doubtful bargain. Now and then he recognizes that he has simply internalized the chorus of editors who reshape every Hollywood script, as well as given himself six more people to please. He told me, "I do wonder, would I be happier if I said, 'Okay, Team, good-bye,' and I went to Maui and wrote twelve first drafts a year, from the heart? Get out of the producer business, the constructive and responsible business. Maybe have some people around just to generate ideas for me, help me figure them out, and then just roll and roll and roll."

I couldn't help smiling at this busman's holiday, which sounds almost exactly like his current life, plus pineapples. Bass caught the grin, and returned it. "I'm also dying to go back to novels, to have something that would appear as I originally wrote it," he said. "The day will come when I've had enough of the tumult, and I'll really go interior and for a year I'll only write a novel." He is silent for a moment. "And three or four screenplays."

Inside his office, Bass runs his hand along the rows of screen-plays on his bookshelves, absorbing memories of frustration, as if the titles, Magic Markered on the spines, were in braille. A binder marked "Personal" lists them by year, like pressings in a vintner's catalog: ninety-five titles in all. And so many lie undone, or redone, such as *Dangerous Minds,* starring Michelle Pfeiffer as an inspirational teacher, which was entirely "re-dialogued," as they say, by Elaine May. "Here's my *Bridges of Madison County,* which Clint Eastwood didn't go for," Bass says. "And *Martine,* about vampires, which is not playing at theaters near you." His voice drops, and he sounds very tired. "*Mao,* the same, and *Children of Angels,* which has guardian angels, like *It's a Wonderful Life.* It's very schmaltzy and sentimental, and nobody likes it but me and my Team." He stands back, gazing up. "There's a lot of heartbreak on this shelf."

Even *Rain Man,* the film that won Bass his Academy Award for screenwriting, was changed that crucial 20 percent. Bass and Barry Levinson, the director who replaced Spielberg, disagreed about the film's last scene. As Levinson filmed it, the Dustin Hoffman character leaves on a train to return to the institution in Chicago and Tom Cruise waves from the platform, having promised to visit him soon. The moment is tender but bittersweet. "In my version," Bass said, "Tom's girlfriend is also there. They'd gotten back together, because I thought Tom deserved that for having made the journey and learned how to relate to someone. So he says good-bye to Dustin, and Dustin starts to get hysterical, really crazy, even though Tom is saying, 'I'm going to be there in two weeks.'

"As the train starts to rumble away, I have Tom looking to the girlfriend, and her eyes say 'Go!' and Tom grabs on to the handhold and swings aboard to take Dustin to Chicago. It didn't change the story at all, but it was the last image I wanted the audience to have. Was the most important truth the connection the brothers would have in the future? Or Barry's image of the lack, the connection they could never have? Both were honest. Barry's choice worked one thousand percent, and—although this isn't why he did it—you're always going to get better reviews if you go out on the minor chord. . . ." His voice trailed off. Having reached the summit of his hopes, the very boardroom of the Dream Factory, Bass still can't make the world as cozy and consoling as he dreamed it should be, long ago in bed. He sighed. "Four hundred and fifty-eight million dollars and I don't know how many Oscars later, the writer still remembers his ending and feels it could have worked, too."

(2000)

PART II

AMERICA AND ITS DISCONTENTS

THE CASE FOR MIDDLEBROW

What can you say about a twenty-five-year-old girl who died? That she was beautiful. And brilliant. That she loved Mozart and Bach. And the Beatles. And me.

—First lines of Erich Segal's *Love Story*

Everything follows from this principle: that the lover is not to be reduced to a simple symptomal subject, but rather that we hear in his voice what is "unreal," i.e., intractable. Whence the choice of a "dramatic" method which renounces examples and rests on a single action of a primary language (no metalanguage).

—First lines of Roland Barthes's *A Lover's Discourse*

Which book would you rather keep reading? Chances are: Mr. Segal's. *Love Story* was a best-seller for seven months, while *A Lover's Discourse* quickly bounced into remainder bins. But which book would you rather be seen reading? Chances are: Mr. Barthes's. The most pernicious modern cultural taboo is the one against admitting that you like middlebrow. Not "like" it. Really *like* it.

We live in a time when highbrow has never been so high—so removed from daily discourse. And lowbrow has never so mesmerized the masses or carried such highbrow chic. What's squeezed in between—the siren call of creamy and proficient pleasure—has never been so decried. We have lost appreciation for the art that was once the mainstay of American culture and the unguilty delight of intelligent readers, listeners, and viewers: the art of middlebrow.

Hounded for years by highbrow derision, by broadsides flowing scornfully from the pens of such culture guardians as T. S. Eliot, Dwight Macdonald, Clement Greenberg, and F. R. Leavis, among many others, we now profess to be above art that provokes only saturated feelings. We disparage "tearjerkers" and "beach reads," fearing that having our tears jerked connotes manipulation, that breezing through a book while basted with Bain de Soleil is somehow less admirable than struggling with a tome we have no hope of understanding. We feel ashamed for preferring Elmore Leonard to Luigi Pirandello, *The Graduate* to *Black Orpheus,* Stevie Wonder to Erik Satie, and for ever watching PBS. But no matter how we lash ourselves to the mast of the "quizzical" and the "refractory," our hearts still quiver when serenaded by pure middlebrow emotions such as sadness and joy.

It's time to bring middlebrow out of its cultural closet, to hail its emollient properties, to trumpet its mending virtues. For middlebrow not only entertains, it educates—pleasurably training us to appreciate high art. It's the spoonful of sugar that makes the medicine go down. In a culture riven by a choice between *Pixote* and *Porky's,* between works contrived to tickle the rarefied palates of the few and those constructed to microwave the permafrozen brains of the many, middlebrow also reconnects the intellectual with the emotional. It provides some unity in a culture where political, social, and intellectual fragmentation is now the norm. To neglect middlebrow is to deal yet another blow to a civilized and informed discourse, one in which we can all participate and have some clue about what everybody else is talking about.

So what are we talking about? Defining middlebrow is a notoriously tricky endeavor, one that depends in part on an understanding of the neighboring realms of highbrow and lowbrow. A recent attempt at boundary marking, Kirk Varnedoe and Adam Gopnik's catalog accompanying the "High and Low: Popular Culture and Modern Art" exhibit at New York's Museum of Modern Art, illustrates the bogginess of this territory. High art, for them, is:

the primary material with which any history of art in this century must contend. Achievements in this lineage have always involved, in one way or another, a consciousness of the traditional "high" ceremonial and religious art enshrined in places like the Louvre, and entailed some sense of obligation—even if that obligation was expressed through emphatic rejection and the urge to start afresh—to the grand manner of art.

In other words, high art is high art.

Middlebrow, in contrast, lacks this self-conscious "grand manner." Where highbrow is mediated and labyrinthine, middlebrow is unmediated and direct. Where highbrow is angst, ennui, schadenfreude, middlebrow is anxiety, boredom, envy. Groucho Marx taking a pulse—"Either this man is dead or my watch has stopped"—is textbook middlebrow. So are Fairfield Porter and Georgia O'Keeffe paintings; the better *thirtysomething* episodes; almost any striking and widely disseminated photograph—Cartier-Bresson's picture of an impish lad carrying wine bottles, Eddie Adams's shot of a Viet Cong prisoner getting his brains blown out; "Me and Bobbie McGee"; and Marcel Marceau's miming a prisoner palming the walls of his cell. Each tells a story in familiar fashion, is memorable, and is readily understood by all.

Middlebrow is distinguished by technical competence, singleness of affect, purity of emotion, tidiness of resolution, and modesty of scope. Thus, in 1939 and 1940, Graham Greene wrote *The Confidential Agent* on benzedrine in the mornings and *The Power and the Glory,* more slowly, in the undrugged afternoons. He considered the former one of his "entertainments" (middlebrow); the latter, one of his "serious works" (highbrow). The essential difference between Greene's brows is that his "serious works" are laden with authorial epigrams like "in human love there is never such a thing as victory: only a few minor tactical successes before the final defeat of death or indifference"; or "innocence is like a dumb leper who has lost his bell, wandering the world, meaning no harm." *The Confidential Agent* lacks only this wintry philosophy to have a full complement of Greene's characteristic virtues: the overmatched protagonists, the punishing dialogue, the murderous, clockwork plots. Without the philosophy, we have smart fun—middlebrow.

—

Context—the frame through which a work is seen—plays a key role in determining its brow. The question "Who farted?" is patently lowbrow—except when Estragon, "recoiling," poses it in *Waiting for Godot,* when it's highbrow. The frames that the culture guardians most often surround otherwise middlebrow work with, thus raising it to highbrow, are the British (consider that Sherlock Holmes and Lord Peter Wimsey seem tonier than Sam Spade, though Sam throws a meaner punch all around, and that the much fawned over *Upstairs, Downstairs* was just *Dallas* with kippers); the otherwise foreign (the Philippines' F. Sionil José and Indonesia's Mochtar Lubis are in; James T. Farrell, despite similar themes and prose, is out); the neglected (it's cooler to be caught reading a dog-eared copy of Poe's *Narrative of A. Gordon Pym* than "The Telltale Heart"); and, especially, the abstruse. Witness the critical pother over Eco's *The Name of the Rose,* which, stripped of its formidable theoretical scaffolding, was just a chilly murder mystery.

Middlebrow is also affected by the sweep of time and taste. Popular entertainment that outlasts its era gets reexamined by new critics, re-presented to a new audience, elevated, and enshrined. Thus Chaplin and Keaton, once middlebrow, are now unimpeachably regarded as high art. So too Harold Arlen, Mathew Brady's Civil War photos, and the movies of *The Godfather, One Flew Over the Cuckoo's Nest,* and *The Shining,* all taken from middlebrow books that remain middlebrow. If Frank Sinatra were dead, he'd be high art; time has already beatified Patsy Cline and Jim Morrison. A populist Rossini opera like *William Tell* or *Barber of Seville* was once clearly middlebrow; now all opera is widely perceived as rarefied and tedious—hence highbrow. (But the classic operas—*Carmen, Don Giovanni*—are really pure middlebrow and all the greater for it.)

Occasionally, of course, the process works the other way, and high art becomes middlebrow. (Some works are born middlebrow, some achieve middlebrow, and some have middlebrow thrust upon them.) So Hemingway, once avant-garde, is now a roasted chestnut. Shakespeare's problem plays (*Troilus and Cressida, Cymbeline, Coriolanus*) rise as worthy of fractious dissertations, and his warhorses (*Romeo and Juliet, Hamlet, Macbeth, Julius Caesar, The Tempest*) sink toward middlebrow, their values diminished—or clarified, depending on your point of view—by constant production. In the old favorites Shakespeare's themes are brilliantly middlebrow, because middlebrow essentially elaborates one strong theme, such as love, revenge, or ambition. The problem plays require intellectually mediated reactions, and our sympathies don't lie as readily with one or two characters. Beethoven's Fifth, Sixth, and Ninth Symphonies have played themselves back to triple-A ball; ditto much of the Mozart and Bach so beloved of *Love Story*'s Jennifer Cavilleri. Her favored Beatles, however, were always hugely popular—middlebrow all the way.

———

The manifold ways in which middlebrow infuses our culture are either ignored or crudely caricatured by culture guardians addled by dainty loathing. In the culture guardians' claret nightmares, middlebrow is exemplified by a grandmother rocking on a porch somewhere near Decatur, Illinois. She wears a hairnet, drinks a glass of Crystal Lite, and furrows her brow over a *Reader's Digest* condensed *Ben-Hur.* In the context of this magazine's readers, middlebrow is much closer to the taste of a well-educated sophomore: Pet Shop Boys and U2 on the stereo; an "encore episode" of *The Fugitive* on A&E (in which rubric it's classier than it was on ABC in 1963); Au Bon Pain croissants in the fridge; and the walls postered with Renoir's boating party and Monet's lilies, Robert Doisneau's photo "Baiser de l'Hotel de Ville, 1950," and a shadowed black-and-white homage to James Dean suffering in leather.

This highbrow stereotyping of the middle stems from cultural and intellectual insecurity—indeed, highbrow may be exemplified by a dinner party at which everyone pretends to have read Richard Rorty. Such stereotyping is rare among those who genuinely respect high art, since they are less threatened by middlebrow than merely uninterested in it. Where high art is work of complex passion—work that may, as we've seen, become middlebrow—highbrow is merely a stance of complexity. It imputes and then fetishizes difficulty for its own sake, as a way of asserting cultural superiority over the less learned. Emotion and passion are largely valueless here because they don't fit a narrative schema, can't be diagrammed, pigeonholed, reduced. This misplacement of priorities leads us to waste time listening to Anton Webern, reading John Ashbery, and watching plays directed by Peter Sellars.

The archetypal contemporary expression of highbrow is high-lowbrow, in which highbrow condescendingly co-opts low. It's okay to "see" the Steven Seagal movie *Hard to Kill* if you make bets on the body count. In the Sontagian sense, it's a trip to summer camp; the highlow sensibility sees all lowbrow in quotation marks. So we can revel in the *New York Post*'s lurid headlines—TEDDY'S SEXY ROMP!—any C. David Heymann celeb bio (*Poor Little Rich Girl, A Woman Named Jackie*), *Gilligan's Island,* and the Archies' song "Sugar, Sugar" without, in any sense of the phrase, a second thought.

This trivia-surfing sensibility leads to intellectualized but fundamentally mindless art, to mere quotation and "de-" and "recontextualizing." Peter Saul takes Donald Duck, paints a jiggly multiple-exposure of him descending a staircase—*et, voilà!* a brilliant emblem of our Disneyfication, a cunning restatement of the Duchampian dilemma, etc.

The problem with art that aims at this highlow sensibility is that it often lacks sympathy for—or belief in—our common humanity. So pervasive has highlow cynicism become that many readers of this magazine would have difficulty even saying "our common humanity" without an ironic edge. Lacking faith that a wide audience will approach their art with trust and goodwill, highlow artists turn precious and diffident.

Martin Amis, Jonathan Demme, Laurie Anderson, David Lynch, and David Byrne all rummage through lowbrow as dispassionately as they would through a clothes hamper, fascinated by unsorted "Americana." While they have had successes—*Money, Something Wild,* the early episodes of *Twin Peaks*—their common failing is a tendency to avoid what they see as the chasm in the middle. But that bellying middle is the funnel through which all great art, either on its way up or on its way down, must pass. So the work of Amis et al. will, in time, seem increasingly marginal; art that is only slumming has no claim on greatness.

Susan Sontag wrote of camp, the harbinger of highlow, that it "incarnates a victory of 'style' over 'content,' 'aesthetics' over 'morality,' of irony over tragedy." Middlebrow exactly reverses that formula—its emphasis is on content, an accessible message. Often that message is just one emotion: being misunderstood (James Dean), dreamy (Monet), in love with someone who wears a beret and reads Roland Barthes (Doisneau). *The Saturday Evening Post* and the *Saturday Review,* the whole idea of catching up with culture on a lazy Saturday afternoon—even Saturday itself—are middlebrow. Redolent of tail fins and Davy Crockett caps, of *Father Knows Best,* of the 1950s and early 1960s, middlebrow hearkens to when we believed we were a happy country. Middlebrow is nostalgic. It is white bread.

In sum, it is never, ever hip. Because ideas and beliefs filter out and become consensual only gradually, middlebrow always trails the next wave. This is actually its greatest virtue: it defines and preserves an enduring set of common American values. The generations that could quote Longfellow's *Hiawatha* are now the generations that flocked to *Dances with Wolves,* but both works reflected and rekindled a longing for the lost American frontier. A great middlebrow poet like Robert Frost or Walt Whitman sings the American ideal: we can all comfortably talk about the mending walls that traverse our body electric. And we can all believe ourselves simultaneously shoulder to shoulder in a great enterprise (Jimmy Stewart) yet iconically solitary (Humphrey Bogart). Middlebrow, which appeals across barriers of age or station, composes our national identity.

To be sure, *bad* middlebrow delivers not truth but "home truths" that sag like Tetley tea bag homilies. For instance, the wretched line from *Our Town* that "there's something way down deep that's eternal about every human being." Everything James Michener has written. Anything issuing from the Wyeth family. Or the cowlicked barbershop boys of Norman Rockwell, the singsong iambs of Joyce Kilmer, and the compose-by-numbers melodies of Andrew Lloyd Webber. All substitute bald sentiment and preachy, phony, or mollycoddling formulas for argument and style. They sink toward lowbrow, which unites us only in leaving our "leisure hours" untroubled by thought, in providing smooth passage from work station to dreamless slumber. They lack verve.

But when that bald middlebrow sentiment is bewigged and given a little thematic styling mousse, you have something wonderfully underappreciated: directness. It is the forcefully forthright that leads to social change. The two novels that have most affected American life—Stowe's *Uncle Tom's Cabin* and Sinclair's *The Jungle*—were crafted with frank middlebrow intent. Similarly, in *The Bonfire of the Vanities* Tom Wolfe takes it for granted that art is engaged with the world and can shake it up. Highbrow, by contrast, often sees artworks as only notional stepchildren of other artworks, as self-portraits in a convex mirror.

Middlebrow's strength (and, of course, its limitation) is its lack of irony. Warhol's Brillo boxes and Lichtenstein's Benday dot comics paintings, originally highlow hybrids, soon became middlebrow icons in the American narrative, thereby shedding much of their intellectual content and their irony. We now experience *Look Mickey* and *Campbell's Soup Cans* with unwrinkled brow; no Brechtian alienation makes us question how and why we're experiencing them, makes us wonder if we need a visa for art's new frontier. So David Hockney, Anne Tyler, and Spike Lee, forceful stylists and passionate thinkers all, are middlebrow by virtue of their accessibility. Where highbrow excludes, middlebrow includes, even welcomes. In a culture of conflicting signals and input overload, where so much art dares you to understand it, this is no small virtue and no small relief. This ease of appreciation leads to another middlebrow virtue: By demystifying art, by bringing it within reach, middlebrow begins a conversation with the viewer or reader that encourages further, more complex and articulate dialogues. We aren't born admiring Debussy and Strindberg; we have to work up to them, apprenticing in the foothills of middlebrow. Chopin's "Chopsticks" leads us to his mazurkas; reading Jorge Amado's magical realism is excellent preparation for Márquez's more demanding pyrotechnics; and much of the luminosity of Cézanne's apples derives from their being unlike any of the round, red, still-life blobs we've previously learned to recognize as "apples."

Middlebrow's tutelary function in turn provokes an attack against it from those who fear, with Dwight Macdonald, that middlebrow values are too seductive; that "instead of being transitional, [they] may now themselves become a debased, permanent standard." This suspicion of middlebrow's allure traverses the political spectrum, from the cranky Right to the dogmatic Left. Frankfurt Schoolers Max Horkheimer and Theodor Adorno were horrified that art could provide pleasure and snorted at the idea that that pleasure might be an inducement to further education. With their usual mixture of condescension and determinism, they declared:

> Fun is a medicinal bath. The pleasure industry never fails to prescribe it. It makes laughter the instrument of the fraud practiced on happiness. Moments of happiness are without laughter . . . delight is austere.

Why the fuss? Aristotle had two criteria for art that haven't been improved upon: that it should entertain and instruct. Great high art does both. The culture guardians' fear is that we—the laggardly masses—can't feel and think at the same time. Of the two, they'd rather we were thinking. Unfortunately, their treasured highbrow tends to lecture rather than instruct. Good middlebrow, on the other hand, offers more amusement and less instruction, but both are present and neither is slighted.

There is, in short, nothing wrong—and a great deal right—with art that is content thoughtfully to amuse. When *Network*'s messianic anchorman Howard Beale says television is "in the boredom-killing business," it's meant as a slam. But to really kill boredom, you have to be genuinely entertaining. And to be genuinely entertaining, you have to appeal to your audience's common humanity—yes—to include rather than exclude, to interest by a considered appeal to intelligence. If you do it badly, people like me will make fun of you. But if you do it well, only the culture guardians will get mad, because you will be furthering the notion that art, all art, should disclose not secrets to the few, but treasures to the many.

(1992)

THE ARMANI MYSTIQUE

Fifty of the world's most beautiful models waited for Giorgio Armani. Wrapped in white housecoats against the air-conditioned chill, clutching bottles of Pellegrino in their thin, lotioned fingers, their hair espaliered in curlers, they sprawled indelicately in the first three rows of Armani's private theater in Milan. Five hundred journalists and celebrities would soon throng in to see them model Armani's spring collection.

Accompanied by an interpreter, Armani strode onto the runway to deliver his credo on deportment. Though Armani was chewing gum and looked customarily casual in a purple sweater and black cotton pants, this traditional session is his high mass. With one hand at his throat, like a man keeping his tie out of the soup, Armani considered the muted palette of women before him, the hair and the skin that rippled from black to chalk white, and he frowned.

Fire-engine red blazed in the front row: Linda Evangelista was still wearing the pouffy red wig she had worn in Versace's show earlier that day. Armani waved his fingers, and Evangelista pulled it off. Armani winced again: her hair was dyed just as red. Daringly, laughing, Evangelista handed her wig to Armani, urging him to put it on. He considered the red tangle in his hand, then gingerly popped it on for two seconds while gesturing to the bank of cameras at the far end of the theater: "No photos!" The photographers never get to shoot the stick-on eagle tattoo on Armani's right forearm, either.

Then, still gravely, Armani said, "Remember, you are women, not young girls walking down the street. This will be very elegant, very simple, and very natural. The makeup is not strong, the hair is not strange"—a glance at Evangelista—"and the clothes are fantastic." He struck an angular pose, his hands braced on his hips, elbows out. "No! Not fashion!" He relaxed: white maned, composed, erect. "Elegance, elegance."

—

"Did you notice the models' hands?" Donald Sutherland asked me after the show, fluting his own hands aloft wonderingly. "Their hands were perfectly relaxed, yet full of energy. There's something about those clothes, and Armani himself, that conveys a self-assurance even to the models." Sutherland grasped the back of his neck, where his dark blue Armani suit lay smoothly: "On every other designer's jacket, there'd be a bump here, but with Armani, never. He captures the flow of the human body." Anjelica Huston, looking like Natasha Fatale in a black Armani dress, leaned over and said, "He's simple, which is the hardest thing in the world."

In the days to come, fashion writers would extravagantly praise his show as the pinnacle of the Milan season, pointing in particular to the way Armani had streamlined his classic cardigan jacket and offered it in unexpectedly bold colors, including raspberry ripple and nectarine, and to his radically different chiffon baby doll dresses. But Armani took greater pleasure from his show's immediate gratifications. His eye flickered eagerly at the curtain peephole throughout, and at the end he bowed with genuine pleasure to the cascading applause, dashing tears from his eyes.

For Armani, at fifty-seven, this adoration was superfluous certification of his vast influence on fashion. When he started Giorgio Armani S.p.A. in 1975, he had $10,000; last year people spent over $1.6 billion for the five men's and four women's lines of Armani clothing and for his accessories, perfume, and eyewear. To complement his mainstay lines—the traditional Black Label and the trendier Emporio Armani—Armani recently launched A/X: Armani Exchange. The December opening of the first store in New York was a huge success, with people lining up to buy T-shirts, jeans, and casual wear for prices mostly under $100: A/X sold twenty-six hundred items in the first two days. Twenty-five U.S. outlets are scheduled to be open by this month. This shark attack on market share, while it may dim the shimmer of the name *Armani,* should further enrich an unlikely billionaire.

After the fashion show, 250 of Armani's most favored guests lingered for dinner in the banquet room of the seventeenth-century palazzo that serves as Armani's office and apartment. The white canopy overhead was speckled with oak leaves, the long tables were illuminated by white church candles and draped in Armani-designed napery, the squadrons of waiters wore trim Cipriani jackets, the cast-iron lanterns were copies of one Armani had bought in Tunisia. Even the Godiva soap in the bathroom was a treat Armani had picked up in St.-Tropez. Everything was just so. Eric Clapton, gazing at the impeccable room, compared Armani with his rival for Hollywood's affections: "Versace is all about sex and rock and roll—very raunchy. Armani is about harmony, harmony in tone and color and fabric—harmony in atmosphere."

Armani himself circulated. Masked by his thin, watchful smile, he ensured that everyone had champagne, that nothing jarred. "I must tell you something grave," Armani would say to me later. "In fashion, everything has been done. The only challenge now is new associations of the same elements—ties, stretch pants, the jackets. It's the way they mix." This instinct for catalytic elements explains, for instance, why Armani hired ex-princess Lee Radziwill as a "special events coordinator": basically, her job is to attend Armani parties and look gauntly fabulous. She was there in Milan. And she looked gauntly fabulous.

Valerio Pinci, a former Armani model, recalled that "we once spent a full evening out at different clubs in Milan, twenty or thirty of us, getting the red-carpet treatment because we were with Armani. At four A.M. he brought us all back to his big house, woke up his servants, and made them prepare a sit-down meal, which they served wearing white gloves. Everyone was trashed, falling all over the place in an interesting chaos. And he sat there quietly, absolutely sober, observing us."

—

"Clothes should transmit sensuality, not sexuality," Armani told me the morning after the show. "Yesterday I was really worried because I didn't want to display breasts underneath blouses or through transparent fabrics. There was a slight *insinuation* of breasts." In fact, I saw at least three full-fledged breasts. "But I didn't want people to say, 'Breasts, breasts, beautiful breasts!' I don't want men to do a 360-degree turn when they see a woman in my clothes, I want men's eyes to go like this—" His eyes darted shyly aside.

We sat in the living room of Armani's apartment, upstairs from his office. The apartment welled with buttery light that soaked into the parchment-white walls, the black doors and black leopard statuary, the sixteen-foot ceilings. The living room had white raw-silk sofas, a bowl of wild white roses and freesia, a silver-topped walking stick reposing against the wall. Designed by Peter Marino, decorated by Armani, it is a cat person's apartment (Armani has three Persians and a tabby), a safe house where nothing bad can happen. "A cat is discretion," Armani will say. "A dog is tenderness." He keeps his white Labradors at his country villa in Broni; when one gets on a footing to see them, one has penetrated Armani's discretion to his humor, his tenderness.

Armani professes to love Milan, its "exclusive and private" hidden elegance, but aside from the red geraniums that float in window boxes high above this least elegant of Italian cities, Milan is hazy and dull. One suspects that the contrast between Milan's massed concrete and Armani's own exquisite niche on Via Borgonuovo is what pleases him. Armani likes contrast.

Thus, in his showpiece living room, the designer sat wearing blue jeans and a blue denim shirt over a white T-shirt, with a blue sweater draped over his shoulders. "I'm communicating simple and clean," Armani said. "It's almost like I'm coming out of the shower, that I've taken a big shower." He smiled. "Clothes, really, are unimportant." One recalls Truman Capote's description of Holly Golightly in *Breakfast at Tiffany's:* "She was always well groomed, there was a consequential good taste in the plainness of her clothes, the blues and grays and lack of luster that made her, herself, shine so."

"They label me the classic designer," Armani said, "but if you look at my clothes, they break every classic rule. On a classic jacket the shoulders fit, the waist is marked, it hits the breasts—my jackets don't do any of that." Different from the start, Armani's jacket-based couture has seen at least three revolutions. Famously, he founded his line in 1974 with the unconstructed blazer—the sloping shoulders, the narrow lapels, the baggy pockets, and the loose-weave fabrics that, unconfined by interior linings, draped so sinuously on both men and women (and often stretched or ripped—the price of flexibility).

At the end of the seventies Armani lowered the gorge, widened the lapels, and extended and padded the shoulders to create the wedge-shaped power suit. In the mid-1980s he abandoned the power suit for the looser, roomier sack suit. But more than the changes, one noticed the thematic continuity: the ideals of understatement and a slouchy androgyny. Armani deconstructs jackets, de-creases pants, deaccessorizes jewelry, and deplores the hair-trigger flamboyance of the stereotypical Italian designer.

"Now," Armani said, running a hand over his suede shoes thoughtfully, "with the Berlin Wall down, it would be offensive to make clothes that are screaming with luxury, screaming with opulence." His Black Label outfits still cost upward of $1,700, but they *look* less assertively expensive. "I have taken things I did ten years ago and corrected them for today," Armani continued. "Ten years ago if I'd done a kimono cardigan, I would have shown it with a geometric hat, a geometric piece of jewelry, to bring it overboard so people would pay attention. Now I almost want to go unnoticed—so for the woman's jacket, my bread and butter, there's a straight, thinner sleeve that caresses the arm and makes the woman feel she is being hugged. And the shoulder is back, but softer. The eighties shoulder was a woman's manager. Now she doesn't need to tell anybody what she is. She *is*."

"More than any European designer," the semiotician Marshall Blonsky suggests, "Armani is a wild, savage semiotician. Through his clothes he's unconsciously educating the people who wear them in the ideology that's coming."

—

"Life is a movie," Armani has said, "and my clothes are the costumes." While demonstrably untrue, this wish helps explain Armani's and Hollywood's mutual fascination. Armani's clothes have decorated movies from *American Gigolo* to *Batman,* emblematizing sleek assurance, and in the last few months alone Armani jokes have enlivened both *Hook* and *Father of the Bride.* Richard Gere and Cindy Crawford were married in December in complementary Armani suits, and actors from Kevin Costner to Jodie Foster, as well as moguls including Mike Ovitz, Dawn Steele, and Sherry Lansing, regularly sport Armani. *Women's Wear Daily* called him "the official outfitter of the 62nd Annual Academy Awards."

"Wearing Armani in Hollywood makes no statement, no, no," Donald Sutherland said in Milan. "It makes you look individual and terrific. And everyone in Hollywood wants to look as individual and terrific as possible." Without necessarily *being* individual and terrific.

Armani studies the way Lauren Hutton and Michelle Pfeiffer wear clothes (often his): "Lauren will wear a very important, expensive embroidered jacket on top of underwear and jeans. Michelle wears a gold lamé suit with no makeup and a pair of black glasses. It's the contrast that consecrates the image."

"Armani is very clever," Eric Clapton mused in Milan. "He's

managed to sell American clothes of the thirties, forties, and fifties, that great Hollywood look, back to the Americans, who think they're buying Italian." Armani, in other words, sells an image of an image, a seductive allusion to a seductive illusion.

In his quest for the perfect sotto voce understatement, Armani dreads vulgarity like death. He will go to extraordinary lengths to frame his creations properly, so they—and he—can never be accused of crassness, of ill breeding. "My atmosphere is everything," Armani said. "If you ask me to design a pillow, you can predict the color, the shape, the amount of puffiness. But because I have a line of thought doesn't make me a monk. There should be frivolousness, but frivolousness in my style.

"Last night's baby doll dresses would make you say, 'Oh, that's not Armani.' But within my context, it *is* Armani. Another designer would have interpreted the baby doll with an aggressive print or an aggressive color, accessorized it with high heels, pearls, rhinestones, or put it on a glamorous girl like Claudia Schiffer or Naomi. But I do it in soft, see-through veils, with flat heels, on an androgynous model, so she looks like a little girl. I love to put masculine outfits on glamorous, made-up women and then give masculine or androgynous-looking girls clothes that don't belong to them, feminine clothes. The contrast is important, otherwise you get an Armani *caricature.*"

—

Armani contends against two familiar criticisms. One was well expressed by a silver-haired man I sat next to at an Armani fashion show at Boston's Isabella Stewart Gardner Museum. As the models strutted in the fall line, this observer, cloaked in a navy Brooks Brothers suit and black Lloyd and Haig shoes, groaned to his wife, "Oh no! . . . Awful! What's that, for chrissake? Shapeless . . . revolting . . . the drabbest clothing I've ever seen." Boston has been a tough sell for Armani.

The suggestion is also made that Armani, who approves even the weight of the stationery in his branch offices, may be overfond of control. When Michael Jackson asked Armani to design the look for his *Dangerous* album and tour, Armani suggested a jazz singer idea, a retrofitted Cab Calloway concept that Jackson seemed delighted with—but Armani withdrew when he discovered he wouldn't be in *complete* charge of Jackson's image.

Gabriella Forte, Armani's executive vice president, interpreter, and lovingly ferocious protector, sat with me in one of Armani's pearl-white offices and preemptively explained—I hadn't asked— that these two charges are absurd. "Armani's clothing system is not monotonous," Forte said. "It is *coherent*. And he's not a control freak. He's a *detail person*. He feels the weight of being. If he sees an ugly flower in a restaurant, he'll move it and then say, 'Didn't anyone see that flower mushing away there?' When he's walking in a park and the grass is too high, he'll tell someone to cut the grass, or if the animals aren't clean, he'll say to someone, 'Wash them.' "

Armani himself passed by during Forte's explanation and, inter- ested, sat down in a rigid and squeaky swivel chair. Looking pained that he couldn't swivel smoothly—and his compelling neediness is such that Forte and I wanted desperately to solve his aesthetic crisis— he said, "Yes, it's a question of respect. I have a house in the country, in the Po Valley, near where I was born. When I moved in, there were two old farmers who were taking care of the garden and the chicken coop and the rabbit hutches. The first thing I did was fix the chicken coop, removing all the dust and feathers and making it into a mini chicken hotel. The old people were in shock, thinking, This new owner is weird. Now, though, they polish *everything,* they're funda- mentally worse than I am. And they do it with great pleasure, because they know that I care, that when I look at the animals it must be calm and soothing."

—

Armani grew up a shy perfectionist in a lower-middle-class family in Piacenza, near Milan. "I think Giorgio was even a fussy baby," one friend said. The middle of three children, he was the most frightened by the bombs of World War II. After the war, on Sunday afternoons he and his older brother would put on meticulously produced marionette shows at the church. Giorgio's mother, Maria, made the puppets' clothing, but Giorgio loved painting the faces and arranging the hair, designing the tickets. "When he was twenty, in Milan," said his younger sister, Rosanna, a model at the time, "he would pay a lot of attention to the way I looked. In an affectionate way, he'd say, 'You should have your hair up, you should wear a skirt instead of jeans, you're wearing too much makeup.' I didn't listen then, but now . . ." She turned her palms up, her hands emerging from a burgundy Armani jacket.

After stints as a department store buyer and a designer for Nino Cerruti, Armani was convinced by his lover and eventual business partner, Sergio Galeotti, to go solo. Armani showed his first menswear line in 1974 and his first women's line the following year; by 1982 he was on the cover of *Time*.

The single defining event in Armani's life since then was Galeotti's death after a lingering illness in 1985. Galeotti was the company's financial wizard, and he had, to an extraordinary extent, protected Armani from the business side of the business. Armani had to begin fresh: like a teenager, he had to learn to carry a wallet, a credit card. Predictions for the company's collapse were widespread, but Armani and his protective circle of intimates, most of them women, revealed unsuspected acumen. The company continued to expand and maintained its astonishing retail margins of 55 to 67 percent. More important, Armani says, is that "since then, I became a human being. Because I understood that you die. I woke up to reality."

—

"My eyes are very expressive, but my body shape is all wrong," Armani said moodily. It was the last of our conversations, and he had slowly lowered his guard. "I usually read people through their body movements, it's my work, but my body just doesn't speak. My shoulders are too big, my face is too big, the calf muscles should be longer, and the thighs should be shorter—and then, fundamentally, there's a certain insecurity I have. I would like to have the physique of Daniel Day-Lewis. He doesn't have such a good body, but he's very sensuous. Or Jeremy Irons, or Matthew Modine in *Birdy*—their bodies speak."

Could you rid yourself of this physical insecurity?

"Yes, if I role-played. If I wore dark glasses and a blue suit, if I played the part of Giorgio Armani the creative entity, the man of success. But I don't want to do that." He paused. "I realize that people love me for my insecurities." He thought some more, and his sad blue eyes glinted with humor. "Probably because I require them to.

"Physically I love loving better than being loved. I love loving someone else's body, feeling someone else's need. I'd rather caress someone else than be caressed."

And through your clothes you caress strangers all over the world?

"Yes!" he said. "Exactly. Do you think they notice?"

Only a man so gifted and forlorn would have such success cloaking the world's needs, dressing its lacks. It is possible and even pleasant to imagine a whole world designed by Armani. The grass would be green and trim, the animals clean; incense would burn in the hallways, people would stride about to dreamy pop music. All loneliness would be soothed, wrapped in the loose weaves of self-assurance. And no one would die except nobly, murmuring, like Chekhov, "It's been a long time since I've had any champagne," or crying out, like Goethe, "More light!"

(1992)

THE SHIRT OFF YOUR BACK

The morning after, she comes from the shower wrapped in a blue towel and considers last night's clothes, rumpled at the foot of your bed. "Can I borrow a shirt?" she asks evenly. She pages through your closet, weighing your taste against her own, and pulls out a blue or white oxford-cloth shirt. It is unerringly your favorite, chamois soft. On her it hangs to midthigh, that ideal spot. Her fingers fumble a little with the reversed buttons, then she rolls up the baggy sleeves and smiles. Your heart constricts oddly; pleasure, yes, but also a tick of unease. She's Daddy's girl now, all right.

When she wears it outdoors as you go for coffee, you glory in the bold semaphore, so reminiscent of college (her wet hair in the dining hall, wearing your rolled-up jeans), even high school (the letter jacket, blazoned with your name). This is our modern way of waving the bloody sheets, of announcing consummation.

But as you swagger like a Visigoth, her mind is already running to intimacy. She is trying out how it feels to walk around in your skin, steeped in your individual scent of sweat and Dial soap. When she returns the shirt, neatly folded, her perfume has insinuated into the weave, and when you press your face to the placket you can summon her up like a genie. A woman once gave me her big navy cardigan, and I adored carrying about her smoky geranium smell, a movable greenhouse of love. Women know that men aren't generally attuned to these powerful nuances, and that they'll panic when they finally catch on: How did we get so deep so fast? This theme lurks in the Arrow ads in which the woman feels naughty, clandestine, for wearing his shirts while he's out.

If you stick at the first borrowing, the threshold intimacy, something's wrong. I once slept with a woman, half regretting it then, and deeply regretting it afterward when she threw on my Icelandic sweater and began to examine the photos on my bookshelves. The sweater tipped the balance: suffocation, anxiety, gloom. It felt much more invasive than having been practically frog-marched into bed.

Years ago a woman borrowed the shirt I'd been wearing when I met her, my cherished blue Sea Island cotton shirt, with its perfect soft, short-pointed collar. She looked great in it as she left—for good, as it turned out. I never heard from her again. As the most plausible explanations were self-wounding, I finally decided she'd slept with me just for the shirt.

And I bet that shirt has since lured other men: a woman in a man's clothes absent the man in question is strangely sexy. When George Peppard first meets Audrey Hepburn's Holly Golightly in *Breakfast at Tiffany's,* she's just emerged from bed wearing only a man's formal shirt with all the studs in place. Whose shirt might this be? We never find out, and the costume retains an endearingly madcap ambiguity—it indicates both Golightly's past courtesanship and her present need to be taken care of.

Similarly, though on a lower plane, when we meet Alison on the very first episode of *Melrose Place,* she is hotfooting around the building's courtyard dressed only in a man's blue oxford-cloth shirt. Again, we never find out whose it is, but we get the message: Where a man has been, a man soon will be. Within minutes she meets Billy, who will become her lover. (The first man's shirt many women wear is their father's; it made a curious formal sense—probably unintended—when in a much later episode Alison recalled having been molested by her father.)

Across a serious love, clothes leak from your closet to hers. A favorite girlfriend loved wearing my denim jacket and, even more, my soft leather jacket so I'd always be with her, enveloping her in my sympathetic magic. Seeing her in my jacket was as intimate as a hug. Hugging her in my jacket was sweeter still. The dangling leather made her seem like a shar-pei puppy—big-eyed, innocent, needing protection. She knew this, and when she felt I was being distant she'd put on my jacket and come stand in the doorway.

When a good relationship ends, you pull the pictures off your desk and determine who gets the dish rack and the CDs, but the borrowed clothes remain on permanent loan. When this girlfriend and I broke up, she took a white shirt and the denim jacket as talismans. She recently told me she still hadn't washed the denim; it was graying, but my smell lingered. It's not likely she'd tell her new boyfriend the jacket's history; we all curate private relationship museums, and women's closets resemble Bluebeard's locked room. One female friend of mine has extracted, from various relationships, eight white T-shirts, six boxer shorts, six pairs of socks, four blue- and one maroon-striped Brooks Brothers shirts, four pairs of tennis shoes, three sweaters, two pairs of pajamas, one black Armani T-shirt, and one car coat.

The most eloquent message of disappointment I ever received was from a college girlfriend, a soft-spoken artist. We had dated for a few months before she took a semester off. When she came back, we met at a party and spent the night together. She was enthusiastic, but I was torn by mixed emotions, having, as usual, no idea what I wanted. She left the next morning wearing my blue oxford shirt tucked into my jeans, carrying her cocktail dress in a brown paper bag.

I didn't call her for a few days. Maybe even a week. (I know, I know.) One evening I came back from class and found the same brown bag on my doorstep. Inside were my shirt and jeans, neatly folded, with a brief note in her terse cursive: "Here are your clothes." If they come back to you, they're yours; if they don't, they never were.

(1995)

WHITE TRASH NATION

"If I hadn't been married, I'd probably have propositioned her myself," Mark Brown says of his sister-in-law Paula Corbin Jones, who is suing President Clinton for sexual harassment. "Paula dressed—shit, *provocative* ain't even the word for it. You could see the crease of her ass, and at least two lips, maybe three. If a woman dresses to where a man is almost *seeing* it . . ."

"She'd wear a black tank top, tight fitting and real low," Charlotte Brown says of her youngest sister, "and leopard-skin spandex shorts."

"Once after she came out of the bathroom with a gob of makeup on her," Mark says, drawing on a Winston, "I got my pocketknife out and I said, 'If you stand real still, I bet I could get three or four jars of Maybelline off your face.' "

The Browns sit under a live oak in front of their double-wide trailer in Cabot, Arkansas. A buzzard drifts overhead. Charlotte wears a rhinestone-spangled COUNTRY BLUES T-shirt, and Mark a denim shirt with his cuffs rolled up to reveal various tattoos: a dragon, a dancing showgirl, a Harley-Davidson emblem. Cabot itself, population 8,319, is one of those uneasy junctions that signpost a changing America. The Cabot Pawn Shop is deep in shotguns and hunting crossbows; funnel cakes are on sale downtown; and rumpled farms with front-yard tire swings quilt the countryside—until they slam into the Tastee-Freez, the sorry subdivisions, the billboard that commands you to FILL YOUR TANK TWICE at Texaco and McDonald's.

The Browns have a foot in each world: Mark used to be a DJ at a Little Rock club, but now he runs a small welding shop. By either standard—old-fashioned country morals, or modern situational ethics—the Browns disapprove of Paula Jones's behavior. They call her a hard-partying gold-digger who pinched men's butts at the local Red Lobster and say she's now trying to capitalize on a flirtation at the country's expense.

"Paula knows the rules, and now she's trying to change them," Mark says. "This is a great country; it's freedom based. I like some white sons a bitches and I like some black motherfuckers. I hate some niggers and I hate some white trashes. Shit, I've worked right beside a welding woman—"

"You didn't sexually harass her, did you?" Charlotte prompts proudly.

"No, I think I did," Mark says. "She didn't take it as sexual harassment, though, so it must not have been. If I'm driving down the freeway and I see a dadgum woman that's got a good set of boobs and she's bouncing around on a dozer mowing down saplings, you bet your ass Mark Brown will stop his damned truck and stare. If her tits is going boom, boom, boom, boom, boom, and bouncing left and right and every fucking thing, you got *rock and roll* going on, man; and she knows what the hell she's doing up there, or she'd have a bra on."

———

American history is a parade of eras dominated by charismatic stock figures. These role players bestride the popular imagination by sheer bravado; they become, for a time, the lodestars by which the rest of the country defines itself. We've had the era of Squanto; that of the Pilgrim; the Minuteman; the Indian fighter; the carpetbagger; the cowboy; the robber baron; the flapper; the doughboy; the organization man; the hippie; and, in the eighties, the soulless yuppie.

Now comes a new archetype to enslave us—and she enters spackled with Maybelline. The male version, "fondling his penis," asks the handiest female to "kiss it"—or so Paula Corbin Jones has alleged. Welcome to the age of white trash.

Traditionally, the label *white trash* has been applied to selective members of the white underclass—a rapidly growing group. In 1990, according to the Census Bureau, 24.5 million Caucasians were below the poverty line, up 29 percent from 17.3 million in 1980 (these figures are somewhat misleading, as they include white Hispanics). "In raw numbers," notes conservative thinker Charles Murray, "European American whites are the ethnic group with the most people in poverty, most illegitimate children, most women on welfare, most unemployed men, and most arrests for serious crimes."

But demographics are only part of the story. What's alarming is not so much the burgeoning number of people with low-rent circumstances as the exponential spread in stereotypically white trash *behavior,* whether exhibited by those in the underclass or by figures like Roseanne Arnold and Bill Clinton.

The term *white trash* is, to be sure, divisive and classist. (The appellation originated among southern racists as a way to explain how certain "different" whites could behave so crudely.) Soon it may be altogether unacceptable. "In six months, no one will say 'white trash,' " predicts director John (*Pink Flamingos, Serial Mom*) Waters. "It's the last racist thing you can say and get away with."

But *white trash* best encapsulates the galloping sleaze that has overrun both rural *and* urban America. And it's also the phrase that best gives voice to the stifled longing of the well-to-do, who covet what they perceive as the spontaneous authenticity of the poor. "In the summer in Baltimore, whole families live outside on their front steps," John Waters notes admiringly. "They watch TV in their bras and underwear, and if someone comes by, they give them the finger. I'm jealous of their confidence and their alarming taste—they're just freer than I am; they don't worry as much."

The allure of guilt-free freedom explains the mainstream intoxication with white trash cultural tokens. The Guess? jeans ads have been only the most visible manifestation of a whole white trash fashion movement: candy-apple lipstick, chipped cherry-red nail polish, fishnet stockings, rhinestone earrings and dime-store barrettes, Candie's mules, and tattoos—of which Drew Barrymore alone has five.

But in truth white trash behavior is a bleak phenomenon, defined well by Ernest Mickler in his book *White Trash Cooking:* "Common white trash has very little in the way of pride, and no manners to speak of, and hardly any respect for anybody or anything." In this light we see white trash's moon face beaming out at us from the Big Gulp lines at every 7-Eleven; from spring break at Daytona Beach; from every graceless winner of the Publishers Clearinghouse Sweepstakes; and from all wearers of T-shirts emblazoned I'M WITH STUPID.

(And Charlotte and Mark Brown, though scraping by on Mark's disability pension, are not, by our behavioral definition, white trash—they turned down a $2,000 offer for an interview on *A Current Affair.* "We could certainly have used the money," Charlotte says, "but we didn't need any money for the truth.")

Trash values metastasize through our cultural lymph nodes: television screens. There's *Cops* and *Jenny Jones* and *Richard Bey* and *Hard Copy* and *Studs;* and there's Fox, which is virtually a white trash network. Of the hottest romance on television's trendiest show, Fox's *Melrose Place,* Grant Show has said that what fuels the passion between Amanda and his character, Jake (whom Amanda has termed a "gold-digging grease monkey"), is that "even though Amanda's got more money than most of the chicks he's gone with, she's still just white trash like he is."

Trash blares from behind the scenes of *Roseanne,* where Tom and Roseanne Arnold jointly "married" Tom's assistant, Kim Silva. As

Roseanne said in her July petition for divorce—from Tom, that is, not from Kim—"I now realize that I have been a classic battered and abused wife." Whatever the truth of that, Tom did sell stories about her to the *National Enquirer,* and he was arrested for public urination outside a McDonald's; she, of course, says she used to turn tricks in the parking lot between comedy gigs. Turning to face the strange, both NBC and Fox are developing fact-based dramas about her life.

A clear symptom of the white trash epidemic is that trash signifiers and behavior have become slipperier, crossing ethnic lines. Consider slaphappy Hungarian Zsa Zsa Gabor; the two Italian Americans John Esposito and Salvatore Inghilleri, who, respectively, were convicted of kidnapping and of sexually abusing Katie Beers; and the voguish Asian-American model Jenny Shimizu. Shimizu flexes tattoos of a blue spark plug and a blonde straddling an eight-inch wrench; she eats a lot of Big Macs and is fond of leaving "You suck" messages on friends' answering machines, using her talking Beavis and Butt-head toy.

And trash now lurks in an upscale guise at the euphemistic "gentlemen's clubs"—joints with a dress code for customers and an undress code for employees. Last year ten million customers spent $3 billion at places like Stringfellow's, where a table dance costs $20 and where men in ties and suspenders watch topless women crawl around "winking, purring, and sometimes barking," as *The New York Times* wonderingly put it.

Even once lofty venues have fallen—the Olympics, for instance, where Tonya Harding stole the show. "Pool-hustling, drag-racing, cigarette-smoking, trash-talking Tonya," as a quickie bio describes her. She of the bleached, permed hair; the blank, cheap eyes; the rabbit-fur coat and the job working at Spud City. She who skated to ZZ Top and whose bodyguard, Shawn Eckardt, drove a 1974 Mercury with missing hubcaps. She whose ex-husband, Jeff Gillooly, just sold the X-rated video of their wedding night to *Penthouse,* which has made it available to a bemused public through an 800 number.

Politics, while often venal, once had a patina of respectability; now it's a vast trashscape. James Carville proudly tells me, "I'm white trash myself," and riffs into a series of jokes about ways to tell if you are, too: "A ceiling fan messes up your sister's hairdo"; "Your brother-in-law is also your uncle"; etc. Whitewater, though numbingly complex, is at bottom a pure good-old-boy scam; the Clintons' former partner, James McDougal, lived up to that tradition when he came to the Whitewater hearings accompanied by one Tamra Meacham, a student from Arkansas's Ouachita Baptist University who modeled bleached-blond hair and a teensy-weensy black dress. Daniel Patrick Moynihan terms Clinton's welfare reform ideas "boob bait for the Bubbas," and we are reminded anew that our president's family tree has bubbas on every branch—his father's acorns, in fact, keep turning up.

Clinton's mom, Virginia Kelley, married four times, wagered furiously at the track, and worshiped Elvis—*the* white trash icon. The president's stepfather Roger, known as Dude, was an abusive alcoholic. The president's ex-cokehead half brother, another Roger and a dude in his own right, parlayed his demigenetic serendipity into roles in such films as *Pumpkinhead 2: Blood Wings* and commercials for Comedy Central set in a mock Oval Office with a faux-leopard-skin chair.

And Howard Stern—*Howard Stern*—ran a bizarre, abortive race for governor of New York.

Then again, there is Paula Corbin Jones. "Paula asked me, 'What would be a good drink that would cost a lot?' " Mark Brown says. "I said, 'Amaretto on the rocks, water back.' You can get a good buzz off it, but mainly it's for women. I said to her later, 'What the hell you wanting to know all this shit for?' And she said, 'I got to find out if somebody's got money or not, if he can pay for this.' "

"She told Mark and myself many times that she would marry somebody with money," Charlotte Brown says. "She has very expensive tastes. She had known him [Steve Jones, now her husband] barely a week, and he bought her a leather couch; he bought her an amethyst ring, a real expensive purse—it's called a Gucci bag—and a matching wallet. She told me they cost $250 apiece." Paula had also sniffed the lingering musk of Elvis: Steve Jones had played Presley's ghost in the Jim Jarmusch movie *Mystery Train.* According to *People,* Paula boasted to a friend, "He looks just like Elvis and talks like him."

Jones has denied the Browns' portrait of her as a loose woman and declared that "some American people have put in their minds that I'm a liar, a lowlife come out of l'il ol' Lonoke, Arkansas." Well, yes. Jones recently accepted $50,000 from No Excuses jeans, apparently unaware of the company's previous campaigns with Marla Maples and Donna Rice. (Tonya Harding is so trashy, even No Excuses turned her down.) When Clinton's lawyer Robert Bennett wanted to disparage Jones's suit, he called it "tabloid trash"—but everyone knew what he meant.

The curious thing about the Browns, the point almost lost in the media fix on them as the skeptics, is that they *do* believe that Jones and Governor Clinton had some kind of involvement in the Excelsior Hotel. "She talked to me about that day in 1991," Charlotte says, "told me that Governor Clinton had dropped his pants in the hotel room, asked her to perform oral sex, and she'd refused. But how she said it, it was like it was flattering."

How did we get to such a pitch of low expectation about our fellow citizens' behavior that this lurid scenario barely registers as a distraction from the O. J. Simpson case? Where we idly watch as the disputed facts are gummed to a gooey cud in the media maw? Jones might not have filed suit if Clinton had prevailed upon his friend the producer Harry Thomason to give her a job in Hollywood. Now, in revenge, we can expect her to sell her story for a movie of the week—perhaps *Kiss It: The Paula Corbin Jones Story.*

In 1916, hobo and Wobblies agitator Harry Kirby McLintock predicted in his "Hymn of Hate": "And *The Day* shall come, with a red, red dawn; / And you in your gilded halls, / Shall taste the wrath and vengeance of the men in overalls." The Day is at hand. Yet the men in overalls have triumphed not because of the puissance of organized labor, but because when it comes to behavior, America is wearing Osh Kosh B'Gosh. Like the urbanites in *Deliverance,* we have found ourselves in the grinning clutches of sexually predatory backwoodsmen. White trash culture commands us to "squeal like a pig!" And we're oinking.

—

Since the first rawboned indentured servants came to America from Europe, a white underclass has simmered on our back burner. These are the Snopeses who live on the poorest land in the South, in Appalachia, in Oklahoma, the ones for whom the certified check of American promise always bounces. "Fierce craving boys," Nelson Algren called them, the ones "with a feeling of having been cheated." "The white world's vermin and filth . . ." W.E.B. Du Bois said, more angrily and less specifically, those "shameless breeders of bastards, / drunk with the greed of gold, / . . . bearing the white man's burden / of liquor and lust and lies!"

White trash has ever been in the eye of the beholder, and as a lay classification, it remains a way to pinion someone to his roots, to deny him upward mobility. In Thomas Harris's *The Silence of the Lambs,* Hannibal Lecter stingingly tells FBI trainee Clarice Starling, "You're a well-scrubbed, hustling rube with a little taste . . . desperate not to be like your mother. . . . But you're not more than one generation out of the mines, *Officer* Starling. [In the movie, it's out of "poor white trash."] Is it the West Virginia Starlings or the Okie Starlings, Officer?"

But even as the term passes into the realm of the unsayable, white trash's connotations increasingly describe America. The country is becoming underclass-laden, illiterate, promiscuous, and just plain fat. A recent report by the Labor and Commerce Departments showed constant-dollar median income declining from 1972 to 1990 by 23 percent for men with less than a high school education and by 5 percent for women from the same group. The well educated did much better. There is a spirited debate over who's responsible for the widening gap between the haves and the have-nots, but the fact is that the number of have-nots is growing. "Trash gets all the working poor who fall out of the middle class—the middle-class boys gone bad," notes Dorothy Allison, author of the novel *Bastard out of Carolina* and the short-story collection *Trash.* "It's the difference between thinking your life is hopeless and *knowing* it is."

The Educational Testing Service reports a drop in young-adult literacy from 1985 to 1992. Sexual-partner numbers are hard to compare because of differing methodologies, but it's suggestive to contrast the 1953 Kinsey Report, in which just 5 percent of females reported having had more than ten premarital partners, with the 1993 Janus Report, which shows 55 percent of women having had more than ten partners—an elevenfold increase.

And according to the government, the number of overweight adults, which had held steady from 1960 to 1980 at 25 percent of the population, suddenly ballooned to 33 percent between 1980 and 1991. We gained a collective 155 million pounds last year, even as Kathleen Sullivan dieted furiously. (The boom in comfort food is very white trash. In *White Trash Cooking,* Ernest Mickler's recipe for a "High-Calorie Pick-Me-Up" directs you to "pour a small bag of Tom's peanuts into a cold Pepsi. Turn it up and eat and drink at the same time.")

Traditionally, to find white trash backgrounds, one looked for "artificial grass, velvet paintings, double-wide trailers adjoined as a sign of status, fish sticks, Spam, muscle cars, John Deere caps, sideburns, collections of dolls or Hummelware, pink flamingos in the front yard, painted tires that hold flowers, and people who like Liberace or Elvis," says Michael J. Weiss, a demographer who draws up cultural maps of the country. His maps of above average concentrations of *National Enquirer* readers and mobile home owners carve out a Trash Belt of the eleven states of the old Confederacy (excluding Atlanta), Maine, Appalachia, strips of rural Texas and Arizona, and pockets of the Midwest.

Hollywood has turned to such maps for clues in its perpetual treasure hunt. Previously we got the risible (Buford Pusser) or the cloddishly endearing (Jim Varney's Ernest character). But now screenwriters are obsessed with the idea of the road-tripping, spontaneous, and often murderous poor. (It is ever tempting for Hollywood to impute authenticity to the ignorant—and to give them bodacious bods.) In addition to the forthcoming *Natural Born Killers,* we've been visited with *Guncrazy, True Romance, A Perfect World,* and *Kalifornia.*

"It's totally about sex," says director John Waters. "Extreme white people"—Waters's preferred term for the white underclass—"look incredibly beautiful until they're twenty, and then they look about fifty. It's a sexual fantasy for people in movies, who don't meet those sorts of people very much—it's the idea of the bad boy, the juvenile delinquent."

Movies give us an airbrushed dream of white trash: alluring and deadly. Television, on the other hand, locks us into a trash feedback loop. "The explosion of tabloid TV sensationalizes problems that were previously repressed and unarticulated, except as small-town gossip," says Mary Matalin, host of *Equal Time* (and wife of James Carville). "Ten years ago, no one would talk about fat, incest, and wife or child abuse. Now, with Tonya [Harding] or the Bobbitts, it's tantamount to why we used to go look at the Elephant Man or the Lobster Boy."

Fittingly, the latest trash scandal involves "Lobster Boy" Grady Stiles Jr. of Gibsonton, Florida, a footless carnival attraction whose two-fingered hands looked like claws. Stiles's wife, Mary Teresa (previously married to a dwarf), was just convicted of conspiring to kill Grady as he relaxed at home in his underwear; Mary Teresa's unsuccessful defense was that he had sexually abused her, head-butted her, and swatted her with his pincer hands. Since Phil Donahue began the genre in 1967, daytime talk has never run out of such gross turpitudes—indeed, the catfights and jaw-dropping catastrophes give Greg Kinnear an endless supply of highlights to smirk at daily on *Talk Soup.*

But most people don't watch to scoff. Penn State sociologist Vicki Abt, who recently studied one thousand hours of *Oprah, Donahue,* and *Sally Jessy Raphaël,* estimates that 90 percent of the guests are illiterate, and suspects that the viewers aren't building their vocabulary much, either: "If you see shows about men who sleep with their mother-in-law enough, people get used to these things," she says. "If you see this all the time, the man who doesn't sleep with his mother-in-law will eventually become strange. . . . A child sees that if he acts terribly, he might get on Phil, Sally, or Oprah."

Indeed, not only is there no manifest reward in our society for behaving well, there is now a reward for behaving badly—the fifteen camera crews on hand to immortalize Joey Buttafuoco's exit from prison after he'd served his term for statutory rape; the reported $500,000 he made from *A Current Affair;* the $200,000 he made from the CBS movie *Casualties of Love.* Witness John Wayne Bobbitt, who has made hundreds of thousands of dollars on a *Love Hurts* media tour featuring appearances where he autographs steak knives and plays Stump the Bobbitt, a contest testing his knowledge of Bobbitt-castration jokes. He has begun marketing a Bobbitt penis protector, made by the Klimax Corporation, and is negotiating with *Playboy* for a photo spread in which his sometime fiancée, former topless dancer Kristina Elliott, shucks her clothes while he, with becoming shyness, keeps his on. Modestly, too, he turned down $1 million last week to do a porn movie featuring his reassembled manroot.

Ponder also Kris Belman, a leader of the infamous Lakewood, California, Spur Posse. Belman had been charged with—and would later be put on probation for—committing lewd and lascivious acts with a thirteen-year-old girl. But after he appeared on *Jenny Jones* and *Inside Edition,* "a lot of girls called," he reported happily. "I went out with them."

And Gennifer Flowers, who in the wake of Paula Jones's accusations marketed her phone call "love tapes" with Bill Clinton for $19.95, was outraged by a caller to a Florida radio show who suggested she was leveraging her own immorality. "You better just shut your mouth!" Flowers shouted. "I'm here to put some factual information to you idiots out there!"

Whatever happened to the useful idea of shame? When James Agee wrote about Alabama sharecroppers in *Let Us Now Praise Fa-*

mous Men (1941), his shame at his comparative social and journalistic advantages was matched only by the sharecroppers' shame at the exposure of their pitiful circumstance. "There was in their eyes so quiet and ultimate a quality of hatred and contempt, and anger," Agee wrote, "toward every creature in existence beyond themselves, and toward the damages they sustained, as shone scarcely short of a state of beatitude."

Nowadays, shame is felt only by those who remain obscure, who never get the call from *Montel Williams.* Jessica Hahn, the then mousy church secretary who was sexually abused by televangelist Jim Bakker in a Florida hotel room and later paid $265,000 in hush money, felt deep shame for years. But the klieg lights of publicity are better than a therapist's couch. Posing topless for *Playboy* in 1987, she said, "made me feel clean again." Hahn's passage from shame to shamelessness ended in white trash nirvana: she became a regular on *The Howard Stern Show,* a featured star in such Stern videos as *Butt Bongo Fiesta.*

As Stern himself bellicosely notes about the shame question: "How many guys have the balls to ask their mom if she takes it up the ass?" More and more, apparently. Stern's pay-per-view New Year's Eve pageant grossed a record-setting $15 million; its judges were Hahn and John Wayne Bobbitt. "If Howard Stern didn't exist," Reverend Al Sharpton has correctly observed, "white trash would not have a superstar."

Stern's compulsions—his fascination with farting, body parts, and some Platonic dream of nympho lesbians—are at trash's root. White trash behavior is defined by childlikeness and the headlong pursuit of easy gratification—quite often, sex. Feral child Amy Fisher said of Joey Buttafuoco that he introduced her to "expensive restaurants and cheap motels." Joey had some difficulties getting to the motel all the time, so Amy shot his wife.

Courtney Love's dark roots and dirty baby-doll dresses are as sophisticated an appropriation of the childlike white trash aesthetic as was the Rolling Stones' homage to black urban style; Love's delight in looking like "a fourteen-year-old battered rape victim," a "kinder-whore," is a nutshell of white trash chic. So, too, are the suggestively named Tease-brand baby-doll T-shirts, which evoke a Lolita-at-the-Dairy-Queen thing. (Real-life Lolita Bridget Hall, the sixteen-year-old model with an eighth-grade education from Farmers Branch, Texas, stayed with Ford Models head Eileen Ford when she came to New York but refused to eat her chili because it didn't come from a can.) The slumming well-to-do believe that by affecting trash poses, they are tapping into authentic despair and alienation, just as certainly as if they had styled a beret and black turtleneck in the fifties.

"The form of trash is attractive," writer Dorothy Allison says, "but the content is not. Americans are into form without content. True trash doesn't care what happens, because we don't believe our good behavior will get us anywhere. So we're dangerous—we don't necessarily care for your life."

—

Tabloid-TV exposure can lobotomize the shame of white trash behavior, but it can't entirely create that behavior in the first place. So where did our rampant trashiness spring from? Liberals and slackers subscribe to the backlash-against-eighties-excess theory. "With *The Cosby Show* they were all doctors and lawyers going off to Princeton and walking around the house with $1,000 outfits," says Mike Judge, creator and voice of MTV's *Beavis and Butt-head*. "All through the eighties I thought there were way too many good-looking people on TV—you just start feeling inadequate. I thought it would be cool to have something on TV where you don't have to be ashamed that you live in a dumpy house and wear dumpy clothes and watch too much TV. Along with *Married . . . with Children* and *The Simpsons,* there's a power-to-the-lower-income-white-people trend."

Then there is the abdication-of-leadership theory, especially favored by Republicans. Harper Lee, author of *To Kill a Mockingbird,* once said that "with two generations of prosperity white trash looks like gentry." Perhaps the reverse also obtains: with two generations of inertial guidance, gentry looks like white trash. "This form of [trashy] behavior is much more prevalent among the bohemians and the hippies, the upper-income groups in the Hamptons," says *Equal Time*'s Mary Matalin. "It goes from the top down. Ernest Hemingway and Scott Fitzgerald and all Max Perkins's writers were total slugs—they all beat their wives and drank like fish and slept around." The conservative view is acute, though hyperbolic. When we abandoned teaching the core values of Western civilization, Allan Bloom argues in *The Closing of the American Mind*, we lost our common mores: "Civilization has seemingly led us around full circle, back to the state of nature. . . ." As Ashley Judd muses in the 1993 movie *Ruby in Paradise*, "Why slave your life out when you can just take? Are there any real reasons for living right, anyway?"

The presenting symptom of our social decline, believes scholar Charles Murray, is white illegitimacy. He unscrolls a dismal statistical litany: In 1991, 22 percent of white births were illegitimate; 69 percent of those single white mothers had family incomes under $20,000; and 82 percent of them had a high school education or less.

An additional stress is rising divorce rates: Of white children born in 1980, only 30 percent will live with both parents through the age of eighteen; those born in 1950 had an 81 percent chance. Families under the poverty line are twice as likely as other families to undergo parental separations, and various studies show that single-parent children are two to three times as likely to have emotional and behavioral problems.

"If the dominant culture deems you a misfit if you drop out, then you plug away," Murray says. "If there is an alternative culture that says, 'Who needs that shit?,' then dropping out becomes an option. And that alternative culture is the black underclass." Of the popular neologism *wigger*, Murray notes, "It refers to white kids who mimic black dress, walk, or attitudes. But what they're really imitating is black underclass attitudes toward achievement. When a large number of males grow up without fathers, then they emulate the local heroes—the drug dealers, who get lots of women, have money, and take no crap."

This argument—that black underclass problems resonate in the white underclass—has had a fierce political valence since at least 1965 (the year of Moynihan's controversial report to President Johnson, "The Negro Family: The Case for National Action," which prefigured Murray). Liberals take obscure comfort from the suggestion, often made by Jesse Jackson and scholar Andrew Hacker, that all races share despair: they find talking about the white underclass a pressure-release valve from coded discussions of the black underclass.

Conservatives, on the other hand, are horrified. "Unless these exploding social pathologies are reversed," William J. Bennett warns in Nostradamian tones about drug use, violent crime, and illegitimacy in his best-selling *The Index of Leading Cultural Indicators*, "they will lead to the decline and perhaps even the fall of the American republic."

Parents, especially fathers, are supposed to prevent us—if not the putatively fragile republic—from falling prey to our impulses. To stop us from acting like children. Kimberly Mays, who last year won a court ruling allowing her to sever ties with her biological parents and remain with her adopted father, this year switched back to her original parents, Ernest and Regina Twigg. The reason, according to one of Kimberly's friends, was her adoptive father Robert Mays's hard line: "She hated him because he wouldn't let her stay out late with her boyfriend."

Fittingly, both Beavis and Butt-head "have single mothers, we've decided," says Mike Judge. "They're from some town like Channelview, Texas, where everyone's parents are welders or work in a big yard where they store pipes. If they had a dad around, there'd be more supervision and they probably wouldn't get away with as much."

The boom in trash behavior clearly owes less to Marx than to Freud, less to the resolution of class dialectics than to simple indulgence of the id. There is, in short, much to be said for repression. "The Zeitgeist of the twentieth century is to throw off the artificial restraints of civilization and etiquette, to express yourself and not control your feelings," says Judith Martin, better known as "Miss

Manners." "It's a pop misleading of Freud, and I abhor it. The moral results are that if you don't like someone, you shoot them, or smash their car, or, if you insist on being law-abiding, sue them over small matters."

The ultimate restraining figure, of course, is the jealous God who has loomed over the American landscape since preacher Jonathan Edwards's early warning that "all children are by nature children of wrath, and are in danger of eternal damnation in hell." White-trash behavior comes not just from the absence of stern parents, but from the masses skipping masses, from all those going cold turkey on religious opiates.

Consider the falls of evangelists Jim Bakker, Jimmy Swaggart, and, most recently, Arkansas's Tony Alamo, convicted of tax evasion and of having wed eight of his followers within the past eighteen months. Jessica Hahn was once a devout Pentecostal, and Roseanne Arnold's father sold 3-D pictures of Jesus door-to-door. Paula Corbin Jones had daily prayer sessions growing up in Arkansas. Of her mother's Bible Missionary sect, Charlotte Corbin Brown says, "They don't wear makeup, no wedding rings, jewelry, no pants for women, no shorts, clothing below the elbows and knees, no movies, and no TV—Mama wouldn't even watch Paula on TV now."

"Miz Corbin is so religious it would embarrass Paula," Mark Brown says. "So Paula went away from all religious-type things. She went away *fast*."

———

White trash behavior is neither a delightful plastic flamingo on the front lawn of American culture nor a glimpse of existential freedom. As Mike Judge says of his own creations, "Beavis and Butt-head are funny from a distance, but I wouldn't want them around a lot. If these two guys came into a restaurant, you'd be thinking, I hope they don't sit over here."

True trash is unsocialized and violent. "[They] are obvious losers, and it bugs them," Hunter Thompson has written of the Hell's Angels. "But instead of submitting quietly to their collective fate, they have made it the basis of a full-time social vendetta. They don't expect to win anything, but on the other hand, they have nothing to lose."

An even more damaged trash response than being chubby and riding without a helmet is serial killings, which are almost exclusively committed by white men between the ages of twenty-five and forty. More serial murders have been reported since 1970 than in all previous American history combined. The commercial response has been swift: there are five lines of serial-killer trading cards; Axl Rose sings Charles Manson songs and *Spin* has the cult leader on its cover; the late John Wayne Gacy's paintings sell for up to $20,000. And Pearl Jam's Eddie Vedder and the ubiquitous Howard Stern have said that they could have easily responded to their childhoods by becoming serial killers.

White trash disproves the notion that we are all infinitely perfectable, that all that stands between us and felicity is a few hours of self-help. White trash is about scars that won't heal. Twice in the past three months, John Wayne Bobbitt has been charged with battering his fiancée. Being unredeemable is "part of the Roseanne-and-Tom shit," Dorothy Allison says. "They're always going to be figures of contempt—there's no reward for not acting trashy, so why shouldn't they do what they want?" Both Roseanne and Tom say they were molested as children; Roseanne has alleged, improbably, that her father would "chase me with his excrement and try to put it on my head. He'd lie on the floor playing with himself. It was the most disgusting thing you can ever imagine." Yes, pretty much. Courtney Love's mother turned her in to the police when she shoplifted a Kiss T-shirt at the age of twelve. And Tonya Harding's vision of the future was also clouded early. She moved eight times as a child; her half brother allegedly assaulted her; and her mother, LaVona, who was married five, six, or seven times, depending on whom you believe, beat her with a hairbrush and called her "bitch" and "scum."

The epithets also flew as Kenneth Lakeberg left a courthouse in Indiana last year after a probation hearing. The wife of a cousin Lakeberg had slashed with a butcher knife shouted at Lakeberg, among other things, "You're nothing but scum." Lakeberg is the unemployed welder whose wife gave birth to Siamese twins and who became notorious after he blew the cash people had sent in to help pay for the risky operation to separate them. Lakeberg spent $8,000 of the contributions on a car, expensive meals, and $1,300 worth of cocaine.

He promised a judge he would quit drugs and reform. And the media did their part to help lick away his shame. His lawyer, Lloyd Remick, sought to sell the family's ordeal as a movie of the week, and did succeed in peddling part of it to the *National Enquirer,* which trumpeted Angela's survival of the operation: LITTLE MISS MIRACLE GETS HER FIRST HUG FROM MOMMY.

Alas, in June, when baby Angela succumbed to an infection, her father was in a drug rehab center in West Lafayette, Indiana. His wife later had to bail him out of jail so that he could go to his daughter's funeral. "Apparently, allegedly, Kenny borrowed a car from a friend, never returned it, and pawned it for drugs," Lloyd Remick told me. "I don't know what he's up to, but the headline is TWINS' DAD ARRESTED AGAIN."

Had he done wrong taking the money? Lakeberg, a walking ad for No Excuses, never thought so. "We ate at nice places," Lakeberg said of his spree. "We traveled good. I think we deserved at least that much." True trash takes what it needs and claims it's what it deserves. True trash is one long boiling tantrum, primed to explode. True trash is the terrible twos forever.

The culture is in a panic to find its collective inner child. Well, here he is.

(1994)

GETTING AWAY WITH IT

As you may have heard, O. J. Simpson walked. And the first thing he did, Disney World being out of the question, was have a party at his Rockingham estate. O.J. would see his small children, Sydney and Justin, the next day in a tasteful reunion, with only the *Star* present to take exclusive photos for upward of $500,000; right now, as Nicole's father said, he had "some wild oats to sow." Near where police had found O.J.'s blood-saturated socks, white-gloved waiters hovered with offerings of shrimp, steak, and chicken. The wingding featured champagne on the balcony; Simpson's mother, Eunice, arriving in a cream Rolls-Royce; and "curvy nude model" Paula Barbieri—as the *New York Post* delicately put it—arriving for the night. The whole fiesta was filmed for later airing on O.J.'s expected $10 million pay-per-view interview. A classy homecoming, in short, one bespeaking the humility that has enabled Simpson to endure these monstrous false accusations.

Wait. That little bubble of sarcasm was wholly inappropriate, and I apologize. I still catch myself thinking that a man who is *manifestly guilty of butchering two people like pigs in a slaughterhouse*

and who should spend the rest of his life vainly scraping at his bars
with a dull toothbrush might give thanks for his freedom in a more
seemly manner. Might even feel a pang of, oh, I don't know, guilt.
But that's old thinking, yesterday's morality. The fact is that
today powerful men walk or do only token time, feel no guilt, and
often cash in even bigger than before. In the old days Fatty Ar-
buckle's career was ruined, Nathan Leopold and Richard Loeb received lengthy sentences for murder, and Robert Mitchum even
served time for smoking pot. Nowadays, punishment, like taxes, is
for the little people.

Witness sculptor Carl Andre (acquitted of pushing his wife out
the window after an argument); John DeLorean (acquitted of drug
possession, conspiracy, and distribution, despite an incriminating
videotape); the director John Landis (acquitted of the involuntary
manslaughter of actor Vic Morrow); Washington fixer Clark Clif-
ford (indicted but never tried—because of ailing health—on charges
of bribery and conspiracy in the secret acquisition of First American
Bank by BCCI); and Senator Alfonse D'Amato (found by the Senate Ethics Committee to have conducted his office in an "improper
and inappropriate manner," but not charged with influence peddling
to Wedtech, Unisys, and many other companies).

Witness also the merry Iran-contra gang: Oliver North and John
Poindexter, whose felony charges were reversed on an evidentiary
technicality; Caspar Weinberger and Robert McFarlane, who were
pardoned by outgoing president George Bush; Bush himself, whose
claim to be "out of the loop" was undercut by Weinberger's handwritten meeting notes; and Ronald Reagan, who gave investigators
three different versions of what he knew and when he knew it.

All these guys knew other guys who knew the guys to know; they
were upheld by their network; they had top lawyers. Lawyers! The
one moment in the Simpson trial when I admired a defense lawyer's
probity was when Robert Shapiro stood in court to denounce Johnnie Cochran for making racist detective Mark Fuhrman the issue.
"Not only did we play the race card, we dealt it from the bottom of
the deck," Shapiro said, apologizing to humanity in general. Oh. My

time line is off—Shapiro said that *after* the verdict, when the race card had already trumped for his client. The piety we heard from so many commentators, including President Clinton, to the effect that the jury system, whatever its flaws, blah, blah, blah, is a dusty civics lesson that shouldn't even be taught in the third grade. The truth is: If you can afford to hire Johnnie Cochran—or Roy Black or Richard "Racehorse" Haines or Gerry Spence or Thomas Puccio or Alan Dershowitz—at $400 an hour, you'll probably get away with it. While Martha "Sunny" von Bülow lies in a coma from insulin injections, her husband, Claus, is a glam socialite with a roguish cachet (yes, yes, acquitted in the retrial with Puccio at his side after Dershowitz won an appeal). We kinda think you did it, Claus, but you're so darn Continental and debonair.

Does anyone doubt that if Susan Smith, who drove her kids into a lake, had had enough money to hire Leslie Abramson, she'd be home right now eating microwave popcorn? Abramson, Erik Menendez's fiercely mothering attorney, would connect the dots of victimization: sexually abused by her stepfather; rejected by her boyfriend; hasn't she suffered enough? Gina Grant, too, suffered considerable abuse before she clubbed her mother thirteen times with a candlestick. But she worked hard, aced her SATs, and was set to go to Harvard until the university caught wind of the whole, um, you know, the thing that happened. If Grant had had Johnnie Cochran, she'd be blowing froth off a cappuccino in Harvard Square.

Of course, both Smith and Grant would have done better if they were men. Guys have license. Judges and juries find their flaws natural and forgivable (of Dershowitz's celebrity clients, Patty Hearst and Leona Helmsley fared least well). But even prominent men need a fortune to be convincing as poor victims. Former House Ways and Means chairman Dan Rostenkowski is having trouble defending against charges that he misappropriated more than $640,000 simply because, after spending $3 million on lawyers, he's broke. Robert Vesco, now languishing in a Cuban prison for marketing a supposed wonder drug, was a fool to flee America. He should have taken the

$224 million he embezzled, hired about five hundred lawyers, and gotten himself off on a technicality like a man.

So clear is it that money buys reasonable doubt that we should simply codify it: Henceforth, anyone who can afford to hire Johnnie Cochran is not guilty. Simple as that. When the prosecutor says, "Isn't this you on the videotape, killing your whole family down to your daughter's gerbils, Puff and Spanky, and then illegally hooking yourself up to a premium cable channel?" you simply say, "May it please the court, my attorney [dramatic pause] . . . Johnnie Cochran!" Pandemonium, and you're escorted home in a white minivan.

Let's allocate society's resources where they can be effective. In the future, we should try only poor people, preferably those with marginal IQs who don't speak much English and have never heard of the *Miranda* decision. And let's reconsider the whole idea of court-appointed lawyers. If Colin Ferguson can do such a masterful (and cheap!) job defending himself—even while missing a few toys in the attic—this is clearly an area where private enterprise should replace government intervention.

In employing the Cochran standard, we will simply be adopting our foreign relations paradigm for domestic use. The United States has expressed distaste for—and finally bombed the positions of— Bosnian Serb leaders Radovan Karadzic and General Ratko Mladic (charged with crimes against humanity for their gleefully announced blood "feast" against Muslims, which required killing two hundred thousand civilians and raping up to twenty thousand women). Yet we winked at the ethnic cleansings carried out by Croatian president and unreconstructed anti-Semite Franjo Tudjman.

So, too, we insisted that Pol Pot's Khmer Rouge, which killed at least one million Cambodians during the seventies, be part of recent election negotiations. And remember George Bush shamelessly toasting the late Philippine dictator Ferdinand Marcos: "We love your adherence to democratic principles"? We brought that policy home in 1990, when Imelda Marcos was acquitted of stealing $222 million from the Philippines and investing it in Manhattan real estate. Somehow, she was able to afford Gerry Spence.

What a benevolent country! The O.J. case was rife with troubling portents about spousal abuse and racist police, but the bottom line is that—finally!—a prominent black reprobate can go as scot-free as a prominent white reprobate. Boxing promoter Don King's odyssey shows how far we've come. Thirty years ago he served four years for manslaughter, but he cleanly beat a 1985 federal indictment for tax evasion. Just charged again with nine more counts of insurance fraud, he'll walk out free and proud.

Mike Tyson and Marion "the Bitch Set Me Up" Barry semi–got away with it. Tyson served three years for the sexual assault of a beauty pageant contestant, but he scored $25 million in a ninety-second comeback fight with a palooka; Barry served six months for an infamous crack possession, then was reelected mayor of Washington. "Get over it," he told old-school moralists. Clarence Thomas mostly got away with it (his nomination to the Supreme Court confirmed, so able to deal a lethal blow to affirmative action, but left deeply embittered). And now Michael Jackson has totally gotten away with a reported payment of $15 million to the family of the boy he allegedly molested. Given the singer's wealth, this is less a punishment than a tip.

In our gorgeous mosaic, any member of a historically disadvantaged group who can afford to hire Johnnie Cochran should now feel free to run amok. Bully for Senator Ben Nighthorse Campbell if he decides to strangle a few liberals to prove his new GOP bona fides. If autograph seekers pester Hideo Nomo, he has our permission to club them like baby seals. And Stephen Hawking—cowabunga!

Instituting the Cochran standard carries little downside, as most of these rich guys have only one or two or three or four spectacular crimes in them. How likely is it, really, that William Kennedy Smith, now a physician with a special interest in fetal-alcohol syndrome, would get another chance to employ his seduction techniques at one of the family compounds? The old "I'm a Kennedy, you should try it" line has pretty much lost its appeal. And the chance that former UN secretary general Kurt Waldheim would join another Nazi unit that commits atrocities in Yugoslavia is near zero, as he's almost eighty and the Yugoslavs want younger, more vigorous soldiers to commit their atrocities. Nor can Lyle and Erik Menendez kill any more of their parents, as they're in jail and, for that matter, orphaned.

And I think we all feel pretty confident that O.J. will be too busy chatting with Larry King, making infotainment deals, and assembling enemies lists to butcher anyone else like a pig in a slaughterhouse. The only ticklish scenario would be if curvy nude model Paula Barbieri makes him really, really mad by, say, disagreeing with him in public, talking to another man in the checkout line, or growing old and wrinkly. And if I were her, I wouldn't.

(1995)

PLEASE DON'T OIL THE
ANIMATRONIC WARTHOG

As I stared vacantly at a lush but empty gorilla habitat of bamboo and palm, a red streak flamed across the corner of my eye. A loud thump followed, and then a scrabbling-fluttering sound. Then silence. A scarlet cardinal lay supine on the path, six feet from the plate-glass window. A dismayed Disney PR handler and I bent over it. The cardinal's head was disastrously askew, and it gasped shallowly, its black eyes locked on mine in an expression I can only call perplexed.

Yes, this *was* Disney's new Animal Kingdom. And the $1 billion playground in Walt Disney World, southwest of Orlando, intends to celebrate our relationship with all animals—real, extinct, and mythical. But only two hundred privileged species were allowed for, only two hundred unpredictable behaviors predicted, as Disney spent eight years planning and planting to transform five hundred acres of cattle pasture into a fantasia of Edens, dragons' lairs, trained bird shows, dinosaur rides, Asian tiger encounters (opening in 1999), and African savanna immersions.

The cardinal—and other local wild animals, including some

pesky opossums and bobcats that were forcibly relocated—wasn't in the plan. But Disney has learned from the lousy publicity it got for killing fifteen unwanted black vultures at Discovery Island in 1989 and shooting feral pigs on its Wilderness Preserve in 1993. Rick Sylvain, the PR man, got on his cell phone and alerted veterinary services, stat: "We've got a downed bird at Gorilla Falls observation window!"

For days afterward I tried to discover the cardinal's fate, but Sylvain said the vets were hard to reach. The bird had vanished into Disney's maw. Ten days later, when I asked yet again, Sylvain reported that the cardinal had been placed in an incubator, "given some medicine," and then released. Hmmm. That's probably true, but after a week in Disney's Animal Kingdom I didn't entirely believe it.

It's not that anyone at Disney would lie to me, exactly. It's just that the company has an uncanny ability to spin animal stories into triumphal myths, to convince you that you're having an authentic experience rather than one manufactured for your pleasure and reassurance. Disney sees it differently, of course. "We're moving away from the cognitive, expository, catalog idea of a zoo, where you randomly access bits of information that happen to be animals," says Joe Rohde, executive designer of Disney's Animal Kingdom (henceforth DAK). "Here we're passionate and personal—we've wrapped the animal interactions in a dramatic experience that will leave you *feeling* connected to animals and *feeling* the importance of our conservation message."

These interactions crescendo as you penetrate deeper into DAK's six "lands," from the opening arcadia of the Oasis, to Camp Minnie-Mickey, where you shake the paw of Safari Mickey, to DinoLand U.S.A., where you take a prehistoric thrill ride, then past a huge "Tree of Life" in the central Safari Village, and—perhaps after a train ride to the research center at Conservation Station—finally to Africa. Here the Imagineers have shifted 1.5 million cubic yards of earth and installed 2.3 million exotic plants to create a 110-acre Serengeti, complete with hippos, rhinos, and lions engaging in "the unpredictable antics of live animals in their own environments," as Disney chairman Michael Eisner optimistically puts it.

Two months before DAK's April 22 opening I spent a week peeking behind the scenes, watching construction workers punch-listing the exhibits and "cast members" learning their scripts, and being hurried into—and quickly out of—interviews with the park's creators. Disney minders bird-dogged me everywhere, wearing worried expressions and having sotto-voce cell phone conversations. The marvels I did see made me confident that DAK will be a great success with Disney World's forty million annual visitors—and, at $39.75 a head, highly profitable. Yet DAK also left me with a lingering unease: its cinematic departure from the taxonomic, geographic, and natural history framework of zoos does facilitate our intimacy with animals, but it also blurs our sense of what, exactly, animals are.

For half a century, of course, Disney has been blurring our sense of other lands and times with rides and tableaux where you are cushioned against culture shock by twin quotation marks. This picturesque compression is what anthropologist Stephen Fjellman has called Distory: thus Epcot's Disneyfied Norway is composed solely of fjords, stave churches, and Viking longboats.

The Distory within the Kingdom is especially insidious, because it's invisible. While elephants have a home range of up to 135,000 acres in the east African savanna, DAK's elephants spend their days in six moated acres. Come evening they're summoned with duck whistles and cow bells and kept overnight in holding barns as repair crews replant the environment—an adult elephant eats 125 pounds of food a day—and whisk away all the manure. The standard of care is excellent by zoo standards, but how "real" are the "antics" of such elephants? As chaos theorist Ian Malcolm said of another such arena, "The kind of control you're attempting is not possible. If there's one thing the history of evolution has taught us, it's that life . . . expands to new territories, it crashes through barriers—painfully, even dangerously."

That arena, of course, was the one occupied so bloodily by dinosaurs in *Jurassic Park*, Malcolm, played by Jeff Goldblum, was the movie's way of allowing viewers to disapprove of man's tampering with nature even as they vicariously enjoyed the fruits of that tampering. A very Disney idea. The company presents animals as a catchall menu: the clownish, farting warthog Pumbaa one minute, a real and "dangerous" warthog the next. "We don't need to reconcile our different messages about animals," says Judson Green, president of Walt Disney Attractions. "Let people connect however they want." And in a sense there is no contradiction, because all the animals here—costumed, animated, audioanimatronic, and real—are presented as treats. The farting warthog is a comic treat, and the live warthog, dislocated from its natural struggle to breed and eat, is a freaky treat.

As I experienced Disney's treats, it became clear that in an important sense this park isn't about animals at all. It's about us, about our wishes and needs. For how we behave toward animals taken from their natural surroundings reveals us to ourselves, as Queen Victoria discovered long ago. During its infancy the London Zoo placed animals in bourgeois surroundings; the apes were dressed in nursery clothes and trained to have tea parties. Watching an orangutan named Jenny drink Darjeeling, the queen felt uneasy, subtly mocked. She confided to her diary the cause of her distress: "He is frightful and painfully and disagreeably human."

———

"The Oasis is the palate cleanser after the hot parking lot," said Todd Crawford as we walked through the lush and soothing understory inside DAK's front gate to begin a tour that involved a lot of ducking under construction ropes and being told we couldn't duck under others. "Here you'll have deer, iguanas, a host of playful birds and colorful ducks," Crawford added. The associate brand manager of DAK, Crawford was a young man with a marketing degree, a tweed jacket, and an air of polite zealotry. He was going to vouchsafe me the official version of my experience: "We uphold the Kingdom's brand image according to our charter, an internal document that sets such matters as our vision statement and the essence—what we want people's takeaway to be."

"And my takeaway will be . . . ?"

"In one word, adventure," Todd said. "Unlike Busch Gardens and Sea World, we're photo-real—you will feel like you're in Africa. And you're a participant, not a spectator. You're immersed in each adventure."

We immersed. In separate habitats I spied a wallaby and a muntjac and felt like an armchair David Attenborough. Widgeons, induced by a tin of food pellets, were being taught to gather by the bamboo fence where visitors—"guests," in Disney vernacular—will be. The most spectacular tool for such operant conditioning lies within Africa's cement "baobabs," which contain lazy Susans that rotate every hour or so, luring the giraffes with willow and acacia shoots—and making it seem that they are eating the trees themselves.

"I got pushback from the higher-ups for telling the lazy Susan story," Rick Sylvain said—he was in the Oasis, too, as my omnipresent minder. (A journalist before becoming Disney World's manager of print publicity, Sylvain sometimes rolled his eyes at the corporate paranoia. He even felt it necessary to apologize for wearing a tie dotted with Mickey Mouse heads.) "They were like, 'You can't reveal the magic!' " he added moodily.

Preserving the magic means controlling the illusion of spontaneity. Ever wonder why trash bins in Disney World are twenty paces apart or why film stands are on the right as you enter a Disney park and souvenirs are on the right as you leave? It's because Disney knows exactly how far you'll walk with trash, and that 70 percent of us instinctively bear right at a crossroads. They know.

Yet that knowledge can also fill us with joy. Later that day I met with DAK's principal landscape architect, Paul Comstock, whose job is to create horticulture-inspired bliss. A shaggy-haired former rock-and-roll drummer who traveled to twenty-eight countries in search of rare and desirable plants for DAK, Comstock was juiced about the Oasis.

"Eden has definite components," he said. "Oh, man! First, a tall canopy, we're using the eucalyptus. Then, at eye level, flowering trees right in your face—the jacarandas and tabebuias. Bridging the gap are vines and lianas. The vital fourth element is water—waterfalls and pools. And fifth are curious little animals, the scarlet ibis and the tree kangaroo, which are like the ornaments on a tree. I went around the world to be inspired by the Almighty's handiwork—a very hard act to follow," Comstock said. "Wow!" He paused reverently. "But I think we can actually say that the Garden of Eden isn't found along the Tigris and Euphrates. It's right here."

With that interloping cardinal still on my mind, I asked about the danger of native plant species reinvading, say, "Africa." Comstock laughed. In the first place, as visitors expect to see flowering grasses year-round—"We're in showbiz here"—Comstock seeded with three hundred different grasses, only seventy-five of them African. Many of the "acacia" trees are actually pollarded sand oaks; seven of the nine mature baobabs are cement. In the second place, given the destructiveness of rhinos and elephants, Comstock expects to re-plant hors d'oeuvres like the Japanese blueberry tree once a month. "If any indigenous plant wants to come back in and can stand up to these animals," he whooped, "I'm buying the beer!"

———

We went next—bearing right, naturally—to DinoLand U.S.A. "Here you're whisked back sixty-five million years in an enhanced-motion-ride vehicle," Todd Crawford intoned. "You're chased by a carnotaurus, a thirty-three-foot man-eating dinosaur, and try to save an iguanodon, the last dinosaur, from the fiery asteroids that spell their extinction." The Countdown to Extinction ride was down, being re-jiggered. (But Michael Eisner got to ride it later in the week—where's the fairness in that?)

So, leaving aside the anachronism of a man-eating dinosaur, I asked if we save the iguanodon. "Do you see any dinosaurs walking around?" Rick Sylvain replied. "No, it just, in a Disney way, kind of . . . fades out."

As I was hustled along, I kept wanting to linger and read Dino-

Land's signs, which are engagingly schizophrenic. For instance, graduate student "Jenny W." declares that a (bona fide) fossil imprint of footprints and eggs shows that dinosaurs had "parenting behaviors similar to birds," while her professor, "Dr. Shirley Woo," counters with a tart note calling that theory controversial and saying, "If you have stronger evidence, you need to present it."

"This whole area will be about analysis versus engagement, order versus chaos," Crawford explained. "Our streetmosphere will be a struggle between graduate students and scientists. The students have graffitied an addition to the restaurant sign so it reads 'Restaurant . . . osaurus!' It's a running battle," he added evenly. "They shoot arrows into the water tower every night." And behold, the water tower is stuck with arrows. It's too rich!

We walked Cretaceous Trail, among flora and fauna similar to that era's: cycads and ginkgos, Chinese lizards and odd birds like the Cape thick-knees. "All these animals lived McMillions of years ago, and they're still alive today," Sylvain said wearily. An apt coinage: McDonald's is the presenting sponsor of DinoLand, and its familiar sign proclaims, "Over 3 Billion Unearthed." Outside a giant gift shop that advertises "prehysterically low prices!" on rubber dinosaurs, Crawford explained, "This is our version of the cheap merchandising stores on Route 192."

What DAK has done in DinoLand is to co-opt all dissent and competition, from contending academic theories to cheapo souvenir stands. It's of a piece with Disney's tentacular reach into every precinct of the lifestyle universe—recently the company has embraced enterprises as far-flung as Cirque du Soleil, Disney Cruise Line, and the eerie picket-fence comity of the planned town of Celebration, Florida.

Yet DinoLand is also the DAK locale least trammeled by necessity—by real animals with real limitations—and it is here that Imagineers had the freest hand. "You can see our longing in DinoLand," Joe Rohde, DAK's executive designer and the man most responsible for its thematics, told me later that day. "There is something poignant about unrequited love for an extinct animal—it will never nuzzle you, you can never set it free to breed. But DinoLand is really about how the science of—the study of—animals creates them. Without paleontologists, in other words, dinosaurs wouldn't exist."

Rohde has a handlebar mustache, a huge Masai-like earring, and the mellifluous voice of a carnival barker—"that face, and that earring, are half our story," Rick Sylvain says gleefully—but his ideas are elegant and fully articulated. He has been pondering his Kingdom since Michael Eisner first proposed it in 1989 and subsequent market research showed that what guests wanted, above all, was an animal park.

How much visitors will grasp and appreciate Rohde's self-deconstructing texts and subtexts remains to be seen, but he certainly has lovely ideas for how DAK *should* work. "There is a great Ages of Man thing going on," Rohde said, fluting his hands aloft. "When we're young we invent dragons to reflect ideas we have about evil in ourselves. So the first way in, the first hook, is humans that look like animals or vice-versa—that's Camp Minnie-Mickey. Then you get cleaned and reset through Safari Village"—a brightly colored animist-feeling area spiced with macaws and lemurs and lots of shops—"and you're ready to experience animals through physical experience, through adventure in Africa and Asia. That's the approach of an adolescent or young adult. Then, as a mature adult, you begin to think responsibly about animals, to recognize our obligation to them, which corresponds to the part of the park you'll probably visit last, Conservation Station."

Conservation Station is an inviting multimedia area garlanded with bracing quotations from E. O. Wilson and Baba Dioum. You put on headphones and listen to a "Song of the Rainforest": animal sounds, then saws, then nothing. One interactive screen shows the globe, labeled a "work in progress," while an animated Rafiki (the mandrill from *The Lion King*) capers about it, urging guests to "Touch the screen / See what I mean." It's an insanely insinuating jingle: I saw two middle-aged construction workers unconsciously singing it aloud.

But Disney is terrified that even this chirpy interactivity will seem too dutiful. " 'Conservation' sounds 'science' and heavy-duty; it sounds like 'Maybe we shouldn't go there,' " said Rick Barongi, director of animal project development. "So we put Affection Section"—a petting zoo—"up there as a hook."

Disney is better at setting a conservation hook than at explaining what, precisely, we're protecting the animals from. Because that's, um, us. "There's an overconsumption message, but no overpopulation message," said Barongi. "It's just too politically sensitive, with all the cultural and religious problems we could have—it's a no-win."

"We don't want to point fingers or be doom and gloom, we want people to leave with a sense of optimism," said public affairs manager Diane Ledder, who one morning carried the struggle over my "takeaway" to my hotel lounge. I noted that in the visitor's experience of DAK's Africa and Asia, ivory poachers and a logging company will clearly be identified as the enemy. "I haven't read the most recent script," she said cautiously, "so I hesitate to say that the poachers are bad guys. I mean, they have families, they may be near starvation. These are complex issues."

—

I eventually found my way into Africa, the park's showpiece—"the center of the wow factor," as Rick Sylvain put it. The section begins with Harambe, a village based on the coastal town of Lamu, Kenya. As we approached it Todd Crawford said, "We hired African students from all over the continent to work in Harambe and in the park as guides, and when we brought them over this bridge, forty out of eighty of them started crying and crying. After they had gathered themselves, they said, 'This is my home—I feel like I've never left.' It's a great testament to what we've done." I especially liked the forty students gathering themselves to speak with one voice.

Yet Harambe, another food and merchandise stop, is an impressive copy. Disney even brought in Zulu craftsmen from Natal to thatch the roofs. The train station is a particular triumph, with ceiling fans twinkling idly, old suitcases and bicycles jumbled in the luggage bays, and a grimy notice announcing that service to Shabi and points beyond has been interrupted due to "an outbreak of kipindupindu." *Kipindupindu,* in a rare flash of mordant Disney humor, is Swahili for "cholera."

Joe Rohde hoped Africa would catalyze genetic *nostalgie de la boue:* "After passing the dense, modern, echoing, hard, geometric town, an intense reminder of our world with its roads and grids, you plunge into nature and feel its sacrosanct quality."

"But Harambe is pure picturesque," I protested. Rohde shrugged, a giant compromised by dwarfs: "Well, yes, that's the Disney slice."

Four days later, after a lot of undignified griping on my part, I finally got to see the savanna. I'd been barred because Kilimanjaro Safaris wasn't finished, wasn't fully overwhelming. "We've only got 38 percent of the animals in," said Tom Hopkins, of animal operations, as we boarded the safari trucks and headed out, past black rhinos rooting in a thicket. The driver radioed ranger Wilson Mutua, who was, imaginarily, in a plane above, directing us to the game. (Actually, it's a set script and a set twenty-minute route on a carefully rutted and grimed cement path known in-house as "the most expensive dirt road in the world.")

I craned to see the animals—crocs, marabou storks, giraffes—as they blurred by, with no intervening bars. It was—or felt—gripping and unexpected. Suddenly we entered open grassland that looked fairly realistic, save for a not-yet-hidden red fire hydrant. Zebras strolled unconcernedly on the road in front of us, but electric fences kept many of the animals from mixing as they acclimatized. "We hope the hot wires will mostly, eventually, be taken down, or they'll be themed," Hopkins said.

"Themed?"

"To look like grass." Meanwhile there was radio byplay about the elephant Big Red and her baby, Little Red. "He trips over [his trunk] with his feet and then he gets very upset and runs to his mama," Wilson Mutua said dotingly. Suddenly the lions' kopje was just above us. The pair of lions lazed, paying as little attention to us as to the bloody zebra head and flank lying nearby—metal facsimiles.

Then the radio announced that poachers had entered the park, and we sped up to catch them, racing through a geyser field and seeing an inert fake elephant off to the left—"Big Red is down!" the radio crackled, and Wilson Mutua cried, "The poachers!" We roared on, chasing the poachers' jeep (in theory) into the wardens' trap. Soon we saw the crashed jeep and an audioanimatronic baby elephant aboard the wardens' truck, waggling his head at us adorably. "Little Red is safe!" the radio said. "We couldn't have saved him without you!" After the instinctive power of the real animals, the ending felt tinny. "Yeah," Tom said, "we all agree . . . it should feel more real."

Even allowing for its incompleteness, the ride was too fast—the bioequivalent of a roller coaster—and though I enjoyed it at the time, my connection to the animals seemed, in retrospect, generic. Disney ballyhoos our "participation," but true participants can change an outcome; we're just along for the ride. I thought of what Paul Comstock said about a research trip to Nepal on which he was menaced by a green viper: "One of the reasons to go to these places is you may be bitten." And of how the only time that Disney Attractions president Judson Green got excited in our interview was when he recalled tracking a leopard couple for five hours in the Masai Mara. "It really made an impression on me," he said. "It took a lot of work and patience, and seeing a leopard couple is so rare."

The implicit contrast hovered in the air. "We don't pretend to be the real thing," Green acknowledged. "But you are going to see many more animals than you would in a typical day in Africa. And frankly, ninety-five percent or ninety-eight percent of our guests will never go to Africa." Adds Rick Barongi, "We don't *want* them all to go to Africa—that would destroy what's left of their environment." Nevertheless, there is already talk in-house of running Disney safaris to Africa.

———

The most honest conversation I had at DAK was an afternoon interview with Barongi. We met in a glum conference room, and I sensed that Barongi, a former curator of mammals at the San Diego Zoo and now Disney's top animal guy, would much rather be outside. He is slight and ingenuous, the voice of reason who says he often had to cajole the Imagineers back to reality. "They wanted herds of wildebeests, and I said, 'No, five or ten is plenty,' " Barongi told me. "And they said, 'Can we have animal babies all over the place? People love to see babies!' And I told them, 'No, you have to regulate breeding. Because babies grow up, and then what will you do with them?' We also discussed whether the carnivores could hunt, and I told them that the park would have to go from five hundred acres to fifty thousand. Also, obviously, it would be controversial."

This exposed a jugular point, and we sparred briefly about just how wild DAK's animals really are. "Okay," Barongi said finally. "There are three kinds of animals: wild, domestic, and captive-born wild. These are captive-born wilds. They look like lions, but they're not—they don't know how to hunt. But I don't think people will notice the difference: our lions are the same as wild ones during the twenty-two hours a day when both are sleeping and resting."

Won't the lions be frustrated, seeing potential prey across a moat? "They're hardwired such that they'll be a little frustrated, sure," Barongi said, adding, "That's only a worry to people who don't know much about animals. For animals, it's really, 'Tell us where the food is coming from, and then don't change a thing for the rest of our lives, and we'll be happy.' Creatures of habit."

This is a controversial position, naturally. As Jeffrey Moussaieff Masson and Susan McCarthy declare in *When Elephants Weep: The Emotional Lives of Animals:* "It is often said of zoo animals that the way to tell if they are happy is to ask whether the young play and the adults breed. Most zookeepers would not accept this standard of happiness for themselves."

Yet Barongi was espousing the latest in captive-animal theory, which places great significance on the fact that animals live twice as long in zoos as in the wild and suggests that they can be happier in captivity. As German philosopher Heine Hediger declared, pointing to the stresses of predation and procreation, "The free animal does not live in freedom."

But Disney's heroic efforts to imitate nature are less for the animals' benefit than for our own. "If the animal appears to be in a calm, natural place, so will the guest," Paul Comstock observed. We'll only stand for the fakery we don't know about. "We had a discussion about just doing audioanimatronic animals," said Rick Barongi. "It would be so much easier. But people expect the large, charismatic megavertebrates—and Disney likes to give people a lot of what they expect."

———

My favorite DAK experience was a late afternoon Discovery River boat ride aboard the perfectly rusted *Crocodile Belle*. The river houses most of the Kingdom's imaginary animals, but the special effects were still being put in place, and so was the trip script. I was the only passenger, and boat captains Lori and Dee practiced their spiels on me in a confiding murmur.

We cast off and approached a white unicorn statue on the left bank. "There'll be mist on that bank," Lori said, "and it'll look like the unicorn is prancing out of it. In the meantime, that red-legged hawk likes to fly in and sit on the unicorn's head."

"Next is the craken," Dee said. "It's like a bug-eyed sea serpent—you'll feel him slithering on the bottom of the boat and trying to tip it over. It'll be scary."

"And over there is a lizard-croc thing," Lori said, gesturing toward a chalky . . . well, lizard-croc thing. "We don't have a name for him yet."

"Is there any story about where all these creatures came from, or what they mean?" I asked.

"No," Lori said. "All we know is that this is the river of no beginning and no end."

Soon we had a splendid view of DAK's symbol and centerpiece, the Tree of Life. The Tree is a towering pleasure: 145 feet tall and 50 feet wide, with 103,000 plastic leaves. Built of concrete cladding around an oil derrick, it resembles an outsize cross between a baobab and a banyan. The crowning feature is the tree's "bark," which is stunningly carved with 325 animals, ranging from a grasshopper to a lion. Jane Goodall declared it a tremendous tribute to biodiversity.

"In the story line," Lori said as we glided past the Tree, "an ant had a seed and he planted it because he wished for the other animals to come take shade under the Tree. The Tree grew with the animals on it, and according to the story they were neither carved nor whatever—they just appeared. It's weird. But it was a magic seed."

"No, no," Dee said. "The ant made a magical *wish*. The seed was normal."

We were enjoying this unscripted twilight moment, trying to figure out an apt myth for the Tree of Life. "Why would an ant want all those animals to come crowding under the tree, where they could crush him?" I asked. They started to laugh. "I don't think anyone thought of that," Lori said.

—

When it comes to DAK's real animals, anthropomorphism like the welcoming ant's is officially in disfavor. "In accord with the movement in wildlife conservation," says Judson Green, "we've made this about systems and habitats—if you go through and here's Max and here's Pete and here's Sally, it just doesn't feel right." The issue is freighted, however, because Disney is the most thoroughgoing anthropomorphizer the world has ever known.

In a 1953 magazine article, "What I've Learned from the Animals," Walt Disney himself wrote, "Some of the most fascinating people I've ever met are animals. . . . The more human they are the funnier they seem to us, and the better we understand them." Referring to Disney's True-Life Adventures nature films, he praised the beaver as "a solid citizen" and disapproved of the seal's polygamous ways as smacking of the "Oriental potentate's harem."

And, in fact, Disney is still cuing us to revere animals or—more often—chuckle at them. DAK publicity releases describe both naked molerats and hippos as "comical," and the Galah parrot as "humorous." The chief reason there aren't any hyenas in DAK's

Africa is that hyenas aren't cute: in *The Lion King* they are vilified as "slobbering, mangy, stupid poachers."

Curiously, Disney also cues us to fear adult humans. One of the most terrifying moments in film is when Bambi's mother pricks up her ears at gunshots and tells her alarmed son, "Man . . . was in the forest." In *The Jungle Book,* Bagheera warns Mowgli that the tiger Shere Khan "is not going to allow you to grow up to become a man—just another hunter with a gun." The seeming misanthropy arises because Disney's Circle of Life worldview countenances no visible killing. (In *The Lion King,* the meerkat Timon tries to point out the idiocy of this idea to his carnivorous friends. Simba just says, "Relax, Timon.")

Yet Disney is not really at fault here. We humans are predisposed to find certain animals and behaviors appealing. It's an extension of our instinctive feeling for human children—for big eyes and round faces and clumsy efforts to walk and play. We are programmed to cuddle, and hence to anthropomorphize. Primatologist Sue Savage-Rumbaugh has observed that apes "express exuberance, joy, guilt, remorse, disdain, disbelief, awe, sadness, wonder, tenderness, loyalty, anger, distrust, and love." If an ape has other, alien feelings, Savage-Rumbaugh doesn't guess at them. How can any of us imagine nonhuman feelings?

———

I returned to Africa's Gorilla Falls one afternoon when the animals were at home. A gorilla named Hope sat next to the window, suckling her baby and fashioning a hay nest with maternal ease. Her graceful hands and somber face seemed familiar, yet her haunchy, slinging movements were strange and her thoughts inscrutable. Why, for instance, did she tap the glass three times right in front of my nose?

"We've got a great picture of them in the newsletter," Rick Sylvain said. "Real madonna and child." I could have watched them for hours, but we headed up the trail and ran into Gino, a huge and smelly 420-pound silverback male. Or rather, we ran into a big family of white people in sherbet-colored shirts pointing excitedly at Gino—they, and he, were models being snapped by two Disney photographers. "There's not a better silverback personality out there than Gino," says Rick Barongi. "He likes people, he plays with his son, he doesn't beat up his females—he's got the whole entertainment package."

Gino beat his chest, thrillingly, and then knuckle-walked to a rock outcropping. "Okay," one photographer murmured, framing the shot, "stop . . . right . . . there." Gino paused on his implicit mark but then kept moving. "Rick, can you make that happen?" the photographer joked, and we all smiled—Disney's control isn't absolute.

But for a crazy moment I had the shuddery suspicion that the "family" of people pointing at Gino with faces of wonder were actually audioanimatronic. It was hard to tell. And it would be so much easier.

—

The core myth in DAK is the story of Big Red and Little Red. It is the same story Disney told in *Bambi* and *The Lion King:* a plucky orphan grows to be king of the forest or jungle. The story, of course, is really about us: orphans from nature, we grow to rule all animals. And like most resonant myths, it is unexpectedly honest, because it enacts our ambivalence and disquiet about poaching upon some dreamy Circle of Life. For we have replaced the survival imperative of the wild with the jaded imperative of pleasing ourselves. Man has become the world's zookeeper, so animals that aren't cute or lively, that don't tug at us the way children do, will pass from the stage.

Claude Lévi-Strauss remarked that the Australian aborigines chose animals as totems not because they were good to eat, but because "they were good to think with." Disney has changed that, crucially, to "good to feel with." Or even "good to feel good with," for DAK is a pastoral, without hunting or sex or famine. The result is that all the animals in it are fundamentally mythical—and, as their full capacities languish, soon to be extinct. Disney's Animal Kingdom is a bright and cheerful museum of loss.

Yet we can't disown this park, for Disney's fractured view of animals is our own. In sight of our former prey and predators, our hearts beat a little faster. We are enriched—and a little frustrated, for we can't quite get at them. We use the animals as catalysts for our genetic memories, as crowbars to pry open our hearts and become, for a controlled moment, wild again.

(1998)

THE GOLD DIGGERS

What to do if you find buried treasure is not a question most of us worry about. It just doesn't come up that much. But anyone who has ruminated on human frailty, or even read *Treasure Island,* knows the etiquette: Shoot the witnesses and shoot them fast. Otherwise, sooner or later, they'll shoot you—because the suspicion and greed that make men bury treasure get buried along with it, and reawaken in those who dig it up.

This story about buried treasure takes place in Sun Valley, Idaho. Like much of the American West, the area was once rife with rustlers and claim jumpers. Now Sun Valley is a recreational haven where men settle quarrels not with Winchesters, but with letters to the editor. So this modern dispute turns out to involve lawyers, depositions, insinuations, and a storm of bluster worthy of Yosemite Sam. Bullets might have been simpler.

At dusk on November 4, 1996, Greg Corliss and Larry Anderson were grading the ground with a skip loader, building a driveway to a new guest house. The guest house was part of Broadford Farm, the

Sun Valley ranch of Jann Wenner, who is the owner of *Rolling Stone, Men's Journal,* and *Us.*

Fifty years earlier, this land—laced with dogwoods and aspens and bordered by a brook full of trout—had been occupied by cows, a woodcutter's frame house, and the occasional mushroom hunter. More than a century ago, Wenner's 117 acres were home to part of the Broadford Townsite, where miners lived in shanties and scratched out a living in the Minnie Moore and Queen of the Hills silver mines. But now every trace of those past uses was gone. The Broadford area had become horse farms, worth more than $50,000 an acre—a landscape where women wearing pearl earrings jogged behind their baby strollers.

As Greg Corliss was examining the trough where the gravel mix would go, he saw a scattering of coins glowing in the fresh-turned earth. He bent closer. "I yelled, 'Fuck, Larry—look, gold!' " Corliss recalls. Anderson, his close friend and the owner of Anderson Asphalt Paving, came running over. "Fuck!" he shouted. "Put 'em in your pocket—we could split 'em."

"Find your own!" Corliss replied. Then Anderson said, "Jesus, Greg—look!" He had spotted dozens of coins nestled in the jagged bottom of a Mason jar, which had apparently been crushed by the skip loader. Seeing the jar, Corliss reconsidered. "Oh, yeah, fifty-fifty," he said. The two men fell to their knees and pawed through the dirt, stuffing five-, ten-, and twenty-dollar gold pieces into the pockets of their jeans. "It was a huge adrenaline rush," Anderson says.

"We'll get a reward!" Corliss shouted. "We're going to be on the cover of *Rolling Stone!*" "Shut up—*he's* home," Anderson whispered, shrugging toward Wenner's Adirondack-style log house two hundred yards to the north. "This is between me and you."

After they had thoroughly sifted the dirt, the two men drove to the Bellevue General Store and picked up a six-pack of Molson Ice, then drove to Anderson's gravel pit, in Poverty Flats. They went into the trailer on cinder blocks that serves as the pit's office, and Anderson locked the door and drew the blinds. Corliss, who had been in a coin club as a boy, filled the sink with warm water and Joy detergent, dunked the coins, then dried them with paper towels. He handled each one delicately, by its edges, admiring the shining images: eagles, Indian heads, and Augustus Saint-Gaudens's striding Liberty.

Greg Corliss is a stocky, cheerful thirty-seven-year-old who is always looking for a get-famous-quick scheme. When he signs his name, he puts two dots inside the capital "G" in "Greg," making a smiley face. Larry Anderson, fifty-three, is a former high school quarterback, a compact figure with a graying mustache that seems to stand sentry over his terse conversation. But flashes of good humor occasionally show through his diffidence, and that night both men horsed around like frat buddies. They puffed cigars and drank the six-pack, and some Smirnoff vodka, and some Crown Royal whiskey. They even mooned the gold. When they inventoried their loot, in a small spiral notebook, Anderson's tally slanted tipsily across the page: ninety-six half-eagles, eagles, and double eagles, minted between 1857 and 1914, weighing four pounds.

"I won't tell my wife; you don't tell your girlfriend," Anderson said. "We won't tell *anyone*." Using half the gold as collateral, Anderson agreed to lend Corliss $5,000, which he needed to avoid bankruptcy. Anderson suggested that they stack the coins in a cigar box and put them in a safe in his garage. As a gesture of trust, Anderson would give Corliss the combination to the safe and to his burglar alarm.

Corliss agreed to everything. "It was Tom Sawyer and Huck Finn," he said later. "We're best friends. We've got our stash."

"You know what I love about you, man?" Anderson said, planting a boozy kiss on Corliss's cheek. "Everything!" Inspired, Corliss pulled out a dull pocketknife and said, "I'm cutting my finger and signing our inventory in blood. Come on—we'll be blood brothers!" Anderson squeamishly declined. "That's when I wondered if he was going to turn on me," Corliss says now. "I mean, it's buried treasure. You got to sign the documents in blood."

—

Two years later, when the gold coins were at the center of a legal free-for-all, Jann Wenner told me, "Greg Corliss is a ne'er-do-well who's milking this for all it's worth. He's a liar and an asshole." Corliss himself says equably, "If you're wealthy, and some dickhead who found coins in your driveway is suing you—I can see Jann's side." He grins as he ventures one of his appealingly muddled analogies: "But you've got to see my side, too—it's like I'm Samson versus Goliath."

Growing up on the shore of Lake Tapps, in Sumner, Washington, Greg Corliss qualified as an Eagle Scout, just as his two brothers had. But he soon shrugged off the burden of what his father, Joe, who is an optometrist and a Rotarian, calls "an old, private, established family." Greg's older brother is a prosperous real estate developer, and his younger brother is an internist, but Greg bounced around the West Coast for years, selling water skis and water-ski boats. Corliss's photo albums from the 1980s show him in a blurry milieu of Thrasher and Shredder wakeboards, Coors Light bottles, wet-T-shirt contests, and sun bunnies in thong bikinis. He dreamed of attaining his customers' freewheeling lifestyle, earning the nickname Worldwide. In 1992, he moved to Sun Valley and opened a Master Craft boat dealership.

A remote two-mile-wide draw cloaked with Douglas firs, Sun Valley is the birthplace of Ezra Pound and—some historians argue—of the hokey-pokey. But for decades after the first miners arrived, in 1880, the valley's residents had little time for poetry or dancing. With the fixity of heroin addicts they tapped the earth's scarred surface, seeking a fresh vein of galena, the silver- and lead-bearing ore. It was a brutal life. One visitor to a nearby silver mine wrote, "The air is scarce respirable. . . . The stenches of decaying vegetable matter, hot foul water and human excretions intensify the effects of the heat." In the mid-1880s in Broadford, on what is now Jann Wenner's land, a dozen saloons served a population of six hundred miners.

The historian Patricia Nelson Limerick has observed, "Mining set a mood that has never disappeared from the West; the attitude of extractive industry: get in, get rich, get out." But in Sun Valley people tended to get in, stay poor, and stay put. By the time the last of the area's mines closed, in 1970, people say that three dollars had been sunk into the ground for every two dollars in metal recovered. And the rare fortunes that men clawed from the earth were often haplessly returned to it. *Sun Valley: An Extraordinary History,* by Wendolyn Spence Holland, tells of silver coins and plate buried for safekeeping by a saloonkeeper, who promptly died; a lost gold vein south of Bonanza City; loot from a stagecoach holdup hidden forever along Bayhorse Creek; and a hundred-pound silver ingot found in 1961 near the Trail Creek toll road, which had perhaps been hurled from a freight wagon in the previous century by a smelting-plant worker who hoped to sneak back for it.

Though prostitution remained legal in the town of Shoshone until the late 1950s, the character of the valley began to change in 1936, after Averell Harriman opened America's first large ski resort, in Ketchum, and renamed the former Wood River Valley to advertise its balmy weather. Fifty years ago, Ernest Hemingway holed up in the Sun Valley Lodge to finish *For Whom the Bell Tolls;* recently, his granddaughter Mariel opened a yoga studio nearby.

An eighty-three-year-old former miner named Rupert House drove me up a precarious weed-grown switchback to the entrance of the old Triumph mine. "This used to be a land for men—we sweated in the mines, head down and ass up," he said. Together, we walked down the shaft until rubble halted our steps. "Before," he said, "you'd ask, 'What do you do?' and everyone would say, 'Carpenter,' or 'Miner.' Now," he concluded, his voice a testy rumble in the dark, "they say, 'I ski,' or 'I jog.' "

Sun Valley's treasure nowadays is real estate. Since 1991, property values have nearly quadrupled. Len Harlig, the chairman of the Blaine County Board of Commissioners, told me, "The billionaires are buying out the millionaires." Local residents include Richard Dreyfuss, Clint Eastwood, Jamie Lee Curtis, Steve Miller, Arnold

Schwarzenegger and Maria Shriver, and Bruce Willis and Demi Moore.

Having settled in Sun Valley, Greg Corliss was surrounded with a taunting vision of the good life. It was during a picnic on Bruce Willis's boat dock that he met his wife, Emily, a spirited, dark-haired woman who is an au pair for a well-to-do family. In 1994, when he lost the backing of a wealthy customer who said he'd help finance a private water-ski lake, Corliss was sued by his boat suppliers for $200,000. He went out of business, had to sell his house, and eventually moved in with Emily, who was then his girlfriend. "I was a kept man," Corliss recalls cheerfully. "In August of 1996, I got $1,300 from insurance because a drunk driver hit my parked truck, and my plan for September was to turn the truck around and hope the guy hit the other side." But when his bank account was down to $4.95—and with more than $60,000 worth of debts—Corliss took a job laying driveways for his drinking buddy Larry Anderson.

Anderson, who was born on a hardscrabble Idaho farm, had built a solid gravel-and-asphalt business in Sun Valley and had raised two sons and two stepdaughters there with his wife, Lexie. He liked cars, guns, and hard work. Despite the differences in the two men's backgrounds, Corliss admired his new boss and hoped to rise to the position of gravel salesman as he worked off his personal debt; he owed Anderson $1,800 for building a driveway to his former house.

Three months later, the two men found the gold. Corliss believed that this stroke of luck would turn everything around. His guesses about the treasure's value kept rising: from $1,160 in face value to $30,000 in gold value, and then on to somewhere between $32,000 and $500,000 in numismatic value, depending on the coins' condition.

The first person Corliss told about the coins was Emily. When he arrived home that night, three hours late and leglessly drunk, she took one look and said, "Pack your shit and get out." Only the story of the gold saved him. So, like a revivalist witness, he kept telling it. Three days later, when Corliss went to shoot pool at Sam's Club, a roughneck bar, he had already informed at least seven people about the coins. But the regulars at Sam's were skeptical, so he returned with photographs. Emily had taken pictures of him and Larry with the gold in Anderson's trailer the morning after the discovery, when the two couples celebrated with Cook's champagne and mimosas. (Anderson had immediately told his wife, too—the first of at least eight people *he* would confide in.)

One of those at Sam's L-shaped bar was Roger Morton, the foreman of Anderson's gravel pit. Morton grabbed the photographs away from Corliss and told him he was a fool for "bragging them up." The next morning, Morton turned the pictures over to his boss, who was furious to hear about Corliss's indiscretion.

Anderson had already confiscated a fortune-cookie fortune that Corliss had been waving around after a Chinese takeout meal—it said "Gold is in your future"—and locked it up in his safe. Now he took Corliss for a ride in his dump truck. "No one will believe you about the gold," Anderson told him. "But they'll believe the photos." He demanded that Corliss hand over all the snapshots and negatives, saying, "You're a dumb piece of shit, and you need me to protect you." Anderson berated him so fiercely that Corliss went home and wept in Emily's arms.

The two men spent nearly all their time together that winter, hauling snow late at night or sitting in Anderson's kitchen drinking beer. Anderson enjoyed the younger man's high spirits, but he worried that his employee was goldbricking on the job. "I like equipment and dirt and asphalt," Anderson says. "Greg could do some shovel work and run the roller back and forth, but manual labor wasn't his forte. He was more of a salesman." (Corliss recalls, "I'd say, 'Hey, lighten up, dude! Why shovel snow off a trailer you're not going to use till next spring? Let's go skiing!' ")

And Anderson was getting jumpy, because he kept being approached by people who'd heard about the gold. "I'd just shine them on," Anderson says now. "I'd say, 'I'm not sure what you're talking about.' But I realized that Jann Wenner would hear about the gold eventually."

Everyone involved had a different idea of what to do, and the recollections of what happened and why are often in direct contradiction. Emily and Greg wanted to tell Wenner; Larry was unsure. Greg trusted Larry, for the most part; Emily didn't. And Larry didn't seem to trust anyone, even himself. When he looked back recently at his diary for this period, he discovered that it was entirely blank. "I felt responsible for Greg, as his employer, to make the decision about the gold, the same way I'd be responsible as the contractor if he drove a tractor into someone's house," Anderson told me. "Only, I wasn't sure what to do. I never thought the gold was worth $10 million, or whatever—I thought at the very top maybe $50,000. And the coins were so beautiful and unique that I would probably never have sold them." He shook his head mournfully. "But I must have been a little bit brain dead to lend him money." After receiving the $5,000 loan in November, Corliss had asked for $2,500 more, "so that I could have a nice Christmas," he recalls. In February Anderson loaned him a further $2,000.

Later that month, Corliss, Anderson, and Lexie took a five-day road trip in Anderson's blue Chevy Suburban. They were headed to Portland, Oregon, to check in on a car that Anderson was having rebuilt, and to Corliss's parents' house in Sumner, to investigate selling the coins. Dr. Corliss had told his friend Jim Jackson about the gold. Jackson, a coin collector and the manager of a Wal-Mart Vision Center, got in touch with a local coin dealer, Andy Stagg, and the two men said that they had lined up a buyer who might be willing to pay $1 million for the coins. Later, the Corlisses came to believe that the buyer was the chairman of Microsoft, Bill Gates. In truth, Gates had never heard of Corliss or the gold.

When the three travelers arrived in Sumner, Anderson announced that he had left the coins in his safe, back in Sun Valley. "I didn't want to be hauling that much gold around with me," he told me later. Gloom settled upon the gathering. Anderson had never quite believed Corliss's boasts about his privileged childhood; now, taking in his hosts' elegant home, with huge glass windows overlooking the family boathouse on Lake Tapps and Mount Rainier beyond, he seemed to feel out of his element. "The Andersons are real friendly, but they're unusual," Dr. Corliss told me later, adding, "Well, they're alcoholics, really." (Anderson disputes this, saying he drinks only as much as the next guy.) Corliss's mother whispered to her son, "I'll fix them dinner, and we can drink the wine you brought, and then they can *leave*."

Anderson was equally disenchanted. "Greg's family was clearly not that overjoyed with him, because he's so obnoxious," he told me. The long drive back to Sun Valley was uncomfortable. "It got to where I could tell Greg's stories better than he could," Anderson says, "and I finally had to tell him to shut up. My friendship with him basically ended on that trip."

———

Legally the coins could fall into one of four categories of found property. The first is abandoned property. But people don't usually abandon gold coins or trouble to bury them if they do. The second is mislaid property—something that the owner has hidden with the intention of recovering but has then forgotten. The third is lost property: objects that the owner has parted with through neglect or carelessness. The fourth is treasure trove, an English common-law term for the riches of the Roman Empire that were buried in English soil when the Romans fled. "Treasure trove" refers to gold or silver coin or bullion concealed for safekeeping. To qualify, the booty must have been hidden long enough so that the owner is probably dead. In England, treasure trove went to the Crown; in the United States, founded in opposition to the Crown, the law was generally modified into a "finders keepers" principle.

Though Idaho had never had a recorded treasure case, other state courts had tended to rule that mislaid property belongs to the owner of the property on which it was found, while lost or treasure-trove property belongs to the finder. But the definitions are charmingly indistinct. As Corliss's lawyer argued in his brief, "The distinction between lost and mislaid property turns on the likelihood that the owner will return to retrieve the property. . . . If mislaid property is mislaid for long enough, it becomes lost." Everything in this precedent-setting dispute could depend on the judge's best guess about the identity and the intent of the original owner.

Locals have speculated that the coins were buried by a whorehouse madam, by Chinese miners, by Basque shepherds, by Jesse James, or by the Sundance Kid. These are typecast fantasies rather than plausible theories: the nearest brothel was miles away, in Hailey; the Chinese had left the area by 1914 (the last date on any of the buried coins); the valley's Basques were very poor; Jesse James died in 1882; and the Sundance Kid died in 1911.

The longtime owners of the Broadford property were not so colorful. From 1890 to 1934 the property belonged to the Peterlin family, Catholics who had emigrated from northern Italy. There were four Peterlin brothers, but census and cemetery records suggest that by 1914 only Charles and Gerolamo Peterlin lived in the property's log cabin. They were reclusive bachelors, who farmed and worked in the Minnie Moore mine, where they were paid four dollars for a ten-hour day. Gerolamo died of pneumonia in 1921, at the age of fifty-five, and Charles died in 1924, at sixty-seven, of "general disability." The property fell to the other resident of the farm, a nephew of theirs named Anton F. Peterlin, known as Frank. Like his uncles, Frank Peterlin was a bachelor loner. Mike Ivie, a retired contractor, remembers Frank as a short, graying, husky man with a weak chin who kept eighty cows. He gave Ivie and other neighborhood kids honey from his apiary, and loved to tease them with homespun magic tricks.

Frank Peterlin had a wire-sided Dodge truck that started with a hand crank. On November 27, 1933, while he was cranking the truck, it plunged forward and crushed him to death against a fence. He was forty-nine and had no heirs. When the sheriff opened a padlocked shed on the property, he was astonished to discover a cache of items that had been reported missing in the neighborhood: mining picks and shovels, chains from the county road scraper, splitting wedges from logging camps, a .30-.30 rifle stolen from a shepherd. "Afterward, we found out from the local store owners that Frank bought more flashlight batteries than anyone in the county," Ivie says. "It was for his night work—he was the slickest thief in the area, and no one had ever suspected it." Frank Peterlin also had a huge jar filled with $100 worth of pennies in his house. He sounds like just the sort of person who might lay his hands on—and then bury—a jar of gold.

—

Back in Sun Valley after the "Bill Gates" road trip, Greg Corliss says, he found himself thinking, I'm getting eight dollars an hour spraying down the inside of dump trucks and hauling snow all night. It's hard work. Emily and I are fighting all the time about whether I should trust Larry. Why don't we just split the gold? One night, as he and Anderson were out riding around, Corliss initiated another of their dump truck dialogues.

Anderson wasn't interested. "These coins are going to be the best thing that ever happened to us, or maybe the worst," Corliss says Anderson told him. "We can't tell yet. But if you got a million dollars you'd just piss it away. I'm going to keep the coins for ten years. After that, nobody will know where they came from." Corliss says that Anderson planned to "discover" the coins on his own property in Hailey in the year 2006—that he was even going to tear up his backyard with a backhoe to lend the tale verisimilitude. Anderson calls this account "complete bullshit."

When the coins were found and Anderson wrote down the combination to his safe, Corliss had thrown away the slip of paper. He didn't want to be tempted to sneak into Anderson's garage, because he was afraid that Anderson would catch him trespassing and shoot him with his deer rifle. Or his shotgun. Or one of his handguns. Now Emily was insisting that Greg get his gold back. But Corliss says that he had become even warier of his boss after the two of them spent a tense afternoon skiing with some of Corliss's family. Eyeing Corliss's sister-in-law from Palm Springs, Anderson had muttered, "That bitch ought to be careful: somebody might bite her ears and fingers off to get those diamonds." (Anderson says he didn't make the remark.)

Early on March 29, 1997, a Saturday, Corliss went over to Anderson's house with $13,000 in cash that he'd borrowed from his older brother to cover all his loans. He carried the money in a fishing hat—"like an offering plate," he says. Anderson wasn't up yet, and Greg sat down on the bed next to him. "Hey, lookit, we've been in bed together on this deal all along," Corliss said, smiling. "So here's the money I owe you, and I'd like my half of the coins." Anderson bolted upright. "Where the hell did you get that money?" he asked. Anderson's surprise soon turned to anger. According to Corliss, he yelled, "Get the fuck out of my house! I declare war on you about the gold! There is no gold!"

When Corliss returned home, crestfallen, Emily got into her car and headed for Anderson's in her pajamas. "I just started screaming at him, huffing and puffing," she says. "He said, 'Nine-tenths of the law is possession,' and told me to get off his property."

Greg decided to quit his job at the gravel pit, and the Corlisses composed a note that Emily slapped under the wiper of Anderson's pickup. This "hit list," as they called it, warned Anderson that if he didn't hand over half of the gold, they would tell Jann Wenner about the coins. Furthermore, they would go to the police and the IRS to relay allegations that Anderson had a pile of undeclared cash in his safe and kept two sets of books for his business. "P.S.," Emily added. "You're not invited to Easter brunch."

"I felt threatened, because I figured they'd do part of it," Anderson told me. "And Greg did talk to the sheriff later." Corliss also talked to Hailey's police chief and called the IRS office in Salt Lake City, but nothing ever came of his attempted whistle-blowing. Anderson went on, "But my business is all aboveboard. I was only worried because I thought Greg might try to break into my house." That weekend, Anderson took the gold from his safe and stashed it in the house of a friend named Ralph Girton.

The day of the confrontation with Anderson, Corliss had called a lawyer friend, Miles Stanislaw, who volunteered to arbitrate the dispute. Corliss phoned Anderson, and that Monday they all held a three-hour mediation session at a local law office. After hearing both men, Stanislaw suggested that the gold be placed in a safe-deposit box for three years and then divided (on the doubtful theory that this stalling tactic would run out the clock on the statute of limitations for found property). Corliss was willing. Anderson considered the idea, then said no. "We had the ball extremely close to the goal line," Stanislaw says, "and if they'd agreed, I think it would all be over with—and Wenner still wouldn't know."

The next morning, April 1, Anderson met with his lawyer, Brian Elkins. Unshaved and looking like a man who hadn't slept, Anderson produced the Corlisses' combative note and asked what he should do. Corliss, desperate to be part of the discussion, had followed Anderson to the lawyer's office and was sitting, with his arms folded, in the waiting room. Elkins ordered Corliss to leave. "Larry wanted to do the right thing," Elkins told me later, "but he was being hounded by this *wild man.*"

Elkins did some research and unearthed a similar case, in Texas, in which the court had awarded the treasure to the property owner; he told Anderson that in Idaho, a conservative, property rights state, the courts would probably rule the same way. With the law seemingly against him, Anderson decided to turn the coins over to Wenner. "I'm surprised it took me that long to come to my senses," he says now, "but I think anybody would have been pulled away by the gold."

—

Later that afternoon, Wenner, back in New York City, heard about the gold from a friend of a friend of Corliss's. Greg's new plan was to offer to split the coins with Wenner. The next day, Wenner received another call about the gold, from Anderson's friend Ralph Girton. Corliss and Anderson, unable to keep their pact with each other, had both scrambled to make separate pacts with the landowner.

Wenner, who says that he was "mildly amused" that the discovery had been kept from him for five months, had his attorney call Brian Elkins on April 3, and the lawyers swiftly made a deal. Late in the afternoon of April 14, Anderson, his wife, and Elkins picked up the coins from Ralph Girton and drove to Wenner's home to hand them over; in return, Wenner indemnified Anderson against any legal claims and agreed to pay his legal expenses. The meeting was brisk, ten minutes at most. "He didn't seem excited by the coins—he was about the only person who saw them that wasn't," Anderson says of Wenner. "I don't remember if he even said 'Thank you.' " Relieved of his burden, Anderson gathered up the photographs and negatives of the gold, the broken Mason jar, the cigar box, and Corliss's Chinese fortune and dropped them in an ashcan at his gravel pit. Then he set them on fire. "I had had all of Greg I could take," he says.

Four days later, Corliss sued Anderson in Idaho District Court for wrongful detention of property. And when Corliss discovered that the coins were in a safe at Wenner Media, in New York City, he sued Wenner, too. Corliss says he called Wenner in late May from Hawaii, where he and Emily were vacationing, to discuss a settlement. (Wenner doesn't recall such a conversation, but phone records from Corliss's Maui hotel show two calls to Wenner's office number.) Wenner had offered Corliss and Anderson a reward of $5,000 each, or 10 percent of the coins' value, whichever was higher. Now Corliss says he told him, "I want my picture on the cover of *Rolling Stone,* and five free copies." Wenner thought he was joking and asked Corliss what he really wanted. "Twenty thousand dollars and six coins," Corliss replied. He says that Wenner countered, "You know what, Greg? I'm getting a little greedy myself."

A few months after the lawsuit was filed, Sun Valley's *Wood River Journal* ran a front-page story about the case. The accompanying photograph—one of several snapshots that Corliss had retained—showed the coins stacked on a postal scale, with Corliss grinning at the camera, champagne at his elbow and his arm around Anderson, who was bent over the gold, beaming.

The article spread the news of the gold to the few citizens of Blaine County whom Corliss hadn't managed to tell personally. Stoney Burke, a ranch broker who had lived on Broadford Farm for years before his wife sold the property to Wenner, was stunned. "We walked over the coins a thousand times when we were starving to death," he told me. LaVona Young, who lived on the farm as a girl in the 1940s and later owned the Mint Bar in Hailey (which she eventually sold to Bruce Willis), was more philosophical. People tell me to go down to the court and get my name on the list, say my folks buried them," she says. "I always laugh. My dad couldn't hang on to money long enough to bury it, and my mother would never have forgotten where she buried it." Treasure hunters began prowling the Broadford area with metal detectors. Richard Sauck, the general manager of the Big Wood Body & Paint auto shop, told me he planned to set up a "nuclear molecular electromagnetic resonator" device "to see if there's any more gold on that man's property."

It's a poignant irony that the treasure Anderson and Corliss found was in gold; Sun Valley was a silver area, after all, and around the end of the last century antagonism between gold and silver forces had been incendiary. President Grover Cleveland believed that the financial panic of 1893 and the subsequent depression resulted from the government's mandated buying of silver. He repealed the Sherman Silver Purchase Act of 1890 and put the country on the gold standard, with the support of eastern bankers, who saw silver as inflationary.

The defeat of silver, which led to the closing of most of Sun Valley's mines, was a major factor in the West's turning Republican and in the flinty attitudes of independence that endure there. Locals are still wary of outside capital—of weekenders such as Jann Wenner. Tom Blanchard, a local historian and former county commissioner, told me, "Given the Y2K problem, and how people still distrust the eastern lenders, I bet a lot of people out here are buying gold and putting it in a sock, figuring the banking system will collapse. Let's hope they remember where they put it."

As the story of the gold coins became a staple of local gossip, most of the valley's sympathies lay with Corliss and Anderson, but this sentiment was tempered with incredulity. "How dumb were these guys?" asked Jim Koonce, a mining engineer, expressing a widely held view. "Obviously, you split 'em and the split buys the other guy's silence—because Jann Wenner needs more money like a hole in the head."

The legal skirmishing—motions to dismiss, changes of counsel, discovery—dragged on through the remainder of 1997 and 1998. During this long period of uncertainty, Corliss took to carrying a picture of the gold everywhere; and, like the Ancient Mariner, he says, "I would tell one person in twenty about it." He even told Demi Moore.

—

Two days after receiving the gold coins, Wenner had them appraised by a pair of New York dealers, who, respectively, valued them at $23,465 and $25,590. Pronouncing himself uninterested in the provenance of the coins, Wenner told me, "They're not worth much, they don't have any historical importance, and they're mine, because they were found on my land."

At a deposition last August, Wenner's tetchy indifference took the unusual form of his choosing to appear without a lawyer. The proceeding was held in the conference room of Corliss's law firm, in Ketchum. Wenner sat across a rectangular oak table from Jon Cushman, Corliss's chief lawyer, and Corliss sat catercorner to them both. Corliss wore a jacket and tie; Wenner appeared in a polo shirt and jeans and breezed through the hour-and-five-minute inquiry. When Cushman asked Wenner whether he had ever gone over and looked around the area where the coins were found, he said, "No."

"Have you sought input from any old-timers about the history of the site at all?"

"No."

"How often are you in Sun Valley? Do you have any general schedule that you adhere to?"

"Generally, I'm here in the winter for skiing and I'm here in the late summer for relaxation, lawsuits—whatever."

Cushman eventually got around to asking, "Is there a price you would accept for these coins?"

Wenner said, "If you want to give me ten million, you've got them, or a million, you've got them."

Cushman professed puzzlement. "You're satisfied with the opinion that they're worth twenty-five to thirty—"

"I have every reason to believe that's the case," Wenner interrupted. Grinning, he added, "But, as I say, I'll take that million. A half a million." When the deposition was over, Wenner turned to Corliss and asked, "What is it that you *want*?" Corliss, startled and under strict orders to keep quiet, made no reply.

When Wenner produced the gold a month later for examination by Corliss's lawyers, their coin expert, Andy Stagg, joined the New York dealers' consensus, valuing them at $25,888. Nonetheless, Cushman continued to tell people that they were worth "half a million dollars." Everyone hoped the treasure would be worth more.

But Stagg did notice something odd when he checked the coins against an inventory that Corliss had secretly made in December 1996. Under the pretext of putting the coins in plastic sleeves while Anderson and his wife were watching TV, Corliss had cataloged the coins' mint marks, which had been omitted from Anderson's original inventory. (Corliss prided himself on a further stratagem. "Because of watching the O. J. Simpson trial," he says, "I figured DNA testing was pretty good, so I put my right thumbprint on the front of all the coins, just to prove later that it was mine." The returned coins had no fingerprints on them.) Stagg discovered that more than twenty of the coins now had different mint marks and that several of the new coins appeared to be less valuable.

"We really believe Larry switched them," Corliss says. "He's a pack rat, a miser. There's no way he'd give up all those coins without keeping *something* for himself." Anderson firmly denies this. Wenner says that there is no evidence of a substitution and that he's content with the coins as they are.

Corliss never got a chance to press this claim, because on January 5 of this year Judge James May ruled that the coins belonged to Wenner. Following a Texas court's precedent—the same decision that Brian Elkins had drawn to Anderson's attention—May decided that the coins had simply been mislaid and that there was "no logical reason to continue the ancient doctrine of treasure trove in this modern age." May cemented his property rights foundation with the point that "Anderson and Corliss were acting on behalf of Wenner and consequently the coins, like the topsoil [that they excavated], belong to the landowner."

Corliss is appealing the decision to Idaho's Supreme Court. Jon Cushman admits that the odds are not good and says that the coins now in evidence—which he believes are inferior replacements— "do not have a value sufficient to justify the continuation of this contest." As was the case with the area's mines, more money has gone in search of the treasure than the treasure is worth.

Larry Anderson, for his part, won't get Wenner's $5,000 reward, because Corliss's lawsuit nullified the offer. Though Judge May awarded Anderson the $11,970 that Corliss owes him, Corliss will appeal that, too. Anderson now regrets that he and Corliss ever met. "There's one road in this valley," Anderson says, "so Greg and I are going to keep passing each other. But I'm not going to say 'Hi.' " Shaking his head, he adds, "Sometimes I wish I'd never found it at all, because it's been such a pain in the rear. I always thought I'd just work, have a family, go through life one day at a time—I never thought I'd be lucky, if that's what you call it. It's like getting in a car wreck: how do you predict when someone's going to cross the white line and smash into you?"

———

Greg Corliss's dreams of glory are more durable. In March, he and Emily attended a benefit dinner in Hailey. After seven or eight drinks, Corliss jumped up onstage during an intermission in the stand-up comedy act. "Hi, my name is Greg Corliss," he announced, as he removed his shirt and lowered his trousers and boxer shorts. "And this is my impression of Demi Moore six months pregnant on the cover of *Vanity Fair.*" He thrust out his stomach and vamped nude for the astonished crowd until he was hustled offstage by the local marshal. Corliss now calls the incident "pretty dumb," but he explains, "Hey, I was just venting, expressing myself. Getting *known.*"

I had a last dinner with Greg and Emily at the Sawtooth Club in

Ketchum. They wore cheery Norwegian ski sweaters and held hands by the fireplace. As we sipped pints of wheat beer, Corliss reflected on the past two years. "My old ten-year plan was to move here and build a water-ski lake, be the hot-shit guy," he said. "That didn't go as smooth as I thought it would. My new ten-year plan is to finish the gold case and work for this boat company and build it the best I can." He explained that he'd taken a job as the national sales manager for Tiger Trax water-sport boats. "I just sold four boats at this show in Seattle," he said, "and this dealer I was helping wrote an order for $710,000. See, I get 5 percent, which is $35,000. So that's pretty excellent." He went on, "I've definitely learned from the gold experience. It made me think you should pick one thing and keep working at it." After a minute his grin spread, and he added, "Hey! If nothing else, I've had my fifteen minutes of fame."

Beneath the cockeyed bravado, Corliss appears to understand that a bond of trust was broken. The matter of which bond, and between which men, is more uncertain. But the defeat of Greg Corliss and Larry Anderson can also be seen as marking the end of Sun Valley's animating myth. Judge May's decision doesn't just make the rich richer; it also gives the haves of the world sole custody of a past built largely by the have-nots. The verdict scotches the "Go West" dreams of the lone prospector, the long-shot player, the self-made man. It signals that the frontier, always less open than advertised, is now truly closed.

Emily Corliss was reflective, too. But she was thinking about how the treasure had affected her friends and neighbors. "It's just amazing, the greed of the gold," she said. "Everyone else acted so badly—but they all call *Greg* the dickhead." As if to demonstrate the unfairness of it all, she concluded, "All Greg wanted was to be on the cover of *Rolling Stone*."

(1999)

THE HARRIET THE SPY CLUB

F̲ive years ago, two friends, Suzanne Kogan and Jenny Linden, went to a minor-league hockey game in Las Vegas. Suzanne started to flirt with the guy in the seat next to hers, a handsome, dark-haired man. Suzanne is a nursing-home executive. She has a way of biting off her words as if she wished you'd get to the point. The man eventually did: he told her that he was a mortician.

Next!

"Everyone I meet is a mortician, or like a mortician," Suzanne whispered to Jenny. "Do *you* know anybody good?"

Jenny, who is an anesthesiologist, is as chatty as Suzanne is terse. "I went out with a guy who's great!" Jenny said. "He's a plastic surgeon, flies his own plane, does charity surgery down in Mexico, scuba-dives, is a gourmet cook—"

"Wow!"

"And he's a great skier, plays classical guitar, doesn't have any children, and he's Jewish. He's perfect on paper."

"So?"

I can't put my finger on it. The conversation didn't flow—it was like being on an international phone call."

"Well, I want to meet him—give him my name," Suzanne said. It turned out that Suzanne had already run across the man Jenny was describing, Dr. Robert Bierenbaum, at the bar mitzvahs and brisses that draw together the city's Jewish-doctor circle. She had noticed that he smiled a lot, seemed to know everyone, and was candid about wanting to get married and have children before he was forty. He was then thirty-nine. "The rumor was that he came on real strong, went through a lot of women. People would say, 'Who's Bob marrying now?' " Suzanne told me. In the course of four years, he gave the same diamond to three different women.

When Bob called to ask Suzanne out, he started talking about Jenny: "You know the girl doesn't like you when she sets you up with her friend." But the conversation picked up, and eventually Bob murmured a seductive phrase in a foreign language.

"Oh, you're bilingual?" she said.

"Actually, I speak eleven languages," he said. Suzanne noted that Bob wasn't particularly shy about his accomplishments. But when they went to an Indian restaurant on their first date, in January of 1995, she found herself having a lovely time. "He was great, fun, too good to be true," Suzanne said. "And I'm thinking, What's wrong with this guy? Okay, he's a little hyper, but a lot of Jewish guys are."

After dinner, they went back to Bob's house in the Lakes, an expensive subdivision west of Las Vegas. Inside, Suzanne observed a peculiar mixture of fastidiousness and disarray. The ground floor was stylishly decorated, and there was a gleaming assortment of professional-quality pots and pans in the kitchen. But upstairs was a mess of unopened boxes. It looked as if Bob, who had moved in two years earlier, had never really unpacked. Later, she noticed that his backyard was still just dirt.

Before long, the couple found their way to Bob's bedroom. Afterward, however, Suzanne became cautious. "I had been married twice, I had a nine-year-old kid, I had plenty of baggage, and I wanted to hear about his baggage," she told me. She asked Bob if he'd ever been married. He said that he had, but then refused to talk about how it had ended.

Finally, after an awkward pause, Suzanne joked, "What'd you do? Kill her?"

"Bob turned about five different shades of color," Suzanne told me. "He said, 'What do you know?' and he's looking at me like, Who the hell have you been talking to?" After a tense few minutes, Bob calmed down. "Finally, he told me his story," Suzanne said. "Years earlier, he was married to a woman named Gail, they were living in Manhattan, he was putting in long hours as a resident, she was a student with a serious drug problem—depressed, having affairs. All this led to a big argument between them on a day that they were to go to his nephew's birthday party. She walked out of the apartment in shorts and a halter top and never came back.

"Years later, her torso washed up on Staten Island, and they identified it because of a distinctive curvature of the spine. He told me he felt strongly that Gail had committed suicide or had fallen in with bad people, but that her parents had accused him of murder." When Bob stopped talking, Suzanne was silent. She felt awful. Then he asked her not to tell anyone about his past. "It was clear he was doing a start-over with his life," she said. "He was trying to leave that behind. I started thinking, Oh, poor you, and I said I'd keep the secret." But, of course, she didn't.

———

The first law of gossip is that you never know how many people are talking about you behind your back. The second law is thank God. The third—and most important—law is that as gossip spreads from friends to acquaintances to people you've never met, it grows more garbled, vivid, and definitive. Out of stray factoids and hesitant impressions emerges a hard mass of what everyone knows to be true. Imagination supplies the missing pieces, and repetition turns these pieces into facts; gossip achieves its shape and amplitude only in the continual retelling. The best stories about us are told by perfect strangers.

When Robert Bierenbaum moved to Las Vegas, ten years ago, he surrounded himself with strangers. "We jokingly call it Second Chance City," says Ernest Sussman, a urologist, who is a close friend of Bierenbaum's. "A lot of doctors who come here had trouble elsewhere—behavioral problems, practices that didn't work, whatever." (The type is epitomized by Jules Segal in Mario Puzo's *The Godfather:* a surgeon from the East who takes refuge in Las Vegas after an abortion scandal.) Bierenbaum had come West from Manhattan at the urging of a childhood friend from New Jersey, Scott Baranoff, who had a urology practice in town. On an all-doctor ski trip to Switzerland, Baranoff and an older plastic surgeon named Charles Vinnik raved to Bierenbaum about the medical opportunities in Las Vegas.

"Las Vegas has a *lot* of plastic surgery," says Dr. Julio Garcia, who stitched up Evander Holyfield's ear after Mike Tyson bit it off. "This is a service-oriented town where tipping is important, so if you're an older blackjack dealer, or a cocktail waitress with sags, it can make financial sense to get surgery."

Bierenbaum made a good impression on many of his new colleagues, who found him to be a skillful surgeon and an easygoing friend. "He was a model citizen, one who just could not volunteer enough of his time," Sussman says. Bierenbaum regularly flew himself to Mexico to perform free surgery on children who had cleft palates. He loved to fly: he often double-dated with his doctor friends, flying a group to Lake Tahoe for a skiing weekend. But he told almost none of his friends about his marriage. "He knew that his wife's disappearance wouldn't add to his panache," a friend of Bierenbaum's told me. "It's not a great pickup line: 'Hi, my wife disappeared, and people think I murdered her!'"

For a time, Suzanne Kogan kept Bob's secret reasonably well; while they were dating, she shared it only with her mother. But after an intense six months together, Bob abruptly broke up with her in July 1995. So, soon afterward, when Suzanne had dinner with Jenny Linden, she no longer felt obliged to be discreet. The two friends met at the Mayflower, a quiet Asian fusion restaurant in one of the city's numerous minimalls, where it is situated both geographically and aesthetically midway between an oxygen bar called Breathe and a Jack in the Box.

Suzanne told Jenny how Bob had been very devoted at the beginning—"Mr. Wonderful, a fairy tale"—but then came to seem increasingly odd. "He could never sit still to read the Sunday paper or watch TV," Suzanne said. (At their request, I have changed Suzanne's and Jenny's names, as well as the names of their relatives and certain identifying details.)

A few minutes later, Jenny said, "I've always been surprised that Bob didn't run for office." A committed Republican, Bierenbaum was active in the Rotary Club and in Leadership Las Vegas, a boosters' group. The one framed photograph in his office, which sat on top of the filing cabinet, was a shot of him with Newt Gingrich.

"Skeletons in his closet," Suzanne replied. "Did you know he'd been married?"

"No!"

As Suzanne recounted the grisly saga of Gail and the torso, and how Gail's parents suspected Bob, Jenny kept saying, "Oh, my God . . . oh, my God."

That night, when she got home from dinner, Jenny told the torso story to her fiancé, Rich Taylor, who also knew Bob. He immediately suspected Bierenbaum. "You dated him!" Rich said. "You dated a killer!"

"If this is *Six Degrees of Separation*," Jenny says now, "then Suzanne is one, I'm two, and Rich is three, and the further out you go, the more convinced the person becomes that Bob did it. Suzanne thought, Oh, another nutty Vegas doctor with a past. I thought, This is really bizarre! And Rich was convinced the guy was an ax murderer."

"There was something with Bob that I've never felt before or since," Rich told me recently. "He wouldn't look me in the eye, and then he looked right through me with the intensity and darkness of an obsessional killer."

This kind of hindsight is a hallmark of gossip. A startling bit of new information about a person, even if it is implausible, prompts a reinterpretation of every puzzling previous interaction. And if the person in question is not someone we know well, the reappraisal is all the more swift and absolute.

For a long time, Suzanne's story was the only clue Rich and Jenny had that something bad had happened to Gail. Additional evidence proved elusive. They went to the library and looked up "Bierenbaum" in the *New York Times* archive, but they didn't find anything. Jenny tried Internet search engines such as Yahoo! and Cyber 411, typing in "Bierenbaum" and "torso" and "missing" and "murder." Nothing came up. Nor did the FBI's Web site mention a Gail Bierenbaum murder.

Then, one night, Jenny and Rich rented *Boxing Helena,* a movie about a surgeon who chops off his beloved's arms and legs in order to keep her prisoner. As they watched, they shouted almost in unison, "That's what Bob did!" Their quest had become a kind of Hitchcockian game—Grace Kelly sneaking into the suspect's apartment in *Rear Window* or Teresa Wright in *Shadow of a Doubt* racing to the library to research whether her charming uncle, Joseph Cotten, could be a killer. Whenever Jenny was getting ready to go to a medical conference that Bob might also be attending, Rich would taunt her about him. "I'd say, 'He's a killer, he's a killer!' " Rich says. He would go so far as to page Jenny at the conference, typing "86776" into her beeper—numbers that, on a telephone, spell "torso."

Rich and Jenny dined out on the spooky tale of Bob and the torso for years. Meanwhile, Bob remarried and moved with his wife to North Dakota. "We weren't finding anything out, and Bob was now out of reach," Rich told me. "I always just figured he would get caught because he'd do it again—that he'd kill his brand-new wife, too."

———

One day early in 1996, about six months after Suzanne and Bob had broken up, she dropped by his small office to pick up some belongings that she'd left at his house. She began chatting with the office manager, Laurie Francis, with whom she'd become friendly. As they commiserated about having to deal with Bob, Suzanne mentioned the story of Gail and the torso.

Laurie was shocked. She immediately passed the details on to the office receptionist, Carol Villanueva. Carol then phoned Sharon Nicholson, Bierenbaum's previous office manager, to tell her the story. All three women went into a swivet of speculation: this astonishing news, even in its most innocent interpretation, seemed to explain a lot about their boss. In contrast to the relaxed fellow his male colleagues knew, Bob Bierenbaum was something of a terror at work. His employees were leery of his high-handedness and fits of rage, traits that had led them to secretly refer to him as "B-dash-B," in reference to the Jewish tradition of spelling God as "G-d."

"Bob was very moody, and he yelled a lot," Laurie told me, adding that his eyes darted about uneasily and that his stomach was often upset. And Carol would later attach particular significance to an incident from 1991. A patient had called her to ask how many procedures of a certain kind—Carol believes it may have been breast reductions—Bob had performed. "He'd only done three, but I knew I was supposed to say 'numerous,' " Carol told me. "The patient wanted an exact number, and I said, 'I don't *know* exactly how many.' Bob was nearby, and I guess he didn't like what I was saying, because he nudged me on the shoulder, not very hard. I turned and saw him throw his hands up in horror at what he had done and then scurry back to his office. Later he came out and said, 'I'm so sorry I hit you. Really, I'm *so, so* sorry.' I said, 'You didn't hurt me—it's fine.' And I looked at Sharon like, What is this guy's problem?"

The story about Gail also seemed to shed light on Bierenbaum's peculiar workplace rules: Any employee who touched the mail—except to pluck out *People* magazine—would be fired. Bob instituted this rule after Sharon Nicholson saw a credit card circular addressed to Gail Katz-Bierenbaum. Employees were also told that they would be fired if they accepted any subpoenas. Bierenbaum refused to advertise his practice on billboards or to have a brochure made up. "I want nothing in print," he told Sharon. "He was the first plastic surgeon who came to Las Vegas and left," his colleague Dr.

Garcia says. "We all wondered why he didn't succeed, because he certainly liked to hobnob, which is how you get referrals."

Bierenbaum seemed more interested in succeeding at a relationship than at a career. In addition to talking ceaselessly about his wish to be married, preferably to a Jewish woman, Bob often gave his staff sexually triumphant morning-after reports about his dates—"First date, first time!" he'd say. Shortly after he'd broken up with Suzanne, he met Janet Chollet. She was a gynecologist, a Catholic, and, as he gleefully told his employees, a virgin. Chollet accepted Bob's proposal of marriage, along with the same diamond he had offered to two other women. (To change his luck, Bob had had it reset in platinum.)

Bob and Janet were married in New York, in the spring of 1996, and that summer they moved to Minot, North Dakota. The town's Trinity Health Center, where Janet's brother worked, had guaranteed Bob a sizable income. The Bierenbaums apparently lived happily in North Dakota: Janet gave birth to a daughter, who is now twenty months old; Bob was written up in the *Minot Daily News* for his bagel and pizza recipes. No one inquired about his past.

A week before the wedding, however, Bob had called Suzanne Kogan and said that his fiancée was having second thoughts. Janet had seen a copy of Gail Katz-Bierenbaum's death certificate, which had come to Bob in the mail from his lawyer. (In order to be married in New York, Bierenbaum had to show proof of his previous wife's death.) Bob had told Janet that his first wife died of unknown causes, so the death certificate gave the prospective bride a nasty shock: in the box marked "Death Was Caused By" is typed "Undetermined (torso)"; just below, the word *Homicide* is circled.

Suzanne says that Bob wanted advice when he called, and she gave him some. "If you'd get comfortable in your own skin, you wouldn't even need to marry Janet," she says she told him. "You hardly know her, she's not Jewish, and North Dakota? For a gourmet cook who speaks so many languages? Please." Bob ignored Suzanne's advice, and she hasn't spoken to him since.

—

In April 1998, investigators from the Manhattan District Attorney's Office arrived in Las Vegas and began asking questions about Bierenbaum and his missing first wife, Gail. The investigators took particular interest in several of Bob's ex-girlfriends, including Suzanne Kogan and Miranda Collier, a dentist who had dated Bierenbaum for three years in the early nineties. News of the investigation spread quickly through the city's small medical community, and was even discussed in operating rooms over anesthetized patients: "Did you hear about Bob Bierenbaum?"

After the investigators went back to New York, Suzanne and Jenny arranged a dinner with Miranda, whom they both knew, to talk about Bob: they all felt that he was possibly, or even probably, capable of the murder, and they wanted to see if together they could turn up some evidence. "It was girl talk with a purpose," Jenny said. "We hoped to help the police, but ultimately we were detectives more in the sense of a Peter Sellers movie than *Mission: Impossible.*"

They met at the Mayflower, and for two hours they traded stories about Bierenbaum. Jenny complained about the way he'd discussed her with all of her friends after just one date: "I told him, 'This is a small community, and I don't want you talking about my private life.' He looked crushed, and he said, 'Oh, I'm sorry. I'm *so, so* sorry.' The response was all out of proportion to the crime."

Suzanne talked about her final trip with Bob, when they'd flown to a conference in Virginia. "He was being very nasty and distant, and he wouldn't tell me what was wrong," she recalled. Finally, she said, Bob came toward her, silently holding his hands out in front of him: they were covered with red spots.

Alarmed, Suzanne had asked, "Are you dying?"

"It's syphilis," he said. (One symptom of secondary syphilis is copper-colored spots on the extremities.) "You had an affair, and you gave me syphilis!"

"I remember laughing, because it was so absurd," Suzanne said.

"But I was really mad. Later, he learned that the rash was something else, and apologized."

Suzanne had treated Bob's moodiness as a foible, but Miranda said that she had grown fearful of his sudden possessive rages. (I have also changed Miranda's name and occupation.) He had never been physically violent, but she was concerned about how he would react when she broke up with him. She waited till she was leaving on a trip and then asked him to move out.

The three women decided to meet regularly to stay on top of the investigation. Their code word was "torso"—as in, "We need a torso meeting"—but Jenny coined the name that stuck. She dubbed the group the Harriet the Spy Club. (Bierenbaum later heard a rumor that the group was called the I Hate Bob Club.)

The second Harriets dinner at the Mayflower, that August, was abruptly canceled. Suzanne's mother, Barb, who had asked to be included, was getting a preparatory facial that afternoon when she reached for her cell phone, rolled off the table, and shattered her right ankle. At the rescheduled dinner, in November, Barb set the tone. As soon as she sat down, she looked at Jenny and said, "I can't believe you fixed my daughter up with a murderer!"

"He could have killed me!" Suzanne said, her eyes widening.

"Hey, I went out with him three times, too!" Jenny protested.

Barb then held forth about Bob, a critique she recently repeated to me in her cottage behind the Desert Inn golf course. A large and cheerful woman with bright hennaed hair, Barb runs a small business out of her kitchen. The day I visited, the table was spread with newspaper and covered with two dozen half-painted figurines of scantily clad women with their legs apart. These Naughty Nellies, as they're called, are souvenir reproductions of a type of bootjack peculiar to Old West bordellos. Barb hopes to sell them in Las Vegas's better department stores.

After we settled in her living room, Barb told me that she'd been suspicious of Bob from the start—not as a murderer, necessarily, but as a lousy potential son-in-law, which, in her eyes, amounted to almost the same thing. Although Bob called himself a gourmet cook, Barb said that when he made paella in her kitchen he "turned it upside down" and all that came out was a "big pot of mess." Then, at Passover, Bob wanted to run the Seder—"He had a lot of balls!"—when, of course, it was Barb's husband, Sol, who would head the table. Bob wanted to piggyback on the family's connections to get high-society clients—"He knew we weren't selling pencils!"—but he made her friends uneasy, and they all went to Beverly Hills for their face-lifts, anyway. Bob had such a "dark energy," she said. "He gave us all a chill."

After Barb had delivered her indictment at the second Harriets dinner, Jenny announced the scant results of her latest Web searches: she'd found a single article Bierenbaum had written, for the *Grand Forks Herald,* about how to avoid snowblower injuries. She was planning to ask friends in New York to look for news clippings on Gail's disappearance, and she might canvas Bierenbaum's classmates from Albany Medical College. Then there was some discussion of how Bob's father, Marvin, who was a cardiologist and whom Suzanne hadn't much liked, had a laboratory in which she heard he did medical experiments on dogs. The Harriets speculated that Bob could have used the lab to cut Gail up. Miranda said that Marvin had told her that "Gail's disappearance was the best thing that ever happened to Bob."

Miranda also said that she kept thinking about what could have happened to her or Suzanne if they'd made Bob really mad. As their musings grew increasingly somber, the Harriets wondered if someone shouldn't tell Bob's new wife about their concerns. No one volunteered.

———

Alayne Katz, Gail Katz-Bierenbaum's younger sister, is a forty-two-year-old family practice lawyer. When I visited her home, in Westchester County, recently, I was met by a slight woman with reddish hair and large brown eyes who carried a folder full of photos, news clippings, and police reports. Although we were discussing events that began two decades ago, Alayne spoke with near perfect recall and referred to the folder just once.

"Initially, I thought Bob Bierenbaum was sweet, intelligent, and good-looking," she told me. "But even before the problems began Gail told me, 'Bob looks perfect on paper—until you meet him, when you see that he's a social moron.' On a double date once, Bob kept putting food in my mouth with his chopsticks, which just seemed weird and embarrassing. And his shirttails were always hanging out, like a ten-year-old's."

Alayne talked about how Bob was a resident at Maimonides Medical Center in Brooklyn, while Gail was pursuing her Ph.D. in clinical psychology at Long Island University. She showed me old snapshots of Bob and Gail in happier times, including a few of them at their wedding, which took place on Labor Day weekend, 1982.

A month before the ceremony, Gail called Alayne at their parents' house in Long Island. She was crying hysterically. "Bob hurt the cat," she said. "You have to help me." Alayne drove into Manhattan, and Gail told her that Bob had suddenly become wildly jealous of her cat and had dunked it in the toilet bowl, apparently intending to drown it, until Gail pulled him away. "She insisted we take the cat to the shelter to save it from Bob," Alayne recalled. "I kept saying, 'Let's not get rid of the cat—let's get rid of Bob!' "

She closed her eyes, then continued: "Gail told me, 'No, I love him.' I think it was partly her feeling that she could change him, make him more secure in her love—and partly that the wedding invitations were out, so the relationship was going to have to work." But it didn't. Gail, Alayne told me, resented her husband's niggling criticisms of her weight, her hairstyle, and her clothing. She'd always worn trendy clothes; as Mrs. Bierenbaum, she began buying conservative wool skirts. But she also rebelled against a life of domestic propriety, and sought refuge in occasional cocaine use and in at least one affair.

"Bob was working a hundred and twenty hours a week, so Gail severely lacked for his attention," a confidant of Bierenbaum's told me. "But she was high-maintenance, a self-absorbed whiner. She loved the idea of being the doctor's wife more than she loved the doctor."

Fourteen months after the wedding, Bob came home one day and saw Gail studying for an exam and smoking a cigarette. Although he'd forbidden her to smoke, she sneaked cigarettes to lose weight. He vaulted over the couch and began choking her. On November 12, 1983, Gail filed a police report—which was never pursued—stating that "her husband did strangle her to the point at which she lost consciousness." (Bierenbaum's confidant acknowledges that "a physical incident" occurred but says it was less serious than Gail claimed.)

Bob seemed remorseful, but Gail and members of his family strongly urged him to seek counseling. Dr. Michael Stone, a psychiatrist, consulted with Gail and Bob separately a total of five times. Alarmed by the hostile dynamic between them, he decided not to take them on as patients. "I tried to convince Gail she should leave him ASAP, but she wouldn't listen," Stone told me.

Stone was sufficiently concerned that, on November 20, he sent Gail a duty-to-warn letter. By signing and returning it, she would acknowledge that she had been counseled to live apart from her husband, and that, "owing to the unpredictable nature of my husband's physical assaults and to the chronic nature of the characterological abnormalities that underlie these assaults, no firm date can as yet be fixed as to when it might be safe to resume living together." The advisory added, "If I do not heed this advice, I must accept the consequences, including the possibility of personal injury, or death, at the hands of my husband."

Gail kept the letter, but she never signed it. She did move out and live with her grandfather for a short period, but she soon returned to Bob. The marriage did not improve, and Gail started having an affair. On Saturday, July 6, 1985, Gail spent part of the day planning a surprise thirtieth-birthday party for Bob—and part of it looking for an apartment for herself. She was twenty-nine.

Bob later told the police that the following morning he and Gail had had an argument, after which she walked out of their apartment on East Eighty-fifth Street. She left her pocketbook behind, telling him, he would later say, that she was just going to get some sun in Central Park. On the evening of July 8, thirty hours after she had supposedly left, Bob reported Gail missing. The next day, Gail's mother accused Bob of killing her. (She would continue to leave messages—"I know you murdered Gail!"—on his answering machine for several years.) Alayne Katz and Gail's lover believed that Bob might have learned of his wife's plan to move out and been provoked into a homicidal rage.

The Katzes told the police enough about the couple's marital history that when Bierenbaum was next interviewed, on July 13, Detective Thomas O'Malley was less gentle with him. Bob had already told the police that his wife had a "history of mental illness" and that she had attempted suicide in 1979. This time he added that "his marriage was in bad shape and he and his wife were always having fights." After recording Bierenbaum's observations, O'Malley continued in his report:

> I then asked him if he ever attempted to strangle his wife, and he said very abruptly he did not want to talk about it. When asked of any incident with a cat, I received the same abrupt-type answer: "No." . . . As we concluded Dr. Bierenbaum said, "This doesn't look right, and people are going to start to wonder." When I asked him what he meant he said, "It's obvious, isn't it?"

Shortly thereafter, Bierenbaum hired a lawyer and declined to speak further with the police.

The police investigation seemed to be languishing, so in 1986 the Katzes asked the chief of the Manhattan district attorney's investigative division to look into the case. The DA's office, too, focused on Bierenbaum. An official there told me that they were troubled by Bierenbaum's response when the police called him a year later, in July 1986, to say that they were holding a woman who they thought might be Gail at the World Trade Center. The police report notes that Bierenbaum "seemed annoyed that I had called him at that hour"—2:30 A.M.—"and was reluctant to respond."

The new team of investigators uncovered a damning piece of evidence. They learned that on the afternoon of Gail's disappearance Bierenbaum had rented a plane in Caldwell, New Jersey—a Cessna 172N, with a baggage allowance of 120 pounds—and flown it for nearly two hours. Bierenbaum had told the police that he'd spent the day waiting for Gail to come home, then had driven to his sister's house in New Jersey for his nephew's birthday party. He never mentioned a plane flight. "That was huge in our minds," one investigator said. "How do you make that omission?"

Bierenbaum's lawyer, Scott Greenfield, says that his client flew the plane to clear his head after his argument with Gail and that he never mentioned the flight to the police simply because Detective O'Malley did an "exceptionally poor job" of asking about his whereabouts on the day of the disappearance.

When police technicians were finally given permission, in 1987, to examine the rented plane and the cars that Bierenbaum might have driven on the day Gail disappeared, combing them for blood and tissue, they found nothing, however. The prosecutors decided that without more substantial physical evidence they couldn't seek an indictment, and the case file went into the archives.

In May 1989, the police found a torso washed up near the piers on Front Street, in Staten Island. It displayed surgical cut marks at the shoulders and pelvis and, although it was badly decomposed, appeared to be that of a white female between thirty and forty years of age. In August, an expert radiologist compared X rays of the torso with old X rays of Gail. He determined that "both sets of films are of Gail Katz." Her missing-person case was officially termed a homicide, and the torso was buried in the Katz family plot in Queens. The Katzes informed Bierenbaum, through his lawyer, that he would not be welcome at the funeral; he did not attend. But he did sit shivah at home. A few months later he moved to Las Vegas.

—

In 1997, Andrew Rosenzweig, the chief investigator in the Manhattan District Attorney's Office, decided to dust off a couple of unsolved cases that had always bothered him. The following April Rosenzweig and an investigator named Tommy Pon flew to Las Vegas for four days to interview Bierenbaum's friends, colleagues, and former employees there. That trip, of course, was the one that inspired Bob's ex-girlfriends to have their first sleuthing session at the Mayflower. The investigators hoped that Bierenbaum would have confessed to a Las Vegas girlfriend; Suzanne, Jenny, and Miranda hoped that the investigators would tell them everything about Bob's past. Neither group was rewarded with precisely the information it had hoped for. But the private suspicions of the women Bierenbaum had dated and the public suspicions of the state were finally linked: both sets of detectives began to borrow from each other's stories and conjectures, braiding them together into a coherent narrative that made sense to everybody.

According to someone who was involved in the official investigation, the interviews with Suzanne Kogan and Miranda Collier "added to things we knew, helped fill in the profile—is he capable of violence, of murder?" Miranda's account of being afraid of Bob, so similar to Gail's, "is the kind of testimony that can have an effect on a jury," and Suzanne's story of her first date "added to our suspicion. His not sharing any details, first, and then his shock at her joke—'Did you kill her?' It connoted someone who'd had a nerve struck."

Although the investigators were careful to appear open-minded, they had a tidy working profile of Bierenbaum—"He has to control everything, but the rage can't be suppressed," one member of the prosecution team told me—and a strong belief in his guilt. The Harriets, who actually knew Bob, had neither. But they were beginning to change their minds. Indeed, once the investigators came to town, the Las Vegas medical community began to reassess affable, civic-minded Bob Bierenbaum. Some of his doctor friends did rise to his defense, however. "Bob doesn't have any capability for that kind of act," Dr. Charles Vinnik told me. "The investigators were interviewing people who barely knew Bob, spreading rumors, and then interviewing people who'd heard those rumors. It was like Chinese whispers."

It wasn't quite that simple. For instance, when the investigators spoke to Dr. Douglas Seip, who co-owned Bierenbaum's plane, they never said that Bob was under suspicion. But they did ask Seip what sort of luggage Bob carried, what might fit into a small plane. They were trying to work out their theory: that Bob had strangled Gail, cut her up with surgical expertise, put the body parts into a bag, and dropped them from the plane into the Atlantic.

Seip drew the obvious conclusions from the questioning, and he mentioned the investigators' suspicions to his assistant, Rod. While Rod was getting some work done by a surgeon named Dr. Resto, for whom Bierenbaum's former office manager Laurie Francis now works, he mentioned the dismemberment idea to her. Laurie then called Sharon Nicholson, her predecessor in Bierenbaum's office, and they chatted about the ramifications of the inferred, thirdhand, get-the-body-past-the-doorman conundrum.

"I think he killed her in the bathtub," Laurie said.

"I could see that, because he's so anal he wouldn't want the cleanup," Sharon agreed. "But maybe he killed her somewhere else in the apartment—he got mad, it was a mistake—and then dragged her to the tub."

Both of the investigations, official and unofficial, were proceeding along the same lines, using inductive rather than deductive reasoning. They started with snippets about Bierenbaum's character and then tried to make the pieces of the puzzle fit.

Naturally, in such an atmosphere, rumors flourished, because they were more satisfying than the uncertain facts of the case. Once, when she was dating Bob, Suzanne had broken a glass while she was unloading his dishwasher. "He started raging," she recalls. "He said, 'This is one of a set, and I can't replace it!' It was just a glass. I pulled eight dollars out of my purse and gave it to him. 'Here, Bob—happy now?' " Suzanne mentioned the incident to her mother, and by the time Bob recounted it to me it had become, "He got violent with her one night and broke glasses!"

The investigators had gone to North Dakota, and on November 30, 1998, they confronted Bob outside his clinic, hoping that the news that they were still investigating Gail's murder would startle him into making a telling remark. But Bob swiftly invoked his right to counsel, and he hasn't spoken with the police or prosecutors since. (Nor would he speak with me.) As this brief encounter passed from source to source, it was embellished until it took on the proportions of *Darkness at Noon.* Last June, Laurie Francis e-mailed me: "The other day I heard from someone who works for a local attorney who is/was friends with Bob Bierenbaum that after four interrogations, he had broken down and confessed and that he had been taken into custody within the past month."

At around the same time, Jenny heard from Suzanne, who'd heard from a cardiologist that the police had found parts of Gail's body cemented into the walls of the couple's Manhattan apartment. Jenny tracked the rumor back to the cardiologist's husband, who'd heard it from an anesthesiologist, who'd heard, somewhere, that Bierenbaum had confessed on *60 Minutes.* Jenny sent an e-mail to *60 Minutes* seeking confirmation, but—as no such thing had happened—got no reply. So Suzanne called the clinic in North Dakota and had Bierenbaum paged, to see if he was in custody. When he answered, she hung up.

Last fall, the rumors dwindled, because a verifiable event was under way: a New York State grand jury had begun hearing testimony about Bierenbaum from a multitude of witnesses, including Miranda Collier. (Suzanne was asked to testify but declined.) In early December the grand jury indicted Bierenbaum for the second-degree murder of his wife, a crime that carries a penalty of twenty-five years to life in prison.

At the arraignment in New York State Supreme Court on December 9, 1999, one of the prosecutors, Stephen Saracco, charged that Bierenbaum "murdered [Gail] in the apartment, that he packaged her body," that he dumped her remains out of a plane, and that "her body still lies on the bottom of the ocean," somewhere between Montauk Point and Cape May. This last claim startled many of those in Las Vegas who had been part of the gossip chain: what about the torso?

When the case was reactivated, the medical examiner had the torso exhumed and ordered DNA tests. In September 1998, the lab determined that the DNA from the torso did not match the DNA in Gail's sister's blood. The biggest break in the story, the famous torso, had proved to be a red herring.

—

One gray afternoon in late January, I finally saw the man I had heard so much about. Bierenbaum, who is out on $500,000 bail and living at his parents' house in West Orange, New Jersey, came to the New York State Supreme Court building for a brief status hearing on the trial, which is scheduled to begin on September 7. He got out of a car wearing a tan raincoat, a blue suit, and small horn-rimmed glasses. As a squad of cameramen surged and blocked his path, Bierenbaum's face remained fixed and blank. In court, he sat with his parents and his wife, Janet. The hearing took two minutes. Scott Greenfield filed the customary motion to dismiss charges—a motion that would be denied three months later—and then everyone filed out.

When I looked at my notes, I realized that Bierenbaum had never said a word, not even to his family. (Nor, after a court appearance in April, would he say anything when Alayne Katz confronted him in front of two TV cameramen as he waited for the courthouse elevators. "Bob, fifteen years I'm waiting to hear you tell me that you didn't kill my sister!" she said. Frowning, he spun away from her.) I also realized that with so much in dispute, a jury might not be certain, beyond a reasonable doubt, that Bob Bierenbaum killed his wife.

In court filings, the prosecutors acknowledge that their evidence is "wholly circumstantial." And a sizable portion of it is testimony about the oddities and anomalies of Bob's behavior—that is, state-certified gossip. When I visited Scott Greenfield in his office re-

rently he seized on this problem: "Let's assume the Bierenbaums had a terrible marriage. And let's assume, for the sake of argument, that Bob almost drowned a cat, that he strangled Gail to unconsciousness, and that some of the women he later dated believe him to be capable of killing her. Still, what has any of that got to do with what happened on July seventh?"

Alayne Katz believes it has everything to do with it. "Bob did a wonderful job of disposing of the physical evidence," she told me. "But what was left behind was his personality—and he couldn't cover that up."

—

The night before the arraignment, a prosecutor called Suzanne Kogan in Las Vegas to tell her that Bob's arrest was imminent. To confirm that he'd been taken into custody, she phoned Bierenbaum's clinic in Minot to ask for an appointment and was told that no appointments were being accepted for the indefinite future. The next day, after the court hearing, Jenny went on-line and typed "Bierenbaum" and "murder" into Yahoo!'s search engine and was rewarded at long last: there was a wire-service story about the court proceedings.

That night, Suzanne set up a conference call among the Harriets. Suzanne and Miranda commiserated because everyone was asking them, "Say, weren't you and Bob, um . . . ?" Then they all grew a little shy. "The mood had changed from that of an exciting parlor game to a scary, real thing," Jenny told me. "It had gone from Bob as a *story* to Bob the *person*. We weren't saying, 'How did he package her?' anymore, but 'Will he go to jail?' and 'He has a baby now.' " She looked deeply unhappy. "I feel sorry for him, and I feel bad for having this prurient interest in him, for spying. I mean, typing 'Bierenbaum' and 'murder' on Yahoo!—there must be something wrong with me, too."

(2000)

PART III

FAR FROM HOME

THE WANING (AND CAREFUL WAXING)
OF THE MARCOS DYNASTY

As I sat down to lunch last February with the Marcos family—that is, what remains of the family in their home province of Ilocos Norte—it seemed clear that the matriarch, Doña Josefa Edralin Marcos, would not be joining us. Still, it comforted everyone that she was resting quietly in the next room, her lipstick a jaunty stitch of scarlet, her face an impasto of Covermark makeup that a high school sophomore would envy. For a woman who'd had her ninety-seventh birthday party earlier in the month, she looked good. For a woman who'd been dead since May 4, 1988, she looked *really* good.

Propped in the hinge of Doña Josefa's open coffin was a small handwritten sign: 298 DAYS 2/25/89. This was not so much for the family as for visitors. Since shortly after her death, Doña Josefa has lain in state in the Marcos family home—a spacious villa that also serves as a Marcos museum—in Batac, a town of fifty thousand in Ilocos Norte. There, she is an indifferent hostage in the struggle over the fate of her son Ferdinand. Ferdinand wouldn't be joining us for lunch, either. The ex-president, seventy-one, was in St. Francis Medical Center in Honolulu, battered by heart, kidney, and respiratory ailments: his doctors were telling visitors he had only a 10 percent chance of surviving the year.

After his mother died, Marcos reached his relatives in Manila and told them not to bury her. It is an Ilocano tradition that the oldest son should bury the mother, and Marcos wanted to use the burial issue to increase sympathy for his plea to return home. (There was also an uncharitable rumor in Philippine political circles that Marcos, who believes in "pyramid power" and that he has a guardian angel, was taking seriously a warning by a fortune-teller that he would die the instant his mother was buried.) It was not working: Marcos remained last winter under U.S. government hold, detained until the Aquino government would permit his return, and further restrained by a federal indictment in Manhattan charging him and his wife, Imelda, with stealing more than $100 million from the Philippine government during their twenty-year kleptocratic rule.

So the vigil in Batac continued. On the veranda I ate adobo, okra, eggplant, and rice with Cynthia Chan, Marcos's niece, who lives in the house, and Colonel Barnaby Aballa (retired), Marcos's first cousin. Chan said that Ferdinand was her favorite relative because he used to bring her chocolates. Then Chan recalled her grandmother's kindness, her passion for mah-jongg, and the thrift that (in Chan's appealing formulation) made Doña Josefa a shrewd businesswoman. Like many of the Marcoses during Ferdinand's presidency, Doña Josefa miraculously became a tycoon, eventually holding monopolies in shipping, timber, wood processing, and food, beverage, and tobacco wholesaling. Even her official photographer somehow ended up with sixteen luxury cars.

"When my uncle was in the senate," Chan said, offering me a glass of coconut milk, "he tried to buy *lola* [grandmother] a car. This was because she was always taking the bus, which was ten centavos. She said, 'No, Ferdie, I don't want to have to pay for the driver, for gas. Just give me the money.' "

Inside the house, six or seven visitors to the museum were settling themselves into chairs around the coffin, quietly paying their respects, as several dozen people do each day. Ilocanos—a tough, thrifty, clannish people—still think of Marcos as their *apo,* or patron. Feeling that they owe him *utang na loob,* the debt of gratitude, to a person they deny he stole or abused his office.

The Marcos legacy in Ilocos Norte is extraordinary, even for a country steeped in the pork barrel. To be sure, goats now graze on the tennis court at Marcos's lavish weekend home in Paoay—where Gina Lollobrigida once took memorable photos of the president in Speedos—and the Aquino administration has shuttered another modest Marcos museum commemorating Ferdinand's birthplace in Sarrat. But more practical monuments remain: good irrigation; electricity even in remote rural areas; parks and municipal buildings; and, most crucially in a country where rural routes are usually just organized mud, cement roads.

Doña Josefa's casket was surrounded by fifteen fresh garlands and a half-dozen pictures of the family, including a tranquil shot of the president kissing his mother on the forehead while she looked sadly at the camera. Three women in white, postulants with the order of Mama Rose, had arrived and were droning prayers—". . . *and* we pray for the return of President Marcos and his family . . ."—while the small, impromptu congregation waved fans across their faces to shuffle the heat.

A few of the visitors dutifully tromped upstairs to view the museum's eclectic holdings, as I had that morning. There were Marcos's license plates, 1950–1966; a copy of the bar exam on which, according to the museum, he earned the highest score in Philippine history; accounts of his successful appeal before the Philippine Supreme Court of his 1939 conviction for the murder of Julio Nalundasan, a political rival of his father's. There were accounts, too, of his eleven-day courtship of Imelda ("When Congressman Marcos played golf at the country club that afternoon, he broke par. . . . But to the congressman in love, breaking par was nothing compared with what he felt when he thought he had a chance of winning Meldy"). I had examined the war medals that made him the Philippines' most decorated soldier; his shoes and racquetball shorts

("The president, mindful of the classical concern over both mind and body, has engaged in different sports exemplified by the sports attire that he has worn"); campaign literature ("Marcos is a simple, friendly man, humble and approachable. To a FAULT"); and newspaper clippings about his promises to end corruption if elected. The displays trail off after 1965, Marcos's first year in office. There is no mention of martial law; the vicious secret police; the death-rattle economy; the cartoon corruption; the revelations that his war record was a fake, that he wore elevator shoes, and that, unknown to Imelda, he already had a common-law wife and three children; or the failing health he tried so desperately to hide. The bright pomade and the sharply handsome features in Marcos's campaign photographs are betrayed only by one small snapshot tacked to the wall: the president in exile, his features bloated, his face resembling an overturned soup plate.

The day of my visit, February 25, happened to be the third anniversary of the EDSA (Epifanio de los Santos Avenue) "people power" revolution that miraculously forced Marcos out of office without bloodshed. In Manila it was a time for speeches and reassessment. The hot topic on editorial pages and on the floor of the senate was whether Marcos should be allowed to return, either to face charges or to emulate South Korean president Chun Doo Hwan with a public apology and the return of stolen millions—in Marcos's case, billions. As issues often do in the Philippines, this one grew somewhat overheated. Imelda wrote President Corazon Aquino an abject, pleading letter. There were demonstrations in front of the U.S. embassy. What seemed like hourly reports blared from radios with news that Marcos was in his final throes, or had made a miraculous recovery. Eight barbers, in drunken argument over the question, began stabbing one another with their scissors.

Surprisingly, the majority of Filipinos I spoke with during my stay in Manila believed Marcos should be allowed to return. "It is the wish of a dying man, and we respect that," Rollie Villanueva, a caretaker at Manila's Chinese Cemetery, told me one morning. "We voted for Cory because we were sympathetic to her loss of her husband, Ninoy. And we remember what Marcos promised to do for us and how he made us known internationally—how he made us *exist*—and we give him the same sympathy. We are a dangerously sympathetic people."

—

Outside the museum, over watermelon, we turned our conversation to tales of Doña Josefa's malefic spirit haunting the town. An Ilocano expression, *tapno saan a mangala ti kaduana,* warns against long wakes "so that the dead won't take along a companion in the journey into the hereafter." After the vigil began, two of Marcos's friends died in Batac, and then a man had a fatal heart attack right across the street from the house. "People talk about it," Chan said sharply, "but they wouldn't dare complain."

Other phenomena Ilocanos attribute to Doña Josefa's prankish spirit include a plague of red tide in the Philippines, a typhoon-free year in Ilocos Norte for the first time in at least fourteen years, and the nine passengers sucked from a United Airlines jet departing from Honolulu, where her son lies gravely ill. Chan said, "Did you see how all her hair is still shiny and in place? It's a miracle."

("It's not a miracle," embalmer Frank Malabed told me later, "it's formalin. As long as the family wants it I can hold the body together. I give her a bath and change her dress every two months, and apply some makeup to keep her attractive—the same makeup my wife uses: Revlon, Max Factor, Covermark." Malabed, who also embalmed Marcos rival Benigno "Ninoy" Aquino after he was shot at the Manila airport in 1983, tries to remain aloof from a politics that keeps requiring his skill with cosmetics. "Professionally, I have to keep my distance. I don't vote, I just embalm.")

Suddenly, Marina Toledo, a Marcos loyalist who arrived from Manila one day asking to work in the museum and was given a job by the family, stepped up to the table and showed me scars—on her arm, face, breast—she said were from stones hurled by anti-Marcos demonstrators. She began speaking, her voice swelling in volume, talking on and on, heedless of interruption; it turned out that one of the stones had deafened her. "Ah . . . the United States kidnapped my president. If President Marcos dies in the United States, I will be the first to kill Cory. I love Doña 'Sefa . . ." She began to cry softly. "I *love* her, and I'm not scared to die. You tell President Bush to bring Marcos home! You have a mother, too? We all have mothers, and we all have the right to bury them."

She was weeping openly now. Colonel Aballa and Cynthia Chan wept, too. Aballa wiped away tears and dried his hand on his white goatee. "If Marcos dies abroad," he said unsteadily, "there may be war. If I gave the word, my two thousand men would follow me. And I would give the word."

Chan stared at her cousin. "He's not going to die. He's not going to die. He's not going to die."

In fact, of course, even Imelda is growing accustomed to the idea that Ferdinand Marcos won't be around forever—at least a Ferdinand Marcos who isn't cold and clammy to the touch. Imelda was saying recently that if her husband dies in Hawaii and the Philippines refuses to accept his remains—many in the government advocate the Napoleonic solution of keeping the body abroad for several years—she'll put his embalmed body on display in Honolulu. (Stand ready, Frank Malabed.)

The "plan" is for Marcos to hang on (alive or otherwise) until 1992, when Aquino's term ends. Then, Imelda says, "I'll bring him home." At which point the Marcos family will finally be able to inter the long-suffering Doña Josefa. But her son won't settle beside her. Imelda says that Marcos's final wish is to be cremated and to have his ashes scattered about the Philippines "to fertilize his country."

(1989)

COCKFIGHTING WITH PAC-MAN
AND THE WEEPING WIDOW

Imelda Marcos click-clacks across the pink marble floor at ramming speed, bursting through the library door so fast that she almost runs down eight Japanese tourists. Gaining speed, Imelda blows by the forty other people perennially becalmed in her $2,000 imperial suite at the Plaza, a group that today includes a bejeweled woman who's been pestering Marcos to help make her governor of Bulacan; three security guards poised to intercept the woman; an ocher-eyed former beauty who was once pursued to the Philippines by a lovesick General Perón; and a very old Filipina from Mindanao who traveled six days to Manila to present "Ma'am," as everyone deferentially calls her, with a live chicken that is now, quite plainly, dead. Before they can all more than rise, Marcos slips past, into the piano room, then onto the balcony.

"Oh . . . ," she cries, fluttering her white handkerchief, transfixed. A quarter mile away the Cultural Center of the Philippines is on fire, its roof boiling with flames and acrid black smoke. Marcos's red nails clutch the railing and her rouged cheeks begin to shine—even her tremendous hair, crouching on her head like a panther, seems stunned. "That's it," she murmurs. "If they burn what's beautiful in us, that's really the end."

The Cultural Center was always Imelda's baby, a powerfully ambiguous symbol of the Marcos years. Built in 1969 for $8.5 million, 80 percent of which was slushed away in kickbacks, the center was the first symptom of Imelda's legendary "edifice complex," her compulsion to build palaces, five-star hotels, and other big concrete things. She was bitterly attacked by her old boyfriend Senator Benigno "Ninoy" Aquino, who decried "a monument to the nation's elite bereft of social conscience," built "to enshrine the name Imelda . . . when the impoverished mass groans in want."

Now, twenty-three years later, Aquino is nine years dead, gunned down, possibly at Imelda's behest, by army thugs at the Manila airport. His clumsy and appalling murder lit the long fuse of revolt that finally dynamited Imelda and her husband, Ferdinand, from Malacañang Palace in 1986 and installed Ninoy's widow, Corazon. And Ferdinand is dead, too, of lupus. Imelda, after five years in exile, has come home at age sixty-two to face eighty-seven civil and criminal cases that charge her with looting the country of up to $10 billion. Blind to irony, she has also come home to run for president.

Below us and across the way, Filipinos costumed for the Cultural Center's National Theater Festival stare at the blaze, which was started by a stray *kwitis,* or homemade rocket, loosed during the opening ceremonies. Among the throng are dancers from across the archipelago's seven thousand islands: festive kings and queens from Parañaque, an epic chanter from Panay, headdress-wearing foot stompers from Ilo-Ilo. Most are holding hands, and many are weeping and crying out in a confusion of the country's seventy languages. In the last few years the Philippines has been battered by a devastating earthquake, a typhoon, the explosion of Mount Pinatubo, and the negotiated departure of U.S. military bases that had brought the country $3 billion a year, more than any of its exports. Many Filipinos detect a plan for divine punishment, and the dancers have instantly identified this fire as the next plague.

Up on the balcony, Imelda whispers, "Oh . . . *oh!*" as the flames tongue higher in the evening sky. Gathering herself, she cries, "The very spirit of the Filipino people is being terminated in smoke!"

—

Luckily, firemen contain the flames that night, and the center sustains only about $200,000 in damages. It seems that the next plague will instead be, as expected, the May 11 presidential election. It is a watershed moment: "The first time in twenty-seven years we can bring about a transfer of power through the ballot," says Vice President Salvador "Doy" Laurel, one of the eight presidential candidates. "But if the massive fraud everyone expects is committed, this might be the last election in the Philippines. It's that serious."

"I don't think history will give us another chance," agrees candidate Ramon "Monching" Mitra.

But the campaign itself has flipped the bird at history. Eerily unconnected to voters and issues, the campaign resembles a Broadway musical dramatizing a squabble about who gets to drive the family car—featuring "but you had it last time and dented the fender" insults, pop stars who serenade audiences with "Feelings," and candidates attempting to outstigmata all comers. The Philippines is 85 percent Catholic, and the candidates include a mass or an altar visit in their daily campaigning, to appear blessed—the Tagalog word *kalayaan* signifies not only political independence, but religious redemption.

These theatrics of pop salvation typify a country bewildered by its colonial legacy under Spain and then America, a history sometimes encapsulated as "three centuries in a convent and fifty years in Hollywood." Only this year, when the Aquino government ended the United States's lease on the Clark and Subic Bay military bases, declaring, "We must slay the father image," did the crippling patronage finally come to an end. Americans, freed as well, could suddenly see that their former colony's democratic processes looked strangely familiar—our own politics instructively reflected in a funhouse mirror.

Imelda Marcos's campaign is particularly edifying, because she takes Filipino political traditions to their illogical extreme. Expected by many to eventually throw her support behind her husband's favorite crony, Eduardo "Danding" Cojuangco Jr., Imelda is easy to dismiss as a political Norma Desmond. Her ideas for resolving the Philippines' problems with population growth, poverty, land reform, and runaway graft are certainly rudimentary. "Her campaign platform," explains Marcos's press secretary, Sol Vanzi, "is reduce the deficit . . . make government more efficient by a reduced but better-paid . . . self-help . . . self-employment . . ." The pauses are getting longer. "Well, it's almost generic."

But Imelda, better than anyone, understands how to capitalize on the Philippine appetite for the gothic. Though Aquino isn't running again, Marcos ceaselessly casts the race as a battle between Imelda and Cory, a "War of the Widows." When she campaigned in her husband's home province of Ilocos Norte, Imelda spent considerable photo-op time brooding over the corpse of Marcos's mother, which has been awaiting burial since May 1988 and was recently put in a meat freezer-cum-display case pending Imelda's imminent retrieval of Ferdinand's body from *his* air-conditioned crypt in Honolulu. Then Doña Josefa and Ferdinand will be buried together—a fitting act of closure, and a real crowd pleaser.

It's a measure of how indelibly the Marcos kleptocracy warped the country's self-image that Imelda can still inflame fabular hopes by flaunting her wealth to those she privately and proprietarily refers to as "my poor, my hungry." When I inquire about the poor's headlong devotion (their frantic caresses leave Marcos's arms bruised), she says, "They know that I too have been disabled by widowhood and deprivation—so a touch, or a kiss, is an act of oneness for them in their desperation. It's a kind of romance."

"There's a very good chance Imelda will win," F. Sionil José, the country's most famous novelist, says gloomily. "The poor don't care about corruption, they don't care about programs. What helps them are dreams, and Imelda lies to them, she presents herself as a goddess, a dream factory—she gives them hope. All the poor, stupid Filipinos. They're their worst enemy."

The candidates' refusal to form coalitions means that Imelda or anyone else who can garner a plurality of about eight million of the expected thirty-five million votes will probably win—and then, mandateless, face accusations of cheating, violent protests, and the strong likelihood of a military coup to restore stability. "Among us Filipinos we don't accept defeat, we don't concede," candidate Joseph Estrada says cheerfully. "We join together to complain about the winner."

"The logical and rational process would be the unification of the Marcos forces' candidates against the anti-Marcos candidates," says Miriam Defensor-Santiago, another candidate. She has enjoyed big leads in three successive countrywide polls on the strength of her graft busting, her youth (she's forty-six), and her cathartic reputation for throwing chairs at employees and calling a congressman "fungus face." "But it won't happen," Defensor-Santiago continues, "because the candidates are power mad. We're all going to carry out the Greek principle: Those whom the gods would destroy, they first run for the presidency of the Philippines."

—

In Imelda's imperial suite, Franco Rossellini, co-producer of the spaghetti-porn film *Caligula,* dreamily sucks on his unlit cigarette holder. Aging, ill, and almost spectral in a collarless white linen jacket, white cotton pants, and espadrilles, he has nonetheless flown in from Tokyo to surprise Imelda. Though best known as Roberto's brother and Isabella's uncle, Franco achieved a certain notoriety of his own as the jester in Imelda's seventies jet-set claque that included Van Cliburn, Doris Duke, Cristina Ford, and George Hamilton.

It's hard now to recall that Ferdinand and Imelda took office in 1965 on an anticorruption platform, styled themselves after John and Jackie Kennedy, and augured boundless promise for a country that was already economically ahead of Malaysia, Indonesia, and Thailand. What sticks in memory is the rank self-indulgence that left the country financially and spiritually bankrupt: Ferdinand making President Nixon promise that Marcos's son "Bong Bong" would be the first Filipino on the moon; Imelda designing "love buses" (which still rattle around Manila carrying their *Partridge Family* heart designs); Imelda spending $12 million on jewelry in Geneva in a single day while two-thirds of the Philippines' sixty-two million people slipped below the poverty line, unable to meet the basic needs of food, clothing, and shelter.

The garish excess helps explain why the world was so taken by the morality play of the bloodless 1986 EDSA revolution, when nuns knelt to block President Marcos's armored personnel carriers from attacking the rebels supporting Corazon Aquino. The housewife from whom Marcos had stolen the election radiated such moral righteousness, she seemed chosen by God to cleanse the nation.

Six years later EDSA is seen not as a revolution, but merely as a change of government, and a small change at that. Aquino's achievements, simply put, are two: She held on to power despite seven coup attempts; and she relinquished power voluntarily after one term, which no previous president has done. But this exercise of constitutional virtue is almost erased by her other achievement—that of making the Marcos era look astonishingly good.

The economy had zero growth and 17 percent inflation last year, and Aquino's ballyhooed land reform program—a crying need for generations in a country where less than 4 percent of the farms occupy more than 25 percent of the land—proved utterly ineffective. Amnesty International estimates that military and paramilitary forces trying to suppress Communist and Muslim rebels have tortured and killed more than 550 civilians for political reasons since 1988—just the sort of "salvagings" involving "zap zap" (electric shock of genitals) and "submarine" (head submerged in a toilet) that made Marcos so infamous. And though Aquino's own probity is unquestioned, she weakly permitted her relatives to become even more heavily involved in graft, gambling monopolies, and illicit barter trade.

Her administration also left the Philippines' endemic distress largely unaddressed. Per capita income is only $700 a year; less than one-third of the urban poor have plumbing or garbage collection; and in Manila, which has two-thirds of the country's cars and trucks, everyone holds handkerchiefs and masks to their faces in a futile attempt to filter the raw floods of diesel exhaust. Population is growing unabated at 2.8 percent annually; by the year 2000 the country will somehow have to find 40 percent more food and sixteen million more jobs. The Mental Health Association of the Philippines recently reported that 50 percent of Filipinos already suffer from mental instability stemming from malnutrition, tension, and economic hardship.

All the candidates save Fidel "Eddie" Ramos, Aquino's former secretary of defense and her endorsed favorite, are running against her presidency, and *sorristas*—those sorry they voted for Cory—abound even in her government. "You just have to keep winning the war," a cabinet secretary says wearily. "I always go back to Exodus, when Moses freed the Hebrews from slavery. And as they left, they began quarreling, bickering, blaming Moses for the deprivations of the desert. They missed the fleshpots of Egypt. Many people feel we gained our freedom too cheaply. If freedom is won in young lives, in blood, you value it more."

"My dear," Franco Rossellini says into the late-afternoon silence in the imperial suite, "everyone here is always going to be corrupt." He fishes in his satchel and pulls out a special issue of "One Thousand Makers of History in the Twentieth Century" from the London *Times.* "This is very favorable about Marcos," he says proudly, passing it around.

A Marcos aide reads it and frowns. "It says he was delusional and the country was going to anarchy."

"Yeah, but he's not being remembered for the bloody murders, he's being remembered for fighting on to the end."

"It's not good," the aide says shortly.

Rossellini takes the magazine back and reads aloud, " '[Aquino] was defeated by a massive electoral fraud. . . .' Well, perhaps not." He puts it back in his bag and leans over confidingly. "Imelda is extremely feminine. She has this secret pillow talk, you understand— she has access to the husband."

While we ponder this, Rossellini continues speaking about Ferdinand in the present tense. "While I was doing *Caligula,* he read the script and made some notes, he said, 'That's not right'—he knew that history like he'd lived it."

The herb doctor who pomades Imelda with ginger and betel nut issues from her chambers, followed closely by the hairdresser who lacquers her roots. This is as good as a trumpet fanfare, and soon enough Imelda herself emerges, resplendent in a green dress with brass buttons and one of her trademark silk scarves (a fortune-teller told her scarves would protect her from assassination). "Ay, Franco!" she says, and sails over. He rises with difficulty to kiss her hand. When Imelda sweeps on, Rossellini hesitantly makes his way out.

She stands with fifteen of the twenty-four candidates on her senatorial slate to be photographed beneath an oil portrait of a young, brash Ferdinand Marcos, and then she takes a few questions. When asked how many of the seven generals on her slate featured in the coup attempts against Aquino, Marcos looks nonplussed. There are snorts from the senatorial hopefuls, boyish giggles.

"None?" she asks them. They look away. "None," she says firmly. In fact, at least two of the seven were coup ringleaders, and another slate candidate, Arturo Tolentino, declared himself the country's acting leader in the first coup, which captured only the Manila Hotel. The rebels were made to do twenty push-ups and sent back to their barracks.

Even when she isn't lying, Imelda's link to consensual reality has call waiting. She has detailed to her simps and flatterers how Chinese adventurers are poised to strike south to reopen Manila's seventeenth-century galleon trade with Mexico, how the Trilateral Commission unseated her husband, and how cosmic force fields protect the Philippines from foreign missiles.

Her wackiness inspired lawyer Pedro Peralta to file a petition with the Elections Commission (COMELEC) to have Marcos disqualified as "an obnoxious political pest" and "an abominable and intolerable nuisance"; Imelda listened to the proceedings with tears slowly rolling down her cheeks. The petition was dismissed.

There is a uniquely Filipino response to such goings-on, a mirthless laugh that is sharply at variance with their prevailing warmth and generosity; it is almost a yelp. "It's not genuine amusement," says Miriam Defensor-Santiago. "It's a way of saying, 'We're suffering, we need help, we're at our wits' end as a people.' "

—

In response to a question at a candidates' forum at the Manila Hotel, former defense secretary Eddie Ramos shifts an unlit, well-chewed cigar around in his mouth and promises to ignite the Philippines' basic economic unit, "the Philippine household, who spend the afternoon sitting on the sidewalk massaging their roosters." Gales of laughter fill the chandeliered room, a giddiness that grows as people look at the chagrined face of Ramos's rival, Monching Mitra. Mitra, the former Speaker of the House, breeds cockfighting roosters. This jab further escalates the battle they've waged since Mitra won the nomination of the ruling Laban Party and Ramos stalked out, formed his own party, and gained Aquino's endorsement. She was known to feel *utang na loob,* or the debt of gratitude, to Ramos for saving her from the seven coups.

Though he drew the most autograph seekers after the Manila Hotel debate, and though he has the support of forty of the nation's seventy-two governors, Ramos's inept campaign seems intent on proving that his greatness was thrust upon him. "At Ramos's kickoff rally," Mitra says gleefully, "they said, 'Region number one, stand up!' and nobody stands. 'Region number two!' and nobody stands. If he can't run a decent national convention on TV, how can this fellow run a government?"

Mitra is fond of noting that Ramos, as a Marcos general, is tainted goods. "I never offered him the vice presidential slot, as has been reported," Mitra says. "If I became president I'd like to be able to sleep nights. As the great Filipino patriot José Rizal said, 'The glory of saving a nation does not belong to one who participated in its ruin.' "

By that standard few could run for president, and Mitra might not be among them. "The president, along with many Filipinos, despises Mitra," says Miriam Defensor-Santiago, who, as one of Mitra's rivals, is admittedly biased. "He made his fortune as a gofer for Danding Cojuangco, Marcos's biggest crony. Mitra is the classic Filipino traditional politician—that is, a crook." (It's worth noting that the Tagalog word for traditional politician, *trapo,* also means worthless rag.)

Under Marcos, Danding Cojuangco became the richest man in the Philippines. He was known as Pac-Man, because he used his control of the $225 million coconut levy to swallow up more than one hundred companies, including a commercial bank, copra trading companies, and the San Miguel corporation, which accounts for 3 percent of the Philippine economy. He also maintained almost two thousand men armed with the world's largest private collection of Uzi submachine guns, and was widely believed to have wiped out scores of his enemies in his home province of Tarlac. "Cojuangco is a Mafia boss," a cabinet secretary says flatly. Cojuangco fled with Marcos in 1986 but snuck back home in 1989 and is now stumping the country, promising to double income in rural households and, sotto voce, to restore Marcosite monopoly economics.

"The Cojuangco clan"—Danding's cousins Cory Aquino and her brother Peping—"cannot allow Danding Cojuangco to become president," Defensor-Santiago says, "because they know he will take vengeance for their stiff measures against him. (Many of Danding's assets have been sequestered, and pending cases seek the forfeiture of $320 million in unexplained income.) The president believes Danding was involved in the death of her husband, so she cannot be appeased. They'll throw everything they have against him, they won't care what happens to the country. There will be carnage, and the Philippines will be a battleground."

—

A Filipino rally is a circus of bread giving, featuring movie stars who are paid $10,000 to lend glitz, and crowds swollen by those willing to endure five-hour marathons for the handouts. "These people are going to be bought for a few bucks," says one campaign manager. "Why? Because they're poor."

There is a tidal ebb and flow in these matters: money pours into the economy during elections—the richest candidates are spending up to $400 million, and Cojuangco is reliably said to have offered Joseph Estrada $8 million just to join him as his running mate—and then the winners suck it back out in graft. "It costs ten to twenty million pesos [$400,000 to $800,000] to even run for Senate, it's *expensive*," says Burton Lozano, whose father is on Marcos's senatorial slate. "But if you *win*! There is a Filipino saying that if you eat *lechon* [roast pig], it will be hard not to get oil on your hands. What is politics for, if not to get rich?"

Though COMELEC has sought to minimize mayhem by banning guns, liquor sales, and cockfighting on election day, trying to stop the influence of "guns, goons, and gold" in Philippine elections is like trying to wall the sea with dental floss. Supporters are paid two dollars to swell the ranks at rallies and are bussed from district to district so they can vote early and often. These "flying voters" explain why, for instance, 4,339 voters registered in Asinan; the population is only 3,073. Reporters and photographers who cover rallies receive envelopes containing $20 or $40, and editors expect at least $1,200 a month to give candidates good play. TV commands an even higher gratuity.

"Anyone with money can fill each of the 170,000 ballot boxes in the country with twenty prefilled ballots, and that's 3.4 million fraudulent votes," says Juan Ponce Enrile, the consummately political timber magnate who was Marcos's secretary of defense before leading the revolt that toppled him and who then became Aquino's secretary of defense before backing a coup attempt against her. "Then, in counting the votes, you read the ballot and say 'Ramos!' or 'Mitra!' when it's Cojuangco. Then you prepare the results: in one precinct in 1987"—when Enrile ran successfully for Senate—"I got 134 votes out of 200, and they just eliminated the first two digits, so I ended up with 4.

"Miriam [Defensor-Santiago]'s strength in the polls is an expression of the people's pent-up frustrations. But she won't be able to convert that popularity to actual recorded votes. In the end, the traditional politicians, the machine, will elect the president. It will be Ramos, Mitra, or Cojuangco."

—

"Young lady, I want to a-*dopt* you," says R. W. Peltier (not his real name), a silver-haired Kentucky tobacco farmer who now frequents the Philippines and who is looking to place a $50,000 bet on Eddie Ramos. But at the moment he is more interested in Rissa, the poolside waitress at the Mandarin Oriental Hotel. As she pours his San Miguel beer, Peltier says confidentially, "I'm going to a-*dopt* you and then marry you, and if you had a sister, I'd adopt her and marry you, but what I'm going to do, I'll fly you back to Kentucky and we'll get the adoption and the marriage annulled and I'll marry you to one of my sons. Now what you say?"

Rissa smiles uncertainly. After she leaves, R.W. cackles, "Hellfahr, I love messing with these baby dolls. I can talk more shit than nine radios." If you believe even half of Peltier's yarns, which would be generous, he has slept with four thousand women, won bets on every American presidential election since Truman beat Dewey, played five-card stud with Johnny Moss, survived three knife fights, and cut nuts big as coconuts off a hog, which he then nursed back to health with uncanny veterinary skill.

"Now, here's how I see it," he says, settling back comfortably in his terry-cloth robe. "Hell, this country's going in the right direction—them Filipinos'll work all day for no *god*damn money a' tall, it's a bidnessman's paradise. And you can buy whole provinces with money, it's just like the old days fixing votes in the U.S. So, then, Ramos's got the army and the farmers, but I'm betting on him because he's got Cory's support—why, man, she got balls of silver. I bet on balls."

Known to most of the bar girls in Manila as a one-night sugar daddy, Peltier is the sort of operator who exemplifies America's vexed legacy here. "All our presidents were elected with the strong support of the Americans and the CIA," says candidate Joseph Estrada, "but now that the bases question is over, the U.S. is no longer interested in Filipino politics." Yet the influence that began in 1898 (Rudyard Kipling wrote "The White Man's Burden" to urge America to grace the Philippines with the bounty of its civilization) remains a vivid template. The elite send their children to American colleges and often complain that life, real life, occurs only in the U.S. Far from Manila, villagers proudly showed me airplane bottles of Johnnie Walker Scotch they had saved as talismanic objects.

America's political heritage here is more tangled. "Our public figures spout Americanisms, but they don't believe them," says Defensor-Santiago. "We didn't learn the meaning of an impersonal system of laws—public officials aren't respected for independence, but for adherence to *pakikisama,* team playing; they must grant relatives favors. We also didn't learn that the function of leadership is to lead and inspire, not to pander. The candidates have to conform to traditional Filipino role-playing, so though I'm no great beauty, as you can see, they insist on almost crushing me for my beauty." (Her left hand throbs in a splint because well-wishers aggravated an existing fracture.) "It's pagan, the need to touch, the need to mystify the public personality so she becomes immortal, a goddess."

Part of the candidates' traditional role-playing is poor-mouthing. "I have a big advantage because in all my movies I play the oppressed, and the bulk of the voters are oppressed," says Senator Joseph "Erap" Estrada, who was born in Manila's notorious Tondo slum but who kicked, punched, and head-butted himself to riches as the Philippines' second-most-popular action-film star. Erap jokes are popular among the elite, who delight in portraying him as a man bewildered by the task of alphabetizing M&M's. "They make fun that my English is crooked, the elite are afraid because I'm so closely identified with the poor and they fear a change that will affect them, these intellectual slobs," Estrada says, perhaps intending "snobs."

The elite in question are the four hundred families that control the country and squabble over the political spoils. They live languorous lives attended by maids, drivers, and their own security guards in "villages" walled to keep out the shanties that encroach everywhere else. "People in Manila think of the other half as the sight they dislike when they look out of their condominium windows, the outstretched hands when their limos are stalled in traffic, but I am one of the other half," says candidate Monching Mitra, who was born out of wedlock and grew up a poor farm boy in Palawan. But a career in politics and friendships with the Cojuangcos of the world change circumstance: though he is always eager to demonstrate that he can still husk a coconut with three strokes of the bolo, as Mitra utters these words he is overlooking Manila through his own condominium windows.

Filipinos, Ninoy Aquino wrote in 1968, "profess love of country, but love themselves—individually—more."

—

Imelda Marcos arrives for her rally in San Mateo's town square four hours late—or rather, as she's usually five hours late, an hour early. She emerges from the six-door gray Mercedes with her familiar stunned look of having just enjoyed a good cry, then moves through the small but loyal throng of a thousand people like a great parade float. ("Look at these crowds," she'll whisper to friends. "Remember how much we used to pay to get these crowds?") As she passes, her crew in their I LOVE IMELDA windbreakers hand out tiny Imelda and Bong Bong photo calendars, and in return people hand Imelda written petitions—"I am a squatter and need a home"; "My husband needs a job"; "We need a toilet and a lamppost." She sees an old woman crying in the crowd and beckons her up onstage. The woman has a land lawsuit; Imelda says magnificently, "Our lawyers will help"; the woman is led away. In the front rows sit other weeping old women, her most devoted supporters, the poorest of the poor, bent and pruned as bonsai trees.

Imelda takes the microphone and improvises a brief excuse about being late because of Aquino administration traffic, then segues into her fifteen-minute stump speech. It begins with a crow of victory—

"I was vindicated in New York in the trial of the century [her acquittal in 1990 on fraud and embezzlement charges], and now I have come home to listen to the people. The voice of the people is the voice of God, and that is the ultimate vindication"—continues with generalized promises about food, shelter, electricity, medicine, lower prices, employment, ecological balance, and garbage collection, and ends with Marcos leading the crowd in a chant of "Marcos! Marcos! Magsaysay! [Her running mate]."

After Imelda finishes, a guitar player thrusts forward onstage and looks at her expectantly. She covers the microphone and clasps her neck. "My throat is scratchy," she whispers. "Oh, Ma'am," her aides and senatorial aspirants coax, "please, Ma'am." "Very well," she says, like a mother granting a special treat.

As the crowd waves V-signs she launches into "Because of You," the Tagalog theme song she and Ferdinand sang from the balcony of Malacañang Palace in 1986 as a farewell to their supporters before they hastily choppered out carrying $10 million in jewels and gold:

> My one desire is to serve you
> And if it were my fate
> That I'd be your slave
> I would do so gladly
> Because of you

No sarcastic laughter spoils the moment; the crowd grants her an exhilarated clemency. There are nothing *but* second acts in Filipino lives.

"The Americans are also astonished that we forgave those who collaborated with the Japanese in World War Two, but that forgiveness is how we survived," says Carmen Guerrero Nakpil, a columnist and close friend of Marcos's. "You look at the Aztecs and the Incas, the proud people who died off, really, of broken hearts when they were conquered. Well, we're still here. We understand that people must compromise, do what is necessary. The most important thing is, we survived."

—

"Cockfighting goes back to Socrates," says Luis Beltran, a jowly cock breeder who is also the Philippines' most influential journalist. "George Washington raised cocks. Abraham Lincoln was a cockfighting referee—that's why they called him Honest Abe. The beauty of our national sport is that the cocks fight and fight, they're all instinct, desire to kill."

"Like the candidates?" teases columnist Lisa Nakpil.

"Except the cocks won't quit," Beltran says seriously. We're sipping punch in a small tent outside Manila's Araneta Coliseum at a party for *Tahor,* a coffee table book on Filipino cockers and breeders. Danding Cojuangco and Monching Mitra, both breeders, are here, as is Miriam Defensor-Santiago, whose husband is a breeder. I had just been inside the stadium, where the bookies, *kristos,* were shouting "*Meron!*" and "*Wala!*"—favorite and underdog—and waggling frantic fingers at each other to indicate the quantity of pesos. They're called *kristos* because with their arms outstretched they appear to be blessing the crowd. When the betting finished, the birds were freed to slash each other with their steel gaffs, leaping and pecking in a flurry of feathers and blood.

Inside the tent the fighting is subtler. "You know," Beltran says, looking at Danding Cojuangco and his estranged cousin Peping, who are on opposite sides of the room, "this is the only forum where Peping and Danding, deadly political enemies, will meet. They won't talk politics, but they'll talk chicken."

"I breed for smartness, the ability to dodge blows, to know when to strike," Peping Cojuangco said when I asked about his cock-breeding philosophy. A slight, self-contained man, he added, "And gameness, you must have the gameness too, because if the cock is only smart, and too smart, he will run away."

And what does Danding breed for?

"Danding . . ." He paused, smiling slightly. "Danding breeds power cocks, real killers."

—

"A Democrat cannot exist in our situation," Danding Cojuangco says philosophically, munching a rice cake. "He is either taken over, or he becomes himself a dictator." We're having breakfast at Cojuangco's house in Quezon City, a beautiful sanctuary with *nara* wood ceilings and two lush courtyards.

Cojuangco and I had met the day before at his rally in Imus Cavite, an hour south of Manila. Among the candidates, his staff work was by far the smoothest: there was a brass band panoplied in Cojuangco's colors, fireworks to announce his arrival in each new part of town, a relentless two-four-beat Tagalog battle song blaring from the loudspeakers, morning snacks, and then a tasty adobo lunch for all.

But Cojuangco himself, badgerlike and possessed of a truculent grace in private, proved a diffident speech maker. "I have to insert the hype, create the aura around him, because he doesn't have it," says Cojuangco's media relations manager, George Balagtas. At Cojuangco's proclamation rally, Balagtas grabbed Cojuangco backstage, put his hand behind his neck, and began shouting, "Fire in the belly! Fire in the belly! Look in my eyes, you have to want it! Why do you want it? Where is the fire?" before sending him on stage, cold-bellied, in a swirl of dry-ice smoke.

At fifty-six, Cojuangco is a reluctant candidate, one running primarily to recover the assets the Aquino government sequestered while he was in exile. "The interests of my children and grandchildren run parallel to the interests of the country," he told me in Cavite—a twist on GM chairman Charles Wilson's famous remark, "What is good for our country is good for General Motors, and vice versa."

Now, over breakfast—where he is gruffly solicitous—Cojuangco expands on the theme: "If this country should go down the tubes, all my investments won't have value, and I would have worked for nothing. I don't know if the other candidates can say that." When

Cojuangco went to see the fifty brood mares on his Batangas farm that had been seized by the Presidential Commission on Good Government (PCGG), the farm was so ill kept that tears came to his eyes. "At one time I wanted to put the horses in a truck and bring them to the PCGG and tie them up outside and let them feed them!" His eyes glare. "But my lawyers advised against it."

"Danding feels, in his stomach, anger at being embarrassed and humiliated," says a senior Western official. "We believe that as he's in the public eye now, he knows enough not to butcher and hatchet his enemies. That is our hope."

The breakfast talk turns to the possibility of a coup and the electoral margin needed to prevent one. "A half a million margin will be enough," says Cojuangco's adviser Tony Gatmaitan, a shrewd, gray-haired investment banker who was a leading Cory supporter in the last election.

"No," Cojuangco says. "More."

"It's just like the U.S.," Gatmaitan says, "where I can lose Arkansas and Georgia if I win New York and California."

"Yes, ten thousand votes in Makati [Manila's financial district] is worth more than ten thousand votes in the provinces."

"The vote of a bank president is worth more than the vote of a farmer," Gatmaitan says. "The thing about Makati is, it's difficult to control votes. You can't brandish a gun, you have to ring doorbells and make phone calls—Western-style democracy. In the provinces, you just need organization. Five to ten percent cheating is doable, but once you're above fifteen percent, the bureaucracy is *killing.* If I've got to change eighty votes in a *barangay* [township district], it will take me a day and a half filling out ballots." (Forty races are being contested in most parts of the country, and the ballot is nearly two feet long.) "And you can't do it beforehand, because you have to wait to know if you *need* to cheat.

"The thing about Danding," Gatmaitan continues, "is with all his business connections, it's like a Honda dealership. You come up with a product and he's already got the distributor network in place. The machine is more important than the message or the media, which pays attention to Ramos, who doesn't have the machine. The machine is about sixty percent, media and volunteer work is forty percent. It's the reverse of the ratio in the United States."

We get into Cojuangco's Mercedes sedan to ride to the morning's rally. As we glide through the slums, Gatmaitan muses, "Filipinos don't love democracy, they just love elections. The fiesta atmosphere, the contest—it's our baseball."

In the front seat, Cojuangco says, "Maybe so, but it's quite a grind, Tony, talking about politics the whole goddamn day. I better start enjoying this." He moodily checks his watch, and I ask what I have been wondering all morning: Is that the gold Rolex President Marcos gave you for being one of the Rolex Twelve? (They were the disciples who planted the bombs and stirred up the unrest that set the stage for Marcos to declare martial law in 1972, sealing the country's decline.)

"No, no," Cojuangco says, animated again, as he was when talking horses. "The gossip got that wrong, we all just got cheap, plated Omegas. At least, I *hope* the other guys just got Omegas." He thinks about this for a second. "But what was valuable about it was his inscription—'Companion in crisis.' I've never been embarrassed about my friendship with President Marcos. This country needed him then, and it needs his kind of leadership now." There is a silence, and we all settle back into the ride. Then he says, "Remind me to look for that watch, Tony. The goddamn government has opened all my safe-deposit boxes, and who knows what they took."

(1992)

THE ROAD TO MOROCCO

The sea of faces at Casablanca airport's arrivals gate had no horizon. Hundreds strained against the barrier to greet the 7:30 A.M. plane. They were quiet but massed; there was no corridor, no polite giving way. I pushed, gently at first and then more brutally, sweating to gain escape room for my luggage, but it was soon knocked aside in the surf of bodies.

And so my first impression here was the one I had hoped not to have, because it was the one Westerners so often have, from Edith Wharton ("From all these unknown and unknowable people . . . there emanated an atmosphere of mystery and menace") to Paul Bowles ("Their faces are masks. They all look a thousand years old. What little energy they have is only the blind, mass desire to live"). The narrative of a trip to Morocco is inevitably the story of a search for resting places, islets of tranquillity.

—

Just as there are dog people and cat people, there are dog cities and cat cities. Fez el Bali, the thousand-year-old medina—or walled town—at the heart of the city of Fez, is clearly the latter; it's all de-vious and intricate six-foot-wide streets, cobbled shunts, and crawl-ways prowled by thousands of stray cats. The labyrinthine feeling is underscored by children who card thread between two nails along the rare straight patches of wall. You feel like Theseus, but the thread is not for you.

As I walked the swarming souks amid the clacking of hand looms, the sheep heads on the butcher's counter, the cedarwood aroma curling out of the woodworkers' shops, the gazelle musk, the live turtles, falcons, and hedgehogs for sale, the mounds of hummus and henna, the ideal eggplants; as I passed the *guerrab,* who rang his bell for the thirsty to drink from his bagpipes-like goatskin bag and who was dressed in a red djellaba and a hat, fringed with cotton balls, that exactly resembled a country-house lampshade; as I skipped to avoid the water sent coursing from the public fountains through the streets to scour them of rubbish and donkey dung, I felt immured in the essence of things.

I moved toward the medina's center on slowing feet, assaulted by a mephitic odor. On a rooftop above the foul, gray Fez River, I gazed down at the big clay vats of the tannery, which brimmed with a child's palette of natural dyes—saffron, poppy, indigo, mint, and an-timony. Flies swarmed over the drying lamb, cow, and camel skins. The nauseating odor was cow's piss, used to treat the leather. My urge to retch was overpowering.

A small child stretched his hand toward my pen and asked, *"Stylo?"* A passing woman in a brown haik, the all-concealing gar-ment, clouted the boy's ear so hard that his water bucket flew from his hand. She called on my guide, Abdelkrim, to witness the boy's impunity, and both berated him. Fez, the ancient city, frowns on begging.

The exchange, though glancing, was an unusual public concord between the sexes. "In the old times," Abdelkrim later said nostalgi-cally, wiggling his toes out of his pointed slippers as we sat to rest, "you could buy and sell your womans like a *tomate,* or even kill them in the ground if they bear a woman child, because it was a famlly dishonor. And still," he rumbled on, as I was heretically going to suggest that the man determines the child's gender, "still, if the wife is pregnant, you must get another wife to love with, and if she is difficult, you get another, quiet wife." Such attitudes are rampant, and women travelers often feel their staring force.

One great oasis of order in Fez, perched above the higgledy-piggledy medina, is the Palais Jamai hotel. Palms and oleander surround an Olympic-size pool aswoop with swifts, and wherever you turn, a white-jacketed waiter pops out with a glass of freshly squeezed orange juice or a café au lait. The food at the hotel's Al Fassia restaurant is some of Morocco's best, particularly the great *pastilla,* a flaky pigeon pie dusted with almonds, cinnamon, and sugar. And Palais Jamai's ashtrays are really cool: I snagged two.

Fez el Bali's other sheltered beauties are curiously Japanese. The roof of the fourteenth-century Bou Inania *medersa,* or student lodging hall, looks from the inside exactly like the *outside* of a Kyoto temple: the same ceramic tiles and cedarwood lintel, the same feeling of enclosed consecration. Pigeons and swallows flew through the purling fountain, and there was peace under this hard-won square of roofless blue sky. Only the Kufic script that covered Bou Inania located me in North Africa. Upon being told the *medersa*'s cost, its builder, Sultan Abou Inan, said, "What is beautiful is not expensive however great the price," and threw the accounts into the river. And so began the credo of Moroccan merchants and the pollution of the river Fez.

———

I lay on a shaded kilim under the tea hut's thatched roof and watched the ceremony with sleepy pleasure: the silver pot raised three feet above the glass; the thin stream of mint tea; the deft wrist flick, no splash. Bluely foaming up beside me were the springs that form the Oum er Rbia, Morocco's longest river, high in the Middle Atlas Mountains. For the last few miles of my passage south, children had run beside the car, pointing ahead and shouting, *"La source! La source!"* The tea was soothingly sweet, almost syrupy—Moroccans have one of the highest sugar consumption rates in the world—and with the locust heat and rushing water I drowsed away.

Then back with a shake on the rough, empty road. The saddles of red earth peppered with corns of rock looked barren; the Atlas cedars have nearly all been felled, and the Barbary apes are gone, too. Only red poppies and buttery swaths of wheat occasionally softened the view. Dark men burrowed, scything the wheat in slow advance, the shocks piling up behind them.

At one turning the illegible signposts finally vanished altogether, and I was . . . not lost, exactly, but puzzled. I stopped my Renault 4 near two crested black-and-brown tents, the *khaimas* of the nomadic Beni M'Guid Berbers. Three young Berber women herded their sheep over to consider me, and I asked whether I was headed toward the local capital, Khenifra.

They hid their faces in their gaily colored cloaks and aprons. Muffled giggles. It soon became clear that they understood neither French—the lingua franca still, though Morocco gained independence from French and Spanish protectorates in 1956—nor my few words of Arabic. It slowly dawned on me as I said, "Khenifra?" and pointed inquiringly ahead and then behind, that they had never heard of Khenifra, the local capital city. Ahead I went by guesswork.

Nine hours later I fetched up in Marrakesh, exhausted by drivers who blast around corners in the wrong lane; by creeping through the abandoned half-built housing projects on the outskirts of every town (a faltering nationwide effort to relieve the constriction in the medinas); and by my absurd Renault, which beeped every time I shifted gears. In my fatigue I simply couldn't breach the vast red ramparts of Marrakesh's old city to locate my hotel, though I circled for half an hour like a Greek commander outside Troy.

Then, finally in, things got worse: a maze of streets without signs, stoplights the size of Christmas-tree bulbs that were invisible anyway in the exhaust-filled gloom, and a churning power merge from all directions—cars, trucks, buses, bicycles, mopeds mewling like teething babies, dogs, cats, pedestrians, donkey riders bellowing, *"Balak!*

nobdol!" ("Out of the way!"), griffons, penguins, mastodons. Perforce,
I adopted the local tactic: gun the car at the nearest diapered toddler
and assume it'll spring aside, creating space. Some forty-five minutes
later my final moped-riding "guide" led me in a complicated Möbius
strip right back to where we started. He showed me the Grand Hôtel
Tazi sign above and stood grinning for his tip.

———

Two nights later I had tea beside the foundations of the house my
friend Abdul was building in the *palmerie,* a 2,500-acre stand of
palm trees just north of Marrakesh. From the road, all one sees are
Abdul's *pisé* walls of sunbaked clay, but inside is a riotous garden
of bougainvillea, roses, date palms, sunflowers, and cypress, and a
Gatsby-size pool.

Hidden splendor is the rule. In the Marrakesh souk Abdul had
bribed a guard lounging under a hand-painted *Union Marocaine du
Travail* poster to take us through a shabby door that led, suddenly,
into the palace of El Glaoui. The cruel and munificent pasha, who
died in 1956 at the height of the sybaritic Barbara Hutton era,
had made this a famous party spot; the huge chambers with their
smooth *tadlekt* walls and intricate mosaic work accommodated
bacchanals at which, by one account, guests were given "literally
whatever they wanted, whether it might be a diamond ring, a present of money in gold, or a Berber girl or boy from the High Atlas."
The palace went on and on, for block after hidden block—deserted,
forgotten, beautiful.

I'd also been delighted by El Badi palace, "the incomparable," a
park-size marvel from the sixteenth century secreted in the northern
medina. Now storks nest atop the *pisé* walls, and pigeons nest
within them, honeycombed in the scaffolding holes, and orange
trees sprout from the old ninety-meter pool. But the space is so vast
and commanding—my guide boasted that Sultan Ahmed el Man-
sour built 365 bedrooms for his 365 wives—that I could easily
imagine the bygone panoply of gold and marble and *zellig* mosaic
tiles, the fountains and strolling lute players.

All visitors perform such acts of imaginative reconstruction at historical sites, yet El Badi's inaugural featured a prescient deconstruction. The sultan was at the peak of his power, having crushed the Portuguese at the Battle of the Three Kings and conquered Timbuktu, and all the sheikhs and caids of the realm, as well as numerous deferential European ambassadors, were on hand to pay homage. After hearing their blandishments, Ahmed turned to his fool for an opinion. *"Sidi,"* the jester said, "it will make a magnificent ruin."

Abdul's two architects drove up and joined us, making the "peace from the heart" gesture. One had brought his five-year-old son, who kissed my hand with great courtesy and very little drool. A long, polite conversation ensued in Arabic about bribes for housing permits. The disagreeable moments were finessed in French. Afterward Abdul took me on a drive, past all the great mansions, country clubs, expatriate hideaways. The night was cool and quiet, the moon bright on the palm trunks.

Abdul was irritable. He has spent ten years selling Moroccan crafts and antiques in America and now resents the bribes required to get anything done here. "Building this beautiful house here is like building a palace in hell," he said. "The officials I must deal with are like the hasslers you must deal with—a virus. A godfather will hire sixteen or seventeen little boys and tell them, 'Go to the hotel and hassle the tourists. Bring them to my shop.' And for them, because they are so poor, this is a useful trade—hustling. And if they are very good at it, when they grow up they become officials."

It's a nasty problem. Step from your hotel, and you are swarmed by young men who drone insistently into your left ear that they must guide you. They must. Really. No, really. Aggressive personal marketing occurs in many countries, but in Marrakesh they never give up. Really. No, really. If a suitor drops away after a few hundred yards, two more take his place to shoulder you toward their uncle's jewelry store.

The only inoculation is to hire one of the gold-medallion-wearing official guides. Their price—$7 for the whole day—is quite reasonable, unfortunately, their spiels are as rapid as they are tedious. And as they get kickbacks of up to 40 percent of your purchases, they invariably land you at an overpriced *restaurant typiquement marocain* for a lunch of soggy couscous, then whisk you, kicking and screaming, to a carpet shop.

Viewed abstractly, the rug merchant's spiel is a performance piece. He unrolls the carpets with a stripteaser's come-hither shimmy, stupefies you with mint tea, and murmurs: "This kilim is the Berber Picasso . . . so tight the threads, your children's children will cherish . . . monsieur has champagne taste"—this is said even if you've pointed to a doormat—"champagne taste, but on a beer budget . . . so what is your top, top price? . . . because you are my first/last customer today, we must accommodate . . . but your price is still sadly low, you are a stonehead, a real Berber. . . ." If you wish to buy, go on a Friday (the Islamic holy day, when markets are empty) and announce that you are a *pauvre étudiant.* He will counter that he, too, is a poor student: when haggling, everyone, even grizzled grandfathers, claims sophomore standing. And so the game begins.

As Abdul and I were griping—Marrakesh being the low point of my trip—I asked about Jemaa el Fna, the medina square famed as a crossroads of theater and miracle. In three nights there, all I had seen in the glow of its hurricane lamps were vendors of fresh orange juice, stale meat, and sneakers; no one even tried to sell me hashish, dammit.

Abdul shook his head. "There used to be acrobats, snake charmers, a plate dancer who spun around with plates and a pot of tea on his head, wonderful storytellers, and a blind man who trained pigeons to do whatever he commanded," he said, "but beginning around 1985, everyone started watching TV. The Jemaa el Fna was the source, the water for our culture to drink from, and now it is dry. . . ."

———

The drive from Marrakesh to the Atlantic coast was desolate. The only people in sight crouched like stones in the scant shadows of the *ksars,* their eyes following the dust devils that whistled across the baked earth of the Chiadma plains. Road's end, in Essaouira, was a revelation: a clean, whitewashed, sun-spanked town, open to the breezes and the gulls, a long, clean arc of beach, and people *who didn't bother you.* *"Bonjour"* was genuine and not predatory; my shoulders and elbows relaxed.

I stayed in the Villa Maroc, where a monkey swung on the terrace and the shutters sang of a deep French blue. The town clock chimed irregularly overhead, and at seven A.M. a local snake charmer who had lost his snakes began clashing his cymbals anyway, hoping to cadge breakfast by sheer force of noise; but otherwise it was a winsome spot, overlooking blue-and-orange-keeled fishing boats brimming with bream and whiting.

In the afternoon I walked the worn fisherman's path on the rocks under Essaouira's old Portuguese battlements and met M'hmad Themi-Alilou, who was looking for a lost puppy. A skinny, barefoot man with white whiskers and sweet brown eyes, M'hmad lived with his twelve dogs beside the tidepools. In very good English he told me a complicated tale of woe: His house in town had burned down two weeks before, and he'd lost his papers and passport in the fire, and he needed twenty dirhams to send a registered letter to his son on Northwood Road in Columbus, Ohio, to begin reestablishing his identity.

It was a fascinating story, with inspired touches, like his wife being an Apache from Omaha who was the niece of the late congressman Senator Ellis. It was particularly fascinating as I knew from my guidebook that he'd been telling variations on it for years. I suggested that I mail M'hmad's letter for him when I returned to America. "You are most kind," he said. "However, I require my insurance receipt, and the letter isn't quite finished to my satisfaction. But, with luck, I will perhaps go to America, where I have not been since just after the World's Fair of 1967, when President Johnson personally called the embassy here, at Senator Ellis's suggestion, to request they allow me a visa to come see my wife."

He never came right out and asked for it, but I gave M'hmad twenty dirhams because he told a great story and because he was so nice. He took me to see his dogs, who were tied up near a steaming pot of potatoes. "I raise them like children," he said. *"Cocha! Cocha!"* He frowned at two of the dogs. "They are having a discussion." The dogs left off nipping each other and looked ashamed. "I must keep them here with me, because they are always eating sugar, which makes their hair fall down. And I must personally show them the rocks, the places where it is safe to go and eat the old fish, and where it is not, because some people here . . ."

He smiled, a wonderfully sad and touching look, and continued in a lower tone, as if he did not like to speak of this and it should remain our secret. "Some people here will throw stones. They will not love them."

(1994)

ATOMIC WASTE: AT SEA IN
THE MARSHALL ISLANDS

At the Kwajalein airport, Steven from army public relations met our group and gave me a limp handshake. "I have been authorized to tell you that we are unable to support your application for admission to Kwajalein," he said, "but we will escort you to the boat to Ebeye."

A dislocated American community dropped in the endless blue of the western Pacific, Kwajalein island is a strange, Strangelovian place whose inhabitants spend their days tracking death machines. The U.S. Army rents the island from the Marshallese government for $9 million a year, and has established a $2 billion American missile-testing base with a vast array of satellite dishes, concrete bunkers, and high-tech installations. Technicians twiddling radar and telemetry equipment track Minuteman, Trident, and MX missiles that are fired from California's Vandenberg Air Force Base, some five thousand miles away. An alert is sounded; the missiles streak palely across the sky, reaching speeds of up to ten thousand miles per hour; and then they splash down in Kwajalein lagoon, where divers hunt for them like water dogs bobbing for wood ducks.

Public relations has rarely let journalists do more than pass through the residential part of Kwajalein since the release of *Home on the Range,* a 1990 documentary about the attempts by local islanders to get their land back when the U.S. lease temporarily lapsed in the late 1980s. The camera followed the island's actual owner into the Kwaj officers' club, where a big sign warned in Marshallese: "No Marshallese are allowed on these premises; anybody caught will face imprisonment and be ruined."

"Do you have a contact point on Ebeye?" Steven asked, referring to the nearby island where most of Kwajalein's Marshallese workers live. I was beginning to dislike him: a short man with dingy, denture-colored hair.

"No," I said.

"Well . . . ," he replied dolefully, shaking his head as if I would be parachuting into North Korea. We got into a blue van, and Steven drove us past the softball fields and tennis courts, down clean asphalt streets with American families in Sears-wear promenading on Huffys and Schwinns.

We stopped at the bakery and bought a bag of rolls. "You will not be able to proceed with that through security," Steven warned me. "It will cause a security situation."

"The bread?" I said.

"Yes," he said. "Because of the political situation. Like that root beer you've got." He stabbed at my soda. "It's only fifty cents here— special rate for Americans. On Ebeye it's a dollar, even a dollar-fifty. *Black market opportunity.*"

I was traveling with Jack Niedenthal, an American who is now employed as the official liaison for the Bikinian people, and his wife, Regina, a stout native Bikinian with a slow, inward smile. Had things worked according to plan, we wouldn't have spent more than a half hour on Kwajalein, but things here rarely work according to plan. We had been scheduled to take a nineteen-seat Dornier straight from Majuro, the capital of the Marshalls, to the now uninhabited Bikini atoll, to dive the recently opened test site where some of the world's first atomic blasts sank nine warships in 1946.

En route to Bikini, we'd bounced westward between the northern and southern chains of atolls, flying low over fringing reefs and bone-white sand spits, then plunging onto rutted coral runways to drop off basketball hoops and Primus stoves for Seventh-day Adventist missionaries who wandered dazedly out of the breadfruit thickets. The Marshallese shyly hung back or were out of sight altogether, harvesting copra from the coconut groves.

The entire country's land area is only 70 square miles—slightly less than the District of Columbia—yet that real estate is scattered among 1,225 islands that stretch over some 350,000 square miles of the western Pacific. It seemed as though we landed on half of them as we hopscotched west. Most were precisely the sort of picture-book Pacific arcadias dreamed by Gauguin, Melville, and Mead. Then, after three hundred miles of island hopping, we hit Kwajalein—and the twentieth century—and stopped. Because Air Marshall Islands had only one working plane at the moment, we'd have to kill a couple of days here before the plane would pick us up again and take us the rest of the way to Bikini. It was a typical Marshall Islands snafu.

We brazenly smuggled the bakery rolls onto the ferry, risking life in the stockades, and made the fifteen-minute trip to Ebeye. As the army transport vessel churned in the lagoon, I noticed the benches were stenciled with admonitions, presumably to the Marshallese: PLEASE CLEAN UP YOUR MESS.

———

The streets on Ebeye were narrow and packed with children, many of them wheeling on a single roller skate while a friend used the other. The tropical heat was merciless, and the sun could not be avoided, since virtually all of the island's palm trees were chopped down long ago to make room for shanties.

I rode in a new air-conditioned Hyundai with Sam Bellu, a

paunchy grocery store owner who wanted to show me around his island. Bellu, fifty-one, wore camouflage shorts and had an air of impatience unusual among the famously reticent Marshallese. He was a proud guide, though, showing me the U.S.-built water tower, the U.S.-built hospital, the U.S.-built causeway to nearby islets. The fourteen thousand people crammed onto this six-hundred-acre island mostly work as maids, cooks, and gardeners for the Americans on Kwajalein. Ebeye owed everything, it seemed, to American largesse. "The U.S. always looks after us," Bellu said. "They say, 'This is how you do it. You have to go to school, you have to work all day, to be a human being you have to live like us.' "

Bellu stopped the car near the island's dump. Children were here, too, playing king of the hill in the mound of trash. He stared at me, perhaps trying to gauge how closely I identified with my country. Then he decided to be frank. "On the bad side," Bellu said, "the U.S. did drop all those bombs here, exposing us to the radiation. It's *theirs,* not ours. How would you like it if I came with a pickup and dropped a load of rubbish into *your* yard?" He killed the engine, and with the car's air-conditioning off, I was immediately drenched in sweat.

Bellu was talking about the sixty-six nuclear bombs that the U.S. military had detonated in the Marshalls between 1946 and 1958, making the chain of islands one of the most contaminated places on earth. But he could just as easily have been talking about America's cultural flotsam, which has likewise irradiated Ebeye and many other islands in the Marshalls and left them without a clear identity—not really American, not really Micronesian, not really anything. At Bellu's store, the JJJ grocery, the aisles and freezers are well stocked with Kool-Aid and Sonic Boom Pops and Shrimp-Flavored Toasted Chips, a QED of why 75 percent of Marshallese inpatients, staggering from shotgun blasts of American sugar, have diabetes. In the sprawling residential warrens of Ebeye, the shanties are tagged with sun-faded graffiti: "Fuck your mama, yes, yes," "Homeboyz," and "Crips," the language of Watts and Compton filtered through Hollywood and rendered, here, merely sad.

—

Like the Philippines, the Falklands, and Vietnam, the Marshall Islands chain has long been a helpless crossroads for the traffic of history. Superpowers, their eyes on farther horizons, have had their way with the place without ever grasping its nature. Named in honor of British sea captain John Marshall, who explored the archipelago in the eighteenth century, the islands became a German protectorate in the late nineteenth century, were taken by the Japanese in 1914, and then, after brutal battles here during World War II, came into American hands. The United States administered them as a trust territory until 1986, when the Republic of the Marshall Islands became independent.

The Marshalls' feudal system has survived democracy: the local *iroij,* or chief, still has absolute power. But American influence pervades, from the Patriot missile casings that serve islanders as washtubs to Rita and Laura, towns on Majuro that homesick soldiers named for Rita Hayworth and Lauren Bacall. The paramount American legacy, however, is nuclear. It began in 1946 with Operation Crossroads, tests ostensibly intended to determine whether ships could withstand atomic attack but at least in part driven by the military's desire to see what its new nuclear toys could do. Bikini was chosen because it had predictable winds and was out of the way. At least, out of *our* way. As Bob Hope once cracked, "As soon as the war ended, we located the one spot on earth that hadn't been touched by the war and blew it to hell."

By far the most devastating test was the fifteen-megaton "Bravo" shot, in 1954. Detonated on the Bikini atoll, Bravo was one thousand times more powerful than the Crossroads blasts; awesomely, it exceeded the combined strength of all the weapons ever fired in the history of humankind. Unfortunately, Pentagon officials proceeded with the test even though winds had shifted east from their customary north. All the men on a passing Japanese fishing vessel fell ill, and one died. On the Rongelap atoll, children played in the "snow" falling from the sky.

"I have had seven miscarriages and stillbirths," a Rongelapian woman told a House committee investigating Marshallese health problems in 1984. "There are eight other women on the island who have given birth to babies that look like blobs of jelly . . . no legs, no arms, no head, no nothing." Bravo made the Rongelap, Enewetak, and Bikini atolls uninhabitable. And for many years the U.S. treated the Marshallese as lab rats, keeping secret the results of "Project 4.1," its follow-up medical program. In 1956 an Atomic Energy Commission manager named Merril Eisenbud declared himself eager to see how radiation affected the Marshallese. "Data of this type has never been available," Eisenbud said in a secret hearing whose transcripts have since been declassified. "While it is true that these people do not live, I would say, the way Westerners do, civilized people, it is nevertheless also true that these people are more like us than the mice."

In 1968 the Atomic Energy Commission and President Johnson himself announced that Bikini was absolutely safe, but the Bikinians, who'd been shuffled between crummy substitute islands for decades, often near starvation, were suspicious. Over the next decade, 137 Bikinians warily drifted back. Their suspicions were soon justified: in 1978 the Department of Energy tested the relocated Bikinians and found that their bodies registered eleven times the normal radioactivity. Panic-stricken, the DOE had everyone reevacuated from the island.

The Bikinians filed a lawsuit against the federal government in 1981, and in 1982 the United States grudgingly established three trust funds, totaling $185 million, for environmental restoration and reparations. It also funded a $105 million cleanup of Enewetak's southern islands and in late 1996 gave Rongelap a $45 million resettlement fund. In 1988 the United States allotted $270 million for a Marshallese Nuclear Tribunal to compensate radiation victims. More than one thousand Marshallese have been awarded damages for troubles ranging from benign parathyroid tumors ($12,500 per case) to leukemia ($125,000).

But the tribunal has also rejected more than four thousand claims.

A number of Marshallese complained to me that too many of their countrymen tend to blame every cough or cataract on the bomb, hoping for personal guilt money to supplement the roughly $70 million a year in general aid that the United States provides under a fifteen-year "Compact of Free Association"—a huge percentage of the republic's $84 million budget. The Compact, however, is scheduled to dissolve in 2001, and Marshallese leaders are now desperately searching for ways to fill the coming void, including entertaining various schemes for siting nuclear waste dumps throughout the archipelago.

J. E. Tobin, an American anthropologist who was studying an exiled community of Bikinians on the island of Kili, foresaw the creation of a welfare culture in the Marshalls as early as 1953. "Positive action must be taken," he warned, "or we will find ourselves with a group of bitter, frustrated, old-time 'Reservation Indians' on our hands, with a dole psychology and a hopeless future."

—

Earlier in the week, I sat with Senator Wilfred Kendall in the boxy, Lego-block-style capitol on Majuro. Kendall was itemizing his republic's problems, which he knows well as the former ambassador to the United States, as one of Majuro's five representatives to the thirty-three-member unicameral legislature, and, perhaps just as important, as the owner of Majuro's Mobil Station. (The country runs like a small town: it's easier to find Foreign Minister Philip Muller at his bowling alley than at the ministry he heads.) "Our reefs on Majuro are all destroyed," Kendall said, sweat coursing down his face. The central air-conditioning was out, indefinitely. "You can't swim in the lagoon, the dump is all filled up, and it stinks, terrible. We've got goddamn diapers floating all over the place. We don't have many tuna left since we started letting the Chinese fish 750 tons a year. We don't have much of anything, in fact." He lapsed into pained silence.

I hesitantly asked about global warming: a fifty-centimeter rise in the sea level, which a UN scientific panel predicts during the next century, would swamp the entire country. Already waves lap over the road if the breeze freshens. "Yeah," he said, sighing. "We'll do something about that. But whatever it is, it won't be good enough."

It was hardly tourist brochure material. And yet for the first leg of my trip across the Marshalls, I'd been invited, along with six journalists from diving and fishing magazines, to "rediscover" Majuro, this long-overlooked spit that Robert Louis Stevenson once called "the pearl of the Pacific." A slim jawbone often only fifty yards wide, the island runs for thirty miles and carries the distinction of having Micronesia's longest road, which, unsurprisingly, is thirty miles long. Majuro is home to more than twenty thousand of the country's fifty-six thousand residents, most of them crammed into low-slung houses bleached by sun and salt air.

Our arrival on Majuro was big news. At the Tide Table restaurant we were toasted by a dignitary who then serenaded us with "Kansas City." The *Marshall Islands Journal* ran a story headlined MAJURO MEDIA BLITZ: "BIG HITTERS" TO MAJURO, just above AUSSIES LIKE CLEAN TEETH. We were ceremoniously lodged at the comfortable Outrigger, a brand-new hotel built as part of the country's ambitious attempts to jump-start a tourist industry. Considering how few tourists have passed through in recent years (in 1995 a measly seven hundred), it's a huge gamble—and one that has already entailed significant sacrifices. While spending upward of $15 million on the new Outrigger, for example, the government canceled the school lunch program to save money. Room televisions at the Outrigger get CNN and VH-1, but it's a tape loop from three months earlier. As of this writing, Outrigger guests believe that Bob Dole is still running strong in the South.

While Majuro itself fails to enchant, the atoll's farther-flung islands are gorgeous and boast some of the finest reef diving in the Pacific. One morning we took the boat to nearby Arno and were escorted by thirty spinner dolphins plunging abreast of the bow. Below, we swam with star puffers, eagle rays, and silver-tipped sharks cruising over chunks of brain coral. When we surfaced, white curtains of rain were drawing all around us, and a single tern sailed over the gunmetal water.

The morning after our dive, I had breakfast with Jim Abernathy, a white-bearded, sixtyish American who had been a longtime consultant to the country's first president, Amata Kabua. We met in the Quik Stop coffee shop, a fluorescent-lit beehive in the heart of Majuro where most of the country's governance actually seems to occur. I asked Abernathy, whose attitude toward the Marshalls veers between cynicism and baffled tenderness, what change he'd like to see in his adopted republic. "I'd go back to the end of World War Two," he said, "and just have the U.S. pass the islands by. If we hadn't come in, they'd have a nice little country." He smoked and stared out the window.

Just then Rick Stinson slid into our red plastic booth carrying the requisite mug of Kona coffee and cigarette. A shrewd, funny Australian consultant with an unshaven face, Stinson had been hired to help reorganize the Ministry of Foreign Affairs.

I asked him the same question I'd asked Abernathy. "You can't change just one," Stinson said. "They have no idea what they're doing. I asked the Undersecretary of Administration to write down what his three most important duties were, and he wrote (1) answering the phone, (2) sweeping the floor, (3) responding to mail. They don't have money for stationery—they don't even have a list of their own staff. They're very friendly, though."

Jiba Kabua came over to our booth. The late president's eldest son, a senator and the scion of an all-powerful *iroij* family, Kabua was selling $5 tickets for a local band's concert, wheedling us in the fashion of a high school raffle. Abernathy and Stinson each bought one. ("If we didn't," Abernathy later explained, "he'd think we don't like him. But he'll just lose the money in a poker game.")

When I asked Senator Kabua what one thing he'd change about the country, his thoughts turned to sex. "When the people's arms and legs are chained in boredom," he said, "this gets free." He put his index finger atop his trouser zipper and waved it about. "It used to be subtle. I would roll a leaf in my right ear to signal the woman,

'Watch out, today is our day.' But the new model is Hollywood. A guy goes into a bar and has a drink and pop, let's go. You bring us all the fatty foods, all the Hollywood pictures—what a job it does on the libido." His finger stood bravely erect, like a planted flag.

That evening, I saw firsthand what the senator was talking about. Around midnight all of us Big Hitters were at the Pub, the darkest joint in Majuro. A local band played bouncy, gecko-bar versions of "Lady Madonna" and "Fly Like an Eagle" as drunks were being stacked like cordwood in the parking lot. I was dancing to "The Locomotion" with a tourism promoter from Hawaii named Heidi when I was suddenly cut in on by a tiny Marshallese woman. She began thrusting her hips against me in a busy, circular motion, buffing my groin like a floor waxer. I leaned away, but she pressed home, grinning to reveal very few teeth. I looked over and saw that Heidi was getting the same from a Marshallese man, as the band played on.

—

Jack Niedenthal is a thirty-nine-year-old man with dark spaniel eyes, the hair of an aging rock star, and an allergy to button-down shirts. Having grown up in Pennsylvania, he fell in love with the Marshalls in the early eighties as a Peace Corps volunteer on Namu, an outer island with only two hundred people and no airstrip. ("NAMU" is tattooed unevenly across the fingers of his left hand.) "The Marshallese were the nicest people I'd ever met," Niedenthal said, fondly recalling his Peace Corps days. "Namu was enchanting. There was no electricity, no running water, and you slept in a little shack with a kerosene lamp and the sound of the ocean roaring in your ears. We'd fish during the day, and at night the guys would come around and play guitar and I'd lie in my hammock, just thinking."

When his Peace Corps duty was up in 1984, Niedenthal moved to Majuro and since 1987 has devoted himself to representing the displaced Bikinian people in all their dealings with the American colossus. Although he looked laid-back, I gradually discovered that Niedenthal was a constant worrier, the kind of man who pursues every stray question to its grave. He doesn't like anyone telling the

Bikinians what to do. He also doesn't like anyone telling him what to do. The two are sometimes the same. At one point Niedenthal told me he expected to die young from brooding over the fate of the 2,200 Bikinians. It wasn't abstract to him: he plans to move back to Bikini himself one day with Regina and their three Bikinian children.

Niedenthal and I rented a tiny skiff from the docks at Majuro and puttered a few miles over to the island of Ejit. Upon landing, we could faintly smell the stench of sewage. Styrofoam cups and USDA beef tins were scattered everywhere on the crushed coral commons. The place had the look and feel of a refugee camp. Two hundred and fifty displaced Bikinians live here, crowded into small tin-roofed plywood shacks (the rest dwell on the main island of Majuro and on the equally grim island of Kili).

As we walked around, we ran into Kelen Joash, a slight man of sixty-six wearing a white T-shirt and a Seiko watch. He was sitting on a plank, watching contentedly as workmen completed his $135,000 cinder-block house as part of a public works project paid for, ultimately, by the United States. Joash was eager to move into his new house and get on with his life here on Ejit, but part of his heart remained on Bikini. Like all Bikinians in exile, Joash kept a bottle containing powdered coral from Wodejabato, a reef head just off Bikini. Wodejabato is believed to be a powerful spirit that banishes evil influences, eases heartbreak, and will eventually ensure the Bikinians' return home.

Speaking in staccato Marshallese as Niedenthal translated, Joash recalled the day the Americans first came to Bikini. "The Japanese had just lost, and we were scared," he said. "The Americans arrived with many, many people and planes and ships and uniforms with stars on them. It was wonderful to watch them come. One guy climbed a coconut tree and blew the top off with a grenade so they could stick an American flag in it. We were frightened—we didn't even know what a grenade was, let alone an atomic bomb."

Commodore Ben Wyatt chose to come ashore and address the wonder-struck islanders immediately following services at the United Church of Christ. (The Bikinians had been converted by

New England missionaries in the nineteenth century.) God and the bomb were often yoked in those days, so Wyatt adopted biblical language. He compared the Bikinians to the "Children of Israel whom the Lord had saved from their enemy and led into the Promised Land." According to the official navy account, Wyatt told King Juda Kessibuki that a "power higher than anything on earth" would bless their move and finally inquired whether they would be "willing to sacrifice their island"—temporarily—"for the good of mankind and to end all world wars."

Probably closer to the truth is the recollection of another Bikinian I met on Ejit, a woman named Binirok who had been a fourteen-year-old girl at the time of Operation Crossroads: "They said, 'Move,' " she told me, "and we moved."

In July 1946 the United States set off two 23-kiloton weapons, Able and Baker, in the vicinity of ninety-five surplus warships that had been gathered in Bikini lagoon. The Baker underwater test hurled a vast column of water a mile into the air and flung the forty-thousand-ton USS *Saratoga* half a mile away to sink, like a toy ship swatted by an ill-tempered child.

The world was electrified by this new atomic power, made giddy. French designer Louis Reard named his new two-piece swimsuit "the bikini," hoping that its effect on men would resemble an atomic explosion. When the Crossroads experiment ended, Admiral William Blandy cut into a ceremonial cake baked in the shape of a mushroom cloud. In those days the lasting effects of radiation were barely understood, and "fallout" was not yet even a word. Army clerk Dick Anderson, marveling at the brilliant pink hue of the Able explosion, said, "It reminds one of cotton candy." Anderson has since had five operations for skin cancer.

Between 1946 and 1958, the year President Eisenhower announced a moratorium on atmospheric testing, the United States set off twenty-three weapons on Bikini atoll. As it became apparent that they still weren't going to be allowed to return home, the Bikinians slowly, against their trustful grain, came to feel betrayed. "The

United States promised they would take care of us like we were their own children," Kelen Joash told me, apologizing if he was hurting my feelings. "They said that no matter where we went, if it was on a sandbar or if we were adrift on a raft at sea, they would take care of us." This exact "sandbar and raft" phrasing is repeated by virtually every original Bikinian, as solemnly as the Twenty-third Psalm.

Now Kelen Joash looked fondly over at his shiny new windows. "It's a beautiful house," he said, "and I do thank America for this. But sometimes we feel like the moneys are not keeping pace with our desires. I don't have beds and furniture yet, so I'll be looking for a budget for that."

"The Bikinians were once the hillbillies of the Marshall Islands," an official on Majuro had told me. "Now they're the Beverly Hillbillies."

—

The Air Marshalls plane finally came to pick up Jack, Regina, and me on Kwajalein, and an hour later the Bikini atoll slid into view. From the air it looked like any other island in the Marshalls, until we circled the Bravo blast area, a deep blue, mile-wide bite in the reef. We landed on Eneu, where the American military observers had crouched in concrete bunkers to watch the blasts, and then took a half-hour boat ride over to Bikini. Everything looked bright and alive on this boomerang-shaped island, with lush groves of coconut, breadfruit, and pandanus. Red hermit crabs scuttled about, intent on sideways errands. But there was also an air of neglect, of ruin. The old houses, uninhabited since the late seventies, were overgrown, and orange cassytha, a parasitic vine, had crept over much of the island, like a runaway soccer net.

The Department of Energy had set up a small base camp on a crescent of white sand. There was a cafeteria, a barracks, a video room, and a few rooms built to accommodate the sport divers who come to explore the spectacular wrecks submerged in the lagoon. Aside from us, the dive masters, and a few Marshallese workers, most of the other two dozen people on the island were DOE scientists from Lawrence Livermore National Laboratory who are studying ways to make the island inhabitable once again.

At sundown the team leader, William Robison, genially offered me a gin and tonic. A handsome, silver-haired man who wore flip-flops, shorts, and a T-shirt, he looked more like a beachcomber than a master of the atom. I told him how odd it was to find a place that had seen twenty-three nuclear blasts looking so normal—so beautiful, even.

Robison agreed, stressing that there was no present risk to us. "The gamma radiation you get walking around here is just natural background radiation, no problem at all." The danger, he said, was not in the air, but in the soil: nearly all the dirt on the island was laced with cesium 137, a radiocontaminant that concentrates in fruits and vegetables grown here. Although not immediately dangerous, cesium 137 can be lethal if ingested over a long period of time. "Let me show you something," Robison said. We hopped into a rickety white truck and drove to an experimental garden in the middle of the island, where DOE specialists run tests on coconuts, papayas, breadfruit, and bananas. We walked over to a trench that had been dug beside a coconut tree, and Robison jumped in.

"This is the story of the island, right here," he said, pointing fifteen inches down to where the rich black humus ended and the dry coral sand began. "The problem is that this soil is very potassium-poor. And cesium 137 is chemically very similar to potassium. So all these plants take up cesium from the soil through their roots instead of potassium, and the cesium concentrates in the fruit. If we do nothing, it will take roughly one hundred years for food grown here to be safe enough to eat."

Robison has been working on the problem for the past twenty years. "Science got us into this mess," he said, climbing back out of the trench, "but it can also get us out. It's a beautiful island. And we owe the Bikinians their home back."

For years the Bikinians wanted simply to remove all the soil from the entire island, a hugely expensive denuding project known as the

Big Scrape. "That gets rid of the cesium, all right," said Robison, "but then you're left with a barren beach." His mouth pursed.

Robison favors a much less drastic approach, one that involves scraping just the soil close to residences while periodically treating the island with large doses of potassium fertilizer. "We figured out that putting adequate amounts of potassium chloride on the soil every five years for the next eighty years will prevent the cesium from being taken up into the plants," Robison said. "Eventually the cesium will radioactively decay and become harmless."

If the Bikinians approve Robison's idea, they could be home in five years. But it is unlikely that more than a few hundred will return, for the exile has, over time, become less about the fading of radiation than about the fading of a way of life. Back on Majuro, I had spoken with a twenty-eight-year-old Bikinian named Alson Kelen, who had lived on Bikini briefly as a boy during the aborted relocation effort in the 1970s. Now he wondered how Bikinians of his generation would fare on their homeland. "If the younger guys were to go back now, they'd probably starve," Kelen told me. "Ninety percent of them would rather move to the States. They just follow TV: for a while they all wore backwards shirts and drooping pants like the two black kids on MTV [Kris Kross]. Now it's a fade haircut and ratty ponytails."

Kelen fondly remembered the stories his father used to tell him of the old days on Bikini. "When I grew up," he said, "I'd use my father's arm as a pillow, and he'd tell me the legends, how to fish using a *jabok,* where you drive fish into shore with a net of coconut leaves. But when I talk to my younger brothers about when I lived on Bikini, about the papaya, about eating lobsters, about how fresh and virgin it was"—he brought his hand to his nostrils, as if sniffing a heady perfume—"after a few minutes they say, 'Hey, I heard videos are on sale.' "

Ironically, argue some DOE scientists, the Bikinian taste for American junk food has made the radiation problem on the atoll almost moot. "Since beer, Coke, and Kool-Aid have replaced coconut milk in their diet, the Bikinians could actually come back right now," soil scientist Earl Stone told Jack Niedenthal and me over a plate of baby-back ribs in the DOE cafeteria. White-haired and nearsighted, Stone spoke with the garrulous frankness common to certain men of research. "Even the Marshallese body shape has changed—not many of them can climb up the coconut trees anymore. The bottom line is, there's no cesium in frozen chicken."

—

One evening on Bikini, as the sun sank with absurd splendor into the lagoon, Jack Niedenthal and I sat on the porch of the DOE barracks and talked about money and values. The Bikinians had recently faced a fateful decision, he said, one that eventually took on the proportions of "a spiritual crisis."

In December 1994, Niedenthal and a group of prominent Bikini leaders met in a San Francisco restaurant with Alex Copeson, a smooth-talking British national. Copeson represented Pan Pacific, a consortium that wanted to use a few islands in the Bikini atoll to store surplus weapons plutonium and spent nuclear fuel, the most dangerous kind of nuclear waste. Copeson's partner, Admiral Daniel Murphy, former chief of staff for Vice President Bush, had already sent President Kabua a letter offering him $160 million for a "suitable atoll."

Copeson screened a six-minute video, *Used Nuclear Fuel Transportation: Safety Every Step of the Way,* which purported to show steel waste containers safely sustaining an 80 mph broadside from a locomotive and being toasted to more than two thousand degrees Fahrenheit in a burning pool of aviation fuel. Then he launched into a vivid spiel about Pan Pacific's plan to bury the 125-ton containers full of plutonium 239—which becomes "reasonably safe" after 240,000 years—deep in the coral reef. One could envision a James Bond–ish techtopia, with men in jumpsuits zipping about on monorails.

After the islanders' half century of experience with nuclear contamination, the proposal might have seemed a black joke. But Copeson stressed that it would enable the Bikinians to determine their own destiny at last. "I said to them, 'Get serious—you're never going to get that many tourists to dive those pathetic wrecks in the lagoon,' " Copeson told me recently from his office in Washington, D.C. " 'But with our project you'll be earning over a billion dollars a year, and you can have your own airline, your own shipping line. Or you can go drinking and whoring—that's your business.' "

Niedenthal found Copeson's presentation terrifying. "Copeson knew I was going to be a problem," he said. "He kept telling me to get over my sixties flower-child ideals, to live in the real world." While Niedenthal knew the Bikinians' desire for money and the good life, having often seen them "turn into demons" at meetings in Las Vegas, he was nonetheless astonished by how seriously they were taking Copeson's proposal. "Everyone was listening to his ludicrous numbers. I mean, this guy was just like the guys who came to us wanting to establish a tire-burning plant or cart out garbage to us from Los Angeles. Copeson was just another scumbag—but they were almost ready to sign on the dotted line."

Although Niedenthal himself is not religious, he found himself adopting biblical language to sway the Bikinians. He told them he could prove from Scripture that Copeson's idea was a mistake: "Read the entire Bible from cover to cover and try to find one verse that says, 'To turn a gift from God into a dump is the work of God.' " And then he added, "I can't stand before you and say, 'I don't care one way or the other.' I'm part of your community. My wife is a Bikinian. My children are Bikinians. I am thinking about my family and the generations to come."

In the end, to Niedenthal's great relief, the Bikinian elders decided to nix the deal and then made a firm decision not to entertain any further dump offers. Copeson remains bitter toward the Bikinians and the Marshallese government. "Their officials started squabbling over money they hadn't even earned yet," he said. "They're all scam artists, banging the tin cup in front of the white man. They'd open a whorehouse and sell their daughters and grandmothers for a dollar. They've never lived so good since that bomb, the fat, lazy fucks. All they want to do is go gambling, drinking, and whoring in the U.S. The only contribution they could make to the world is to give someone their islands [for waste] and take a hike—be an absentee landlord for world peace."

Instead the Bikinians are insisting that the U.S. government carry out a full environmental restoration of the island, and they harbor hopes of returning in the next few years. This December they decided to "seriously consider" Bill Robison's plan for limited scraping and periodic fertilizer drops over most of the atoll. But after visiting Regina's family's homestead on Bikini, Jack and his wife began to have some reservations about even a limited scrape, wondering if they really want to bulldoze the coconut and pandanus off their property: it all looks so lovely as it is.

—

Deep in the midnight-blue water of the Bikini lagoon, the USS *Saratoga* seemed impossibly large and strange. It was swaddled in sea fans, its twenty-millimeter guns plugged with tampions of white whip coral. Jack, Regina, and I were following the huge figure of Fabio Amaral, our jolly Brazilian dive master, into the aircraft carrier's very maw, a dark elevator shaft that bottoms out 130 feet below the surface and a half century into the past.

Our halogen beams lit up the hangar deck, which remained pocked and buckled from the 1946 blast. Three Navy Helldiver aircraft were perched in the gloom, their wings folded up casually as if still ready to sortie. We hovered over the cockpits, observing the dials forlornly frozen in position, and then spiraled up through a school of saddleback groupers and three unicorn fish that cocked their horns at me quizzically, like exclamation points.

As we plunged below one hundred feet I kept imagining I was hearing the faint, deadly tingle of nitrogen bubbles popping into my bloodstream. Diving at such depths always poses dangers, of course, and there's little margin for error. Getting the bends was simply not an option, since the nearest hyperbaric chamber was on Kwajalein, and the nearest plane was, well . . .

Fabio beckoned me to the compass bridge. His bulky form

slipped through two dark, narrow doorways as effortlessly as the banded sea snake I just saw knifing by. I followed gracelessly, banging both doorways, battering my way into the tiny room. Suddenly I was overcome with a wave of claustrophobia. We hung in this watery dungeon, gazing through the tiny window holes as a batfish glided past. Fabio grinned—there was just enough light to see his teeth—and flipped the toggles of the ship's navigational lights panel. In my dreamy state I half expected the ship to light up and surge forward again, rejuvenated from its fifty-year nap.

Back on the dive boat—named the *Bravo,* wryly enough—we chattered exuberantly about the bombs, the fish, the exquisite play of colors. A diver pays $2,750 for a week here, a fair price for some of the best diving in the world. Certainly it doesn't translate into much of a windfall for the Bikinian people: even when the operation is running at full capacity—twelve divers a week—the 2,200 Bikinians will stand to gross only about $300,000 a year. But having tasted the fleshpots of America and seen how quickly they could get rich if they sold everything that matters, the Bikinians have chosen, for now, anyway, to enrich themselves slowly. In their wanderings they've concluded that it's better to live off a nuclear wreck than a nuclear dump.

That evening, Jack Niedenthal and I found ourselves staring at the moonlit lagoon, still rhapsodizing about the dive, while Regina sat cross-legged in concentration, weaving herself a headdress of frangipani blossoms tucked into a pandanus leaf. There was a Bikinian flag snapping in the breeze outside the barracks, and I noticed how oddly similar it was to the American Stars and Stripes, with twenty-three white stars for the islands they hope to return to and three black stars for the islands blown to smithereens. I idly mentioned the similarity.

"It looks *just like* yours, goddammit," Jack snapped. Then he grinned. "That's the point—we're part of you forever."

(1997)

ZAMBEZI DREAMS

I'd arrived in the Zimbabwean town of Victoria Falls stunned after two days of flying, needing to nap. But the Zambezi's roar, rattling windows from a mile away, drew me like the summons of an angry god. I slipped away from my newly met companions toward the noise, passing from wide, hot streets through dry savanna and at last into a cloud chamber of ficus and lianas as the booming grew and the temperature plunged.

Suddenly I was on a vast precipice. A mile across and a hundred yards deep, Victoria Falls is twice as wide and high as Niagara. Cat-footing as near as I dared on the slippery black basalt—this is Africa: no railings—I stared down, down, down into a churn of froth so maddened that the mist rebounded into the air above to fall again as rain.

Off to the east, the huge basin below narrowed to a thirty-yard-wide ribbon that coiled through four sheer gorges in five miles, like a stomach draining into an intestine. Tomorrow I was going to be drained down there myself; I was going to be digested. The rafting I'd done in Colorado and Alaska now seemed like dips in the baby pool. And the sadness I carried, having left New York the day my ex-girlfriend was getting married, was swallowed up by fear.

—

After crossing the Zambian border to hike down to a spot just below the falls—the river divides Zambia and Zimbabwe—we plunged into the first rapid, a level five monster known as Boiling Pot. (Rapids, which are graded in difficulty on a scale of one to five, are christened like rodeo horses: Widowmaker signals danger; Butter-ball, a soft ride.) Most of our group hadn't rafted before, and we were about to embark on the 70 toughest miles in the Zambezi's 1,700-mile meander to the Indian Ocean, but the instruction had been skeletal. Paddle forward or back per the call of Kulu, our raft's guide and the trip's leader; brace your feet under the inflated side and center tubes; if you fall out, hold on to your paddle and keep your feet in front of you so they, not your head, bounce off the rocks.

Just before we dropped into the fifty yards of heaving white water, I glanced around: everyone was wide-eyed and rabbity, as if preparing to be shot from a cannon. Boom! We immediately hit a hole—a vacuum between waves—that knocked me facedown onto the raft's flooded bottom. My cheerful Irish raft mate, Tom, landed atop me an instant later; everyone was flung down, prostrated. And before we could even write a will, we were into the second rapid and that roller-coaster terror again: Here we *goooo* . . .

When you are bouncing between being fried and being soaked, between panic and jubilation, you learn about one another fast. All told, we were twenty in two paddleboats and an oar-propelled supply boat: sixteen rafters, three guides, and Ali, the trip photographer. The rafters were mostly British, with a few Irish and New Zealanders; average age, twenty-five. I was the only American. As a group, the Brits were much given to sucking candies, to boozing, and to terming any phenomenon "top"—as in "That's a top-rank chicken/top-notch life jacket/top-hole hiccup."

A gung ho group. And quick studies—so much so that by the third day of our eight-day trip, as we drifted toward roughly the thirtieth of the trip's sixty significant rapids, we donned helmets and life jackets almost casually. This was a level three no-brainer known as Let's Make a Deal. And even on the level fives, we'd had few "swimmers"—usually Tom, who exploded out of the boat like popcorn at the slightest jostle. We'd learned to paddle in unison, to grasp the luggage ropes like subway straphangers, and that, all in all, a fifteen-foot raft piled with food and gear is a sturdy thing.

I was thinking that we were certainly doing a lot better than Sobek, the American travel company that in 1981 seized on the invention of the self-bailing raft to make the first successful journey down the middle Zambezi. The trip was filmed for ABC and, for now-obscure synergistic reasons, included LeVar "Kunta Kinte" Burton (not an African, but he played one on TV). On the first rapid, Sobek president Richard Bangs's boat slammed the wall and capsized; ours hadn't. They portaged the fourth rapid; we ran it. At the fifth rapid, which we'd also run smoothly, they hit a pour-over wrong. LeVar Burton went for a long swim, and in the rock-strewn current one Grant Rogers broke four ribs and suffered a collapsed lung. He was airlifted to a hospital, and another rafter wrote, "Some would have flown out with Rogers if they could." And that was before a crocodile attacked and disabled one of their boats.

But what we hadn't yet grasped was the difference between Sobek's exploring and our adventure travel. A river is a text, and just as reading Joyce's *Finnegans Wake* is easier than it was sixty years ago, running even a severe challenge like the Zambezi is easier now that the safest narrative line has been explicated. If you stray from that line ever so slightly, suddenly you're no longer the river's master but its plaything. As we were about to find out.

"Where the river levels and goes left, wave pushing us right into the right bank, we avoid it," Kulu mumbled, explaining Let's Make a Deal. Everyone smiled at this boilerplate, tickled by his nonchalance and the local accent, in which "bank" sounds like "bink" and "levels" is stretched like a rubber band, then snapped: "layyyvv-ls." "Falling out, flipping," he continued, "grab the paddle and back to the boat. If not, have a nice ride and see you on down the bottom." We mimicked his slurry cadences: "Seeyouondown the bottom."

Kulu grinned and slithered his body backward from the stern to plant his paddle as a rudder, his bare feet waggling under a retaining strap for balance. "Left turn," he said, and we stroked but kept sliding right, right, and Kulu shouted, "Hard left!" but the raft slammed the wall. I was in the right bow, sliding up the wet rock toward the sky. "Oh, my goodness," Kulu said—and we flipped.

I fell toward Barry in the left bow and hit him in a jumble of helmets and paddles, and then we were deep underwater and pelting downstream, cocooned in cold thunder that cuffed the breath from my body. I was never going to surface; I was drowning. I finally bobbed up, but my head wasn't fully clearing—I was under the overturned boat. A gasp in the air pocket and I ducked out, surfacing yards from the boat, now ringed by the other rafters. A loose paddle clonked my helmet, so I grabbed it, but with both hands holding paddles, I couldn't fix my Teva sandals, ripped open by the current. I was flotsam, spinning toward the left bank. Ali, the photographer, put down his camcorder and rowed the oar boat toward me, calling, "Watch the bink!" I finally clutched his extended oar and flopped to the bottom of the raft, dead, gasping into the white sky. Two Egyptian geese flew low overhead, honking derisively.

Meg, who'd been resting in the oar boat, came back to Kulu's raft with me, crowing, "What a bunch of plonkers!" Brown eyed, with a corolla of blond hair, Meg was all nubile spunk. Sitting close behind her in the raft, I brooded about her soft back and the blue-and-white bikini strap that marked its equator. Her boyfriend, Andy, was affable and handsome, with little spaces between his teeth. In a game we all played of "Who would you most like to be?" he chose Alan Greenspan. Not the sort to drown, alas. "Top flip!" Meg said. "Brilliant!" The rest of us were muted, reassessing the dangers as we thawed and dried.

Sensing our mood, Kulu taught us to sing "Shosholoza," a Zulu freedom song. It was a subtle reminder of how far southern Africa has come. Under British rule for almost a century, Rhodesia was notorious for its oppressive mines, known to blacks by such names as Makombera (You're Closed In) and Maplanki (Planks for Punishment). It wasn't until 1980 that Zimbabwe was born, when black rebels finally closed out a brutal war against Ian Smith's white-pride government. Now, less than two decades later, I was going down a river on a trip—organized by a New Zealand company, Adrift, and its American representative, Africa-Tours—with a black Zambian trip leader and a black Zimbabwean photographer. And a group of white tourists, visiting the old colony.

As the sun set, we came to Chimamba, a cataract as slick and slender as a water slide. A spiky ten-foot tree trunk was surfing along just behind us, ready to club anyone who fell out. For this we could thank the Rambo brothers, so nicknamed by Ali: Adam and Christian, two muscular lads from Manchester who sported matching camouflage pants and a surly machismo. They had manhandled this mopani trunk downhill when we'd stopped to gather firewood for camp and then, upon learning we already had enough, hurled it into the river.

We sat tense and quiet as Kulu slipped us in perpendicular to the fall line. Over the lip, and we shot through a boil toward the right wall. "Back paddle!" he shouted, and we dug in reverse but nailed the wall anyway and bounced off hard. The river paused, deliberating our fate, then spun us downstream. Everyone echoed Kulu's happy cry of *"Iwe!"*—Shona for "Hey, you!"

But then straight into another class five, the famously daunting Upper Moemba. We could hear the grinding roar before we rounded the corner. The idea is to thread two large boulders at the top of the narrow channel and then hang on for the plunge into a standing wave that knocks the boat straight up, the swoop into blinding foam, the climb up into a second wave of equal ferocity, and the long, swirling cascade out.

The first wave knocked Meg from the boat. She floated for a second, then disappeared beneath us. After the second wave, we still couldn't see her. Finally she popped up, gasping, behind us. She'd cracked her back on a boulder and was finding every breath painful. We pulled her in and paddled wearily to shore. Dark fell with tropical swiftness as Meg shivered and blinked back tears. When we set up camp in the gloom, I gave her two Advil and, leaning on the power of suggestion, told her that they were potent American anti-inflammatory drugs. She swallowed them solemnly.

Though the next day was our layover day, we would try to run Moemba fifteen times—the result of a drunken bet made the first night, when Ali insisted our group couldn't break the record of fourteen runs set by guides two years ago. The stakes were collecting all firewood, doing all dishes, and bringing the winners breakfast in bed. After a chicken dinner that first evening, we'd boozed around the campfire, getting acquainted. Meg and Andy led everyone in a round of "Do You Take It in Your Mouth, Mrs. Murphy?" Southern Comfort brought out the pirate in Barry, a modest, black-haired pharmacist from Northern Ireland. He crooned "Beat the Drum Slowly" in a fine baritone, then took it into his head to climb a steep, shaley outcropping. He was halfway up when his foothold crumbled, and he slid and rolled, almost into the fire. Anne examined Barry's bleeding knees with a tender hand; they were on their honeymoon. Adam and Christian, deep in vodka, began ragging him: "You give up pretty easy, Paddy," Christian muttered thickly. "A real Irishman would be up that rock like a rat up a drainpipe."

"Right, then," Barry said, and bounded up to seek a new foothold. Anne grabbed to restrain him but only pulled down his shorts, leaving Barry in a spread-eagle moon. Shaking with laughter, Anne maintained her grip. "Free up me arse!" he shouted. She finally did, but made a basket of her arms beneath him in case he fell again. He somehow scrambled to the top, where he stood, weaving, headlamp flaring, a pie-eyed firefly.

From his perch, Barry began ragging Ali about his adventures on rapid number nine, Commercial Suicide. The river narrows there to a fifteen-yard-wide torrent that plunges into a seething pool. We had all walked around, but Ali took it on. His red kayak vanished into the hole like a drop of blood into a blenderful of cream. Seconds passed. Ali finally ripped out with an Eskimo roll, but the current had snapped his paddle like a toothpick.

Then he took the oar boat through and broke an oar. "I'll raft number nine with you any day, Ali," Barry said now. "And I won't be the death of so many paddles."

Ali began dancing round the fire, gesturing with a burning brand as he proposed the bet. "We will see how brave you whinging Brits are when we come to Upper Moemba," he said.

"All right, all right," Barry said, "I'll wash your dishes and kiss your arse for you, you mad dog."

Ali stiffened. "What do you mean, 'mad dog'?" He was sensitive, mercurial, given to proclaiming that he was the rightful king of his tribe and to teaching us to greet Kulu by saying, *"Yebo, indwangu"*—Ndebele for "Hello, baboon"—yet also prey to abrupt melancholies. "We will see who is the madder dog," he said. "The *nyaminyami,* the river spirit, will decide." He leaned forward, scowling: "Maybe it doesn't like you."

———

During the day's flat stretches, as we drifted and drank iodine-laced water, I'd study the trees, dull gray baobabs fat as milk bottles, figs threading through the black rock to drink from the river. They guarded their water at sentries' intervals, surrounded by grass tawny like a lion's skin. Old-fashioned riddles also helped us forget the heat. "A man lies dead in a telephone box with glass all around him," someone would say. Or, "A man lies dead in the desert, holding a twig. What happened?" The guessers would ask yes-or-no questions, hunting the bizarre truth. The Irish always wondered, "Was it a bomb?"; the Africans, "Was it a snake?" As I lay in my sleeping bag on the sand, listening to Moemba's drumming fury, it occurred to me that all the riddles were about death.

Death, the mother of beauty, haunts the river. The Scottish explorer David Livingstone felt this when he happened on Mosi-oa-Tunya (the Smoke That Thunders) in 1855 and renamed it Victoria Falls after his queen. But he gave the river's dark power a sentimental spin, declaring, "On sights as beautiful as this, Angels in their flight must have gazed." Livingstone's statue stands on the falls' Zimbabwean side, his bronzed left hand grasping a canteen and a Bible for succor. He believed that the Zambezi would be "God's Highway," a trade-and-missionary route bringing light to "the Dark Continent."

He was wrong, of course, about everything. The British arrival brought only greater darkness (the Zimbabwean government is currently removing LIBERATOR from the plinth of Livingstone's statue). And though Livingstone praised the river's navigability, he never even saw the rapids we'd run, because he twice took the easier land route east. The Zambezi's white water refused to part, even for evangelists.

Have tourists taken the missionaries' place in the rolls of the misguided? I wondered drowsily. And so to sleep. In the middle of the night, Nikki woke us with her yells. In her dreams, the river had turned and flooded the camp, drowning us all.

———

The next afternoon we reluctantly tackled the bet. I had hoped to avoid being in the eight-man crew, but no one else much wanted to do it, either, and American honor was vaguely at stake. We portaged the boat up to the eddy pool atop the rapid, along a ledge so narrow and pitted with bore holes that we had to raise the raft at a crabbed angle and heave it forward a few yards at a time, again and again. The life jackets made for clumsy work and chafed our sun-torched skin. From the eddy pool, we stroked hard into the current, made a swinging right turn, and tried to split the two rocks. On the first run, we knifed between; on the second, we went right; on the third, we hit the left boulder and hung there for a yawning moment. Yet we stayed afloat. Each time, I felt a moment's charmed relief, then the return of anxiety as we bulled the boat back uphill.

On the fourth run, we tipped left on the first wave, rocked sideways into the second—and went over. I just had time to snatch a breath before I was trapped under not only the boat, but Andy. The current locked us together in a foaming boil, and it took enormous self-control not to start clawing through his flesh. When we were finally ripped apart, I tried to swim toward the oar boat but got nowhere. By the time Kulu picked me up fifty yards downstream, I was beat, my left hand a palsied claw. And the world looked too bright—my sunglasses, a gift from my ex-girlfriend, had whirled away in the confusion.

Exhaustion and fear. We dug in glumly for the long paddle upstream, heaved the raft onto the ledge, then paused to watch three Shearwater rafts negotiate the rapid—the final test in their shorter trip. They scouted it nervously, dithering. The first two boats made it, and the third crept forward. Our Italian guide, Marco, started a chant of "Flip! Flip! Flip!" which they mistook, in the din, for encouragement. They flipped instantly, and we shouted and high-fived as Ali bucked his hips at the swimmers in copulatory thrusts, shouting, "Oo, oo!" Giddy with schadenfreude, we started working together, even the Rambo brothers. We got in six more runs, hurling fists into the air after each one, before dark. Only ten trips, but we learned that it's really the teamwork and harmony that matter. Or so we tried arguing to Ali. He didn't buy it.

We celebrated anyway, pickling our unstrung bodies with a whiskey, lemon juice, and iodine-water punch that tasted like Pine Sol. Meg and I fell into quiet conversation. She was intrigued when I correctly guessed that she was the youngest of three children. So I told her how rare she was in having no apparent dark side. She was silent. "When I get angry at people who cross me, it's like I have a little green light glowing in my stomach," she said at last, staring into the fire. "And sex provokes dark feelings. It's quite primal, isn't it?" I considered the implications of this and looked at her, but she was looking at Andy across the way.

—

Sin's wages came due the next day: an early-morning portage around Lower Moemba's twenty-foot waterfall in a daze of heat. We heaved our hundred-pound food barrels and dry bags up a rise of blistered basalt, then lowered everything on ropes to the rafts. An hour later we had a longer portage across a flood platform at Chibongo Falls— a stunning cataract strangely neglected in historical accounts. But it will vault into prominence if the Zimbabwean government has its way and builds a dam there; the reservoir would flood back to rapid number five and kill the rafting forever.

After lunch we lowered the boats and gear into the foam below Chibongo. I was feeling cranky and lethargic, rather like Major Alfred St. Hill Gibbons, who led an 1898 expedition up the Zambezi in a steamboat, taking nineteen men and—ah, England!—a Great Dane. "It would be difficult to exaggerate the almost deathlike dreariness," the wonderfully named St. Hill Gibbons wrote of the sweltering gorges. After he brought his African crew back from desertion at gunpoint, "the boys were in better spirits," he wrote, "no longer victims to an imaginary discontent." No doubt. St. Hill Gibbons quit before reaching our stretch of the river, having exhausted his rations and enthusiasm. Another failed conqueror, he surely would have favored a dam to tame these waters once and for all.

We came to the last big class five: Ghostrider. After two of their first three boats had flipped on this long whirligig of boils and fretful waves, the Sobek expedition sent its fourth boat through unmanned, hence the rapid's spectral name. We checked chin straps, clenched paddles, wedged feet deeper under the tubes. "Stay riverright," Kulu said, "hit twostanding waves headon, bearleft and hitthethird wave at an angle so we miss thebigledge and eddypool ontheleft. Fallingout flipping seeyouondown the bot-tom." He didn't add, but Ali already had, that a big croc lurked in that pool.

Two hooded eyes just above the surface, then a great V wake as the croc surged to snap its evil jaws—an ugly prospect. A kayaker was killed above the falls recently in just that way. So, paddling in grim unison, we hit every wave dead-on. Glad shouts of "*Iwe!*" A feeling of carefree felicity, of riding a perfect, never-breaking wave into the future.

—

At six A.M. the sun sprang up and pierced my sleep. I had been dreaming about Julia Roberts. With tears in her eyes, she had run her light, frank hands through my hair, consoling me. Prints in the sand and fresh scat showed that baboons had passed among us in the night. We rose and floated on. The basalt walls gave way to low sandstone hills, and a hot wind licked upstream so that steady paddling gained us only ten yards a minute. Basking six-foot crocs became a regular sight.

But the real danger in the calmer water was hippopotamuses, which kill as many people in Africa as the next five animals combined. Though they're vegetarians, these two-ton oddities are extremely territorial. One of our rafts bore bite marks from an enraged hippo during a previous trip, and the guides cautioned that we shouldn't linger for good camera shots. I did hope to see one defecate, though: to mark their band of river, they waggle their hind parts around, flinging feces in all directions.

On our last day, the river widened and grew much shallower. Reeds thronged the shore and housed thousands of chirruping weaverbirds, along with the odd skimming, squeaking plover. And just before the last small rapid, we saw five hippos wallowing about two hundred yards to the left as we crept along the right shore. Then three of them vanished, so we picked up the pace. They can stay submerged for five minutes as they swim or run along the bottom.

Two minutes later a chocolate shape popped from the water thirty yards to our left. It regarded us, treading slowly closer, its head the shape of an old Packard convertible. Another head emerged twenty yards away, on the same line—close enough that we could see slimy dark pink beads of sweat on its face and the bristles on its pig ears. We were really digging now, and Nikki was screaming. Then the third hippo surfaced, only ten yards off the left bow. I barely glanced over because I was paddling in a blurry panic. Even Kulu raised his voice: "Hard, hard!"

We made it to the rapid—an unexpected refuge from greater terrors. But their flanking movement, as choreographed as the hippos' dance in *Fantasia,* left me deeply shocked. Trespassing, we'd been warned.

—

On the final night, we camped in Zambia near a tiny village of round mud huts and got hammered again. Tom and Ali danced to Dusty Springfield's "Son of a Preacher Man" over and over. Meg and Andy cuddled and then disappeared. Christian and Adam got tanked. A sadness fell around midnight, an awareness of leavetaking. "Everyone lie on your back and be quiet and look at the stars," Barry commanded. We lay back, but people were giggling. "C'mon, dammit now," Barry said indignantly. "Just shut up and listen to the silence of Africa!" The Southern Cross glittered in full splendor, diamonds on black velvet, and the frog chorus swelled—clamorous, insistent, exhilaratingly strange. It seemed to be the voice of the *nyaminyami,* the river spirit, speaking just beyond the reach of comprehension.

Christian staggered up the hill toward his bed, his camouflage pants shimmering in the dark. The group still by the fire began singing "American Pie" as a lullaby. Christian's voice rolled down: "You fooking spud-eating, Guinness-swilling, coontlicking Paddy bastards!" He repeated the insults, howling, in the whiskey-fueled bellow of the past.

"Ah, put in your Tampax, mate," Barry replied mildly. "Don't make me come up there and kick your arse into the river."

"All you fooking Kiwi, Irish, Yank bastards, you're not English," Christian said, still at high, slurred volume. "You're not English, and you're just jealous of the English empire. The English empire. The English empire . . ." He trailed off, crawling into his sleeping bag and curling up and falling, like the empire itself, to sleep at last.

(1997)

UNO . . . DOS . . . TRES . . .
URRRNGGGHHH!

In a dusty pelota court in the old Basque village of Arcangues,
Migueltxo Saralegi squares his shoulders and throws his hands to
the sky. Wearing blue shorts with white thigh pads, a leather waist-
coat, and two black tummy belts, he cuts a heraldic figure. Saralegi's
reach is actually to expand his lungs, but his aspect makes one imagine he's summoning ancient gods.

Now the stone lifter bends over a lead-filled block of granite.
Grasping handholds on its far side, he bucks the awkward object
onto his padded thighs, his face crimsoning as his lungs explode in
a *whoosh*. The stone weighs 250 kilograms—550 pounds. Saralegi
slides his hands to the stone's base and then jumps back while lev-
ering it end over end to his chest. For the third combination in this
dance of balanced force—Saralegi should be the hero of every
mover who ever schlepped a grand piano—he drives his torso back
again and boosts the stone to his left shoulder. He cradles it there,
then removes his hands and pirouettes before shrugging the stone
onto a foam hassock.

Two hundred tourists give Saralegi a polite golf clap. Rich Germans and Brits sprung from four gleaming buses, they are kitted out in red "Basque" berets and cloth belts, and everyone carries a glass of rum punch. After witnessing dances, a pelota match, and woodcutting, they are in a folkways frame of mind—curious to see more Basque exotica, but emotionally disengaged. Saralegi has a parallel view: he drove two hours into France from Pamplona solely for the money. He gets about $400; the tourists get a show. No harm done.

Yet the twenty-nine-year-old actually holds the world's stone-lifting record of 326 kilos, or 717 pounds, and in three days he'll attempt a new mark of 327 before an entirely different audience: knowledgeable Basques primed by a daylong "festival of hunting and fishing." To the Basques, these *herri kilorak*—"rural sports," derived from clearing the land and from farming—epitomize their manly culture. Such contests include log chopping, scything, handling oxen and donkeys in stone-dragging races, running with two-hundred-pound sacks on one's shoulder, tossing hay bales over an elevated rope, and, most impressively, the *harrijasotzaile,* or stone lifting. Stone lifting is "no longer a folkloric exhibition, or for circus strongmen," the local *Diario de Navarra* editorializes proudly. "It requires much more strenuous training than a weight lifter['s]." In November and December, when Saralegi bulks up for the following summer's record attempts, he lifts 88,000 pounds *per day.*

To put it in terms that every American can understand, Saralegi's record of 326 kilos is equivalent to hoisting seven supermodels. Indeed, Saralegi calls the record stone La Gorda—the Fat One—as if it were a fleshy but fickle mistress. In cold weather he wraps her in a blanket, and if she refuses to come to his shoulder, he mutters, "She didn't want love today." If she balks repeatedly, he calls her *culebra!* (snake) and *puta!* (whore).

Now Saralegi rolls out a granite ball that weighs only 220 pounds, and the announcer invites the audience to give it a try. Three men come and strain at the sphere, then slink off to general giggling. No tourist has ever lifted it above the instep of an Italian loafer. Saralegi, who's maintained a fixed expression throughout these indignities, whisks the ball to his shoulder in one pull and whips it around his n**o**olt **s**ix ti**m**e**s**. Th**e** appl**a**us**e** i**s** **m**uch mo**r**e appreciative; their representatives' humbling has given the audience a connection to the feat. Afterward, as the tourists are herded off to a ghastly "Basque" feast, I try the granite ball myself. By straining till my eyeballs fill with blood, I nudge it perhaps six microns. "How much does he think I could lift?" I ask Edurne Percaz, the voluble brunette who works at a Pamplona gym with Saralegi and who is serving as my translator. (Saralegi, who suffers interviews warily and whose Spanish has an elementary school flavor, is happiest conversing in Euskara, the k-, x-, and z-riddled tongue spoken by one-fourth of the 2.5 million Basques.) His surprisingly gentle hand envelops my biceps; next to his 290-pound Clydesdale frame I feel like Ichabod Crane. "Fifty kilos," he says in Spanish, "but tell him seventy to make him happy.

"I'm sorry," he adds pityingly, "but we are just stronger. It's the race." The Basques believe they are Europe's oldest people, having inhabited the land straddling the Pyrenees since at least 4000 B.C. They have the world's highest percentage of Rh-negative blood and claim to be bigger and stronger and braver than any arriviste Aryans, Franks, and Normans, claim to be the world's toughest soldiers— claim, in fact, to have landed in America before Columbus. "We do our tasks," Saralegi says. "We have a history with the stones. An Italian man with the same muscles can't pick up our stones— because he has no reason to."

And with that Saralegi picks up his stones, slides them onto a handcart, and dollies them up wooden planks into the back of his beat-up Peugeot van. Then the world's greatest stone lifter takes a push broom and sweeps up the woodcutter's sawdust, working steadily with workmanlike strokes until everything is tidy, until the job is done.

———

The streets of this Pamplona neighborhood are full of Basques who are sweaty and cheerful and rather drunk on *kalimotxo*, their dignifying name for red wine mixed with Coca-Cola. I am equally sweaty and cheerful, and just possibly more drunk. A spontaneous festival has broken out here in Milagrosa: teenagers thread in and out on stilts; dancers click fingers and shake leg bells as they sing "Azuri Beltza"; children parade in pointed hats crowned with feathers, wearing twin cowbells attached to the backs of their wool doublets. When they hop in unison, the streets ring. A man inside a mechanical bull's body that shoots out sparks chases the children about in a cloud of smoke and happy screams.

At midnight we pause for dinner at the Sorgintze bar. We've already hit the Sorgintze four times, acquiring new friends with each pass. I am surrounded by grinning Saralegi supporters gobbling up trenchers of greasy cod and toothsome asparagus. Meanwhile Saralegi, preparing for the record attempt in two days, has already been asleep for three hours at his mother's house in nearby Leitza. In his home village Saralegi can ramble with the dogs and feed the cows and never answer the phone. He can dream tidy dreams. If he raises the stone, he will reward himself only with a gigantic ham sandwich.

"Migueltxo is a champion, a monster," says Josu, shaking his head at such self-denial. "But all Basques can lift 100 kilos—how much can you lift?"

"One hundred kilos, at least," I say, made rash by *kalimotxo*.

"I can lift a hundred and fifty kilos," says Zube. I am astonished: Zube works at the Volkswagen factory, but he is as soft and mild as a tub of sweet butter. "But just now I have a bad back," he admits, having caught my eye.

"Men are always boasting about these sports because they have nothing to do, really," Percaz whispers to me before addressing the table: "Women are the kings of the Basque household, and men are the kings of nothing." All the men groan and roll their eyes.

About two A.M. the kings of nothing lead us down the street to an outdoor concert for Basque independence. The black eagle of freedom flutters on yellow pennants, and the square is thronged with *jarrai*, the radical young separatists who last year rampaged through the city of Bilbao, burning banks and buses. The women have brightly hennaed hair, the men a punk look: shaved heads with rat-tails, piratical earrings, and Che and *Amnistía!* T-shirts.

Some five hundred of the older colleagues of the *jarrai,* the Marxist-Leninist Euskadi Ta Askatasuna, are in prison. A terrorist group whose name means "Basque Homeland and Liberty," the ETA has killed more than eight hundred people since it was founded in 1959 to battle Franco, who seemed intent upon genocidal revenge for the Basques' having opposed him in the Spanish Civil War. First Franco's German allies bombed defenseless Guernica in 1937; later Franco exiled two hundred thousand Basques, put one hundred thousand in prison, and outlawed the Basque language.

But when I ask about the ETA, everyone frowns. Their extremism is out of favor now that their pressure has led to limited self-determination: today the Basques have their own schools, television, and police force. Zube gestures to the crowd, as if to say that tonight everyone just wants to drink and throb around. "That is the stereotype Americans have," says Percaz, "that we all shoot people. And your other stupidity is about running the bulls at San Fermin."

Pamplona's eight-day Fiesta de San Fermin, beginning every July 6, was first made traveler's legend by Ernest Hemingway in *The Sun Also Rises.* Hemingway described an unlucky runner being gored to death, and nearly every year nowadays, as the men flee the rampaging bulls in the daily race through the streets, a drunk American stumbles, forgets to hurl aside his rolled-up newspaper—bulls charge at movement—and gets himself ripped a new one.

Handing me another scarlet drink, Percaz explains that for the Basques, this chase down slick flagstones is a way to triumph over death, to feel life coursing through your veins. "You have to grow up watching it to truly understand. That man trains all year long to run the bulls," she says, pointing to a slight, potbellied gentleman whose training protocol seems to be chugging *patxaran* liqueur until it dribbles down his chin.

"I could run the bulls as well as that guy," I say. "And next year I will." This is the *kalimotxo* working its ruination, yet my brainstorm seems fiendishly plausible. I will run every morning of the fiesta, hoping to survive till the somewhat easier *encierro,* the *encierro de la villavesa:* all the bulls are dead, so the proud warriors lope in front of a bus.

"*You* can't run the bulls," Percaz says, tossing her hair. "Not really."

"Anyone can *run,*" I say.

"You don't understand anything," she says. "Nothing. And tell me this while we are speaking of Americans who have no good ideas in their head: Why don't you have topless bathing?"

I mumble something about our Puritan forebears. "Here I can kiss my friends on the lips in public," she interrupts.

"But not with the tongue," I counter.

"Yes," she says. "Sure, why not? You are a hundred and fifty years behind us sexually."

"Maybe in public," I say, hazily trying to mount a defense of American debauchery. "But in private we are tremendous bedroom athletes."

"No," Percaz says decidedly. "No, I have been to America."

—

The next afternoon we drive to Lumbier for a village sports festival. Beside the road an occasional red-tile-roofed village shoots up from the swaths of green wheat and then is gone. They are somehow dustier and more insular than other Spanish villages, and more helter-skelter than French Basque villages. Poplars line the river course and hills crowd in, unsettling the eye like a bunched-up quilt on an unmade bed.

In Lumbier we are nearly bowled over by a parade of fifteen-foot-high papier-mâché "giants," including Ferdinand and Isabella. We follow a huge, sad Don Quixote through the stone alleys to the square. (Quixote was far too inept to be a Basque, but he makes a splendid costume.) Every Basque town has an annual festival, seizing any reason to party: honoring the Virgin Mary, celebrating fishwives, or simply seeing who can pull the head off a greased goose. Lumbier's festival, for instance, is to celebrate expatriates from the Navarra province, none of whom seem to be here.

Yet in the square the presentation of rural sports has attracted per
haps five hundred people. First is the *sokatira,* the tug-of-war, which
the Basques claim to have invented. Then comes the *aizkolaris,* in
which two men race to chop through a succession of wide beech
logs, teetering atop them with their axes flashing in the hot sun.
Then a special exhibition: Nartxi Saralegi, Migueltxo's thirty-
seven-year-old brother, places his six-year-old son, Ruben, atop a
small log and hands him a George-Washington-and-the-cherry-tree-
size ax. Nartxi points to a spot on the log, and the boy makes the first
cut. Nartxi touches another spot, lower down. And so it continues
for hundreds of tiny blows, including one that narrowly misses
Ruben's toes as he slips off the log. When the beech finally splits,
the applause is warm and generous.

Finally the announcer introduces Iñaki Perurena, a butcher from
the Saralegis' home village of Leitza and a legendary stone lifter: he
raised the single-lift record from 250 kilos all the way to 318 and
still holds records for lifting 267 kilos with one hand and for re-
volving the 100-kilo stone around his neck thirty-six times in a
minute. Perurena is forty now, his gingery hair and beard thinning.
He is a little chubby, perhaps, and his brow shines with sweat. But
he takes the microphone eagerly: "Friends, thanks for gathering to
see our countrymen's work made sport. I am happy to see so many
of you here, because it means we will never lose the traditions. And
it is our traditions, special to us alone, that make us who we are." He
stretches his hands to the sky, pauses dramatically, and then runs to
the 200-kilo stone with the quick steps of a lover.

As he lifts it four times to gathering applause, I talk with Nartxi
Saralegi, who holds his son tenderly but looks a trifle grim. The
Basques love Perurena's gusto and still consider him the sport's em-
inence, though Migueltxo topped his single-lift record four years
ago and has raised it six times since. "Perurena is a showman,"
Nartxi says, "grabbing the microphone though there is already an
announcer. I only wish they were the same age, just once, so everyone would see that Migueltxo is *better.* Still," he acknowledges,

"Migueltxo would never be able to make that speech." Migueltxo is like Ferdinand the Bull, possessing none of the I'm-the-man braggadocio required to cross over from athlete to cultural (and advertising) phenomenon. "I try and try to get him to talk, to gesture to the crowd," Nartxi says, "but I cannot even get him to tell *me* about his feelings."

Ten years ago Nartxi, a Navarra champion in woodcutting but never world-class, saw his youngest brother's career languishing in Leitza. Migueltxo's only training was lifting the stone, as it had been since age eleven, when he spied a 65-kilo stone around the house and found it "a temptation." At eighteen he was stuck on the 280-kilo stone. So Nartxi installed Migueltxo in his house in Pamplona, had his wife cook him special fat- and sugar-free lunches and dinners, and built him a training area in his garage, where he would lift stones regularly with Nartxi when he wasn't lifting weights with his trainer. Nartxi became almost a father to Migueltxo, even more so since their father died last year.

"I control everything," Nartxi says simply. "I am sharper, more open-minded, and I have more concentration—many times I have made Migueltxo lift when he is not feeling like it." Nartxi's frustration is evident: to make ends meet, both men must work at the Gymnasio Jolaskide, Migueltxo as a fitness trainer, Nartxi as a receptionist. Nartxi believes that he himself could go much further in the sport, for he has the mind and passion of a great lifter—but it is Migueltxo who has the body.

That body has been reinforced like a missile silo. I later ask Saralegi's trainer, a slim, bullet-headed man named Jose Luis Tovias, what I would need to do to become a stone lifter. He laughed for a while. "Go to Lourdes," he said at last, ashing a cigarette. "Seriously? Well, first get your weight up to a hundred and thirty kilos," he suggested, plumping me up 50 kilos, "but by eating only proteins. No hamburgers, no lamb. No alcohol. Then the basic exercise is the squat, because the most important muscles are the quadriceps and the back. Migueltxo does five hundred kilos"—1,100 pounds—"five times in a row." Ouulegi also bench-presses 450 pounds and curls 200 pounds. Eight years ago he totaled his car but emerged unscathed. The doctor told him, "Your body was ready for a big shock."

"Migueltxo doesn't have the quick strength in the wrists and the knees to be an Olympic weight lifter," Tovias said. "He has a slower force. But it's mentally more difficult. He has time to think between the three movements, time to feel his body falling apart." Saralegi knows he has only a few more years to make records and hopes to reach at least 330 kilos before his knees give way.

Here in Lumbier comes the hope of the future: Perurena's thirteen-year-old son, Inaxio, will lift a 90-kilo stone four times. His father hovers nervously as Inaxio makes the sign of the cross and tips the stone back on shaky, coltish legs. Perurena can't resist helping a little on the final lift, so the referee requests a relift. Inaxio staggers under the weight but ultimately raises it, to sustained cheering. Then Perurena lifts 250 kilos four times, huffing and clutching his lower back in between reps so that the audience bends and jerks with him in silent unison, willing the stone up. After the last hoist he spreads his arms in happy exhaustion. "I want to be like my father," Inaxio tells me, his face reverent.

Perurena then comes over to talk, crowding me cheerfully with his elbows and stalking the conversation like a boxer, his blue singlet soaked with sweat: "We are not force men only—we have feelings," he says. "The stone gives me everything. The view of my life always has the stone in the middle of it." He folds Inaxio in a sideways hug. "When he was three I let him start touching the stones— and it's important that he's listening to this interview. It's not just the lifting; it's the life. Lifting and teaching Inaxio to lift are different pages of the same book."

And Saralegi? I ask. "We are very different," he says. "My son should learn from Migueltxo how to train, which I never did so much. But Migueltxo's focus is to hold the record stone—that is his only goal, his only interest in this task of ours. For me, I will do this the rest of my life. Even when I have no hair, when I am as bald as the stone, I will be lifting with pride in my job. And the people will come see me to encourage, and to relish the effort."

—

Migueltxo Saralegi eyes La Gorda nervously, as if his mistress had picked a fight. Two days ago he added a kilo to it and spray-painted the new number in red: "327 K." He also lifted it in practice. But now he stands on a small platform in the Salburua fields outside Vitoria at five-thirty on a hot, still Sunday afternoon with several thousand people watching. It is a strange, jerry-built venue, removed from the rest of the festival happenings. Basque television broadcasts all of Saralegi's record attempts, so the stage bustles with cameras and technicians and is further checkered by five sponsors' banners, including Volkswagen and Kaiku Milk. For the record attempt he'll be paid about $12,000—enough to buy a new van.

Saralegi rosins the stone's edges as if he were dusting it with diamonds. Incongruous *trikitixa*, Basque accordion ditties, play on the loudspeakers. "We have to be very quiet for the moment of the great deed," the emcee bellows, "quiet like we are in church." Saralegi grimaces—all that silent expectation only increases the pressure. His best friend, a plumber named Ibon, towels Saralegi's red, sweating face.

Nartxi fixes his brother with his fierce green eyes. "You are going to do it," he commands. Migueltxo scuffs at the floor with his special red-and-white shoes, and Nartxi, who misses nothing, insists, "The floor is not as bad as we thought—you are one hundred percent!" In fact the stage is much too bouncy, and its planks are dangerously far apart. After Nartxi checked out the footing yesterday he told Ibon privately, "Migueltxo won't do it."

"It is too hot, and the floor is very bad," the TV announcer intones, and Nartxi whips around, glaring. But Migueltxo's concentration is such that he hears none of this. He turns to stare out the back of the stage into an empty green field, taking huge breaths that echo through the microphone. Two black eagles rise above the field, circling on the convection currents. He mimes the lift to himself, picturing where the stone will touch his body. Beside him Nartxi shadows the movements in tandem, leaning in as if to merge his strength with his brother's.

Then Saralegi turns and begins. He hoicks the weight to his thighs, his eyelids closing over with the effort. The huge stone seems to be squeezing him. After a steadying pause, he jumps back and pulls it to his chest. This is the lift's crucial maneuver—akin to balancing a plate on a stick with your nose and jumping back to steady it, only the plate is top-heavy and weighs 719 pounds. But Saralegi's heel catches in a crack and his body shivers sideways. Nartxi, miming alongside, has his notional stone shoulder-high, but Migueltxo's stone hovers just out of control in midair. Ibon and Nartxi leap forward, but Migueltxo has already thumped the stone onto the tuffet.

The applause is generous and encouraging, and he gives a scrunchy-faced wave. But he stares angrily at the stone, measuring its edges with his hands. As Ibon wipes his face again, he murmurs, "The floor is a whore." Only once has he nabbed a record on the second try—the first effort saps 20 percent of his energy—but Nartxi doggedly psyches him up: "Breathe, breathe!" Migueltxo braces and heaves, but the stone makes it only halfway off his thighs. He waves again but looks crestfallen.

Nartxi tries to spin the failure. "In a way it's good," he says afterward, "because the people need to see that this is not easy to do, that he requires good conditions." Meanwhile, a Viscayan stone lifter named Zelia is metronomically hoisting a 150-kilo stone, aiming at his own record of fifty-two lifts in ten minutes. Zelia has asthma, and by the time he has broken the record with fifty-six lifts, he is utterly out of air and topples sideways into his handlers' arms. The crowd loves it, the drama as much as the record.

But Migueltxo, who hasn't much use for Zelia, remarks that "that record is easier, because the man can always lift the stone. In my record, sometimes the winner is the man, sometimes the stone." Rendered smaller and more loquacious by defeat, he now sits readily for an interview with *Diario de Navarra.* "The first problem is that the stone was very heavy," he explains—a funny line, were his intent not so methodical.

Almost drowning out Migueltxo's plain talk are the hugely amplified announcements of Tom Knapp, an American trapshooter in the neighboring field. Knapp throws two clay targets into the air, shoots one, ejects the cartridge, shoots it, and then shoots the other target. His buttery voice rides over the cheering, announcing, "A *muy rápidas* Berelli! And so easy-loading!" It becomes clear that the exhibition is purely an ad for the Berelli rifle. Knapp mentions Berelli thirty times in a minute—"It's like having two Berellis in one—a semiautomatic Berelli and a pump Berelli!"—as he blows balloons and vegetables to smithereens.

Nartxi listens to all this odious persuasion—"I have a new product from Berelli for the ladies of the house only!"—with surprising care, sifting, within his manager's role, for promotional tips. "If Migueltxo were an American, it would be the best," he says at last. "He would understand. . . ." He gestures delphically, a glyph of love and frustration. "He would understand that part of the job is to sell himself." But Migueltxo pays it no mind at all, only rolling his eyes and waving good-bye as he's ushered off for his urine test.

(1997)

LOST IN MONGOLIA

In a tepee high in the mountains of Mongolia, Frank Kimball was very ill. He couldn't catch his breath or keep anything down, even water. He lay restless and semiconscious under reindeer skins, only dimly aware of the Tsaatan children who peeped in to stare at his leg stumps, of his son, Ivan, trying to spoon tea with reindeer milk past his clenched lips, and of the Tsaatan shaman who'd arrived to divine Frank's future.

The shaman was a thin, gray-haired man who cast a dozen thumbnail-size rocks near the iron stove. He studied the patterns with his head cocked, like a tracker examining hoofprints, then began to murmur about Frank. The villagers' mood underwent a subtle change. But Batmunkh, the young Mongolian wrangler who'd stayed behind with the Americans, didn't seem to want to translate. Finally, Batmunkh told Ivan, "Now this special man is going to see when the helicopter will come."

This was Tuesday morning. The other dozen of us had ridden out of the mountains very early Monday, hoping to use a satellite phone

at the base camp eight hours away to summon an emergency helicopter. Baagi, the Mongolian trip leader, had told Ivan, "I'll do
everything I can to get a helicopter in Tuesday." Ivan knew Baagi as
a man of his word.

But the seer now shook his head: "The helicopter will not come
today." Still, Ivan knew that a helicopter had long been scheduled to
arrive Wednesday to fly us all back to the capital, Ulan Bator. The
shaman sifted his stones, serene in his possession of what was to
come. At last he said gently, "It will not come tomorrow either."

As an electrical engineer, a man at ease with power grids and deductive logic, Ivan comforted himself with the thought, The guy's
reading *rocks,* after all. But he was alone at ten thousand feet among
the frozen Sayany Nuru Mountains with sixty nomadic Tsaatan who
knew no internal medicine and followed no compass but the wanderings of their reindeer herds. His father clearly needed a saline
drip to rehydrate, for starters, but Ivan was a hard three-day horseback ride from the nearest town, where there wasn't so much as a
tongue depressor, anyway. As his Tsaatan host stoked the fire, Ivan
kept a hopeful ear cocked for the chop of a rotor but heard only the
snow softly melting down the limestone crags. This, he thought despairingly, is not how an adventure trip is supposed to turn out.

Yet the delirious man who was the cause of Ivan's anguish might
have disagreed. Frank Kimball had kept many secrets over the
years, and his closest held was why he had chosen to come here
from Charlottesville, Virginia, now, at age fifty-five. Certainly, visiting Mongolia had been a dream of his since he was a small child.
A passionate horseman who in a life of duty had never rambled
abroad, Frank was eager to roam an unfenced frontier. And this
country, lodged like a walnut between the mighty jaws of Russia
and China on the other side of the world, was about as far away, both
geographically and culturally, as you could go.

At the same time, the Mongolian countryside matched Frank's
own inner landscape. It was fierce and stubborn, a vastness where
travelers were few. Like Frank, its flinty people could spark great

loyalties. And, above all, it was full of horses. In an empty land twice the size of Texas, one-third of the 2.3 million Mongolians are nomads who ride to move, to stay alive.

But as to Frank's ultimate goal—well, he kept his true hopes secret to the end, perhaps even from himself.

—

The fourteen of us, Americans all save one Canadian, had gathered in Mongolia for a ten-day trip into the northern mountains bordering Siberia. Led by the Montana-based Boojum Expeditions, we were going to seek out a band of the Tsaatan, or reindeer people, who number only five hundred. In truth, most of us didn't know beans about these remote wanderers and just wanted to ride, to test our inner resources in rugged country, eager for whatever would come.

Or so we assured one another. No one wanted to slow the group down, to be embarrassed—or to get badly hurt trying to keep up. So as we flew from Ulan Bator, known as UB, to Mörön, in the northernmost Khöwsgöl province, there were many polite inquiries about the others' experience on horseback. Some could really ride, but the rest of us were products of dude ranches and recent frantic lessons. I spoke nonchalantly about having saddled up in Australia and Argentina but was secretly nervous: Mongolian horses are notoriously short and wild, and I am notoriously tall and tame.

In the initial sniffing out, we formed a fast impression of Frank. Not to put too fine a point on it, he struck us as a pain in the ass. During the cramped three-hour flight to Mörön, Frank shifted his gaunt, bearded frame to and fro, threatening to "disassemble," and it was murmured around the plane that he limped so because he had two plastic legs. It was also said that he had diabetes. After landing, we loaded our duffels onto a Russian transport truck that had a white school bus body grafted on back. Janet, a retired Montanan, couldn't find her water bottle: "Oh, I forget where I put it."

"That happens to older women," Frank snarled, leaving an uneasy silence. Though tender with his son, Ivan, whom he called "Doodle," and intimately savage with Lynne, a cheery horse trainer friend of Frank's from Charlottesville, he was otherwise often churlish. He reminded me strongly of my lame grandfather, Tom, whose creaky hips and hectoring voice—"How can you not understand the difference between a weed and an onion?"—shadowed my childhood. For years I had stepped lightly around Grandpa Tom, fearing the claims of his baffled affection as much as his fury.

We'd left the last road behind in Mörön, and it was jolting travel: the 120 miles north to Rinchinlhümbe, where our horses were, took two and a half days. After we'd been driving a few hours, I saw Frank drop his head into his hands with his eyes squeezed tight, and I realized he was in agony. And I saw that his torment had become a stamp of character, like a gang tattoo: He was an initiate in the secret society of those who spend their lives in pain; we were not. He would neither explain his condition nor suffer our sympathy. So we mostly ignored him.

The first afternoon, the truck broke down twice and the rains came, soaking through the roof. Then our support jeep skidded down a muddy bank and flipped, ending crumpled upside down in a culvert. By a miracle, the passengers were only badly cut up. Led by Mishig, our pint-size driver and man Friday, most of us slid into the sloppy, dung-filled ditch to reflip the jeep. Frank, excused by his bad legs, just stared impatiently north.

Later we took a "shortcut," which soon narrowed in the woods until we were wedged between two larch trees, swarmed by greenhead flies and mosquitoes. I laughed with the others in disbelief— we were fucking up so much, it had to be an adventure. Then a voice growled from the back, "I didn't come all this way to spend all this time in a dipshit forest": Frank.

In the morning, Kent Madin, Boojum's director, tried to relaunch the expedition by pasting "Boojum" labels on the truck's doors in both roman and Cyrillic letters. There was great consternation among the Mongolians: a mistake in the Cyrillic version of "Ulan Bator," which means "Red Hero," made it read, instead, "Red Shit Man." "Oh, why not some other mistake?" Kent muttered, fixing it with tape and a black marker. We shared a tent, and I liked his laconic derring do. Gray haired and rangy, he told funny stories about being a finalist in the selection of a new Marlboro Man.

As we wheezed along, fording rivers and crossing mountains, a group spirit began to emerge, a teasing familiarity. "How do you pronounce the sound Mongolian cows make?" Geoffrey, a New York lawyer, asked our translator. Gongor looked blank. "Moo?" Geoffrey suggested.

"Yes, moo," Gongor said.

"And cats?"

"Moo."

Amid rising laughter, Geoffrey persisted. "What about roosters?"

"What is a rooster?" Mongolians keep only herd animals, so they don't know poultry.

"A male chicken," Geoffrey explained.

"Oh yes," Gongor said. "That is also moo."

General mooing and hilarity. "If they're picking on you," Frank called, "you come to me and I'll take care of you."

"Thank you," Gongor said. "That is very reassuring." A prankish man with a shaved head, Gongor perfectly resembled a Mongolian Christopher Walken. He had the same quick smile under flat, dreaming eyes. As a child, in a Russian school under a Russian puppet government (that was thrown out at last in 1990), Gongor was often punished for ripping out the pages in the history books that showed valiant Russians slaughtering cowed Mongols. I enjoyed his deadpan humor enormously, and he and Frank and Ivan grew very close. Frank was drawn to the Mongolians, to the dauntless attack embodied in their axiom "If you are afraid, don't do it; if you do it, don't be afraid."

When we finally arrived at our wrangler's log cabin outside Rinchinlhümbe, I drank Chinese beer with Ivan by the truck under the huge, starry sky. Barrel shaped, twice his father's girth, Ivan told funny sex and golf jokes and in conversation paused a moment before speaking, giving each reply his best attention. Ivan told me something of his father's life: Frank had been a 440-yard runner at the University of Virginia as well as a three-goal polo player. After veterinary school, he became a small- and large-animal vet. He loved his job and was always running and riding from place to place. But in 1969, at twenty-seven, he caught brucellosis from a cow and then came down with mononucleosis; the combination damaged his pancreas and gave him insulin-dependent diabetes. His circulation was gravely impaired, and when another cow stepped on Frank's right big toe and he kept working hundred-hour weeks against his doctor's advice (he feuded with doctors, who asked too many questions and gave too many cautions), gangrene set in. He had his first amputation, of the toe, in 1978. He then developed ulcers on both feet, and over the next ten years he had seven more amputations, whittling both legs to the knee, chopping his six feet five inches to a mere five feet. To Frank's bitter disappointment, he could no longer work as a vet, and after two divorces he settled in Charlottesville, where he kept three horses and a Great Dane and turned to harness making.

"He had a kidney transplant in '92," Ivan said. "And just recently he broke his neck playing polo, lost one finger from arthritis and lost another in an accident with a horse. And he was hit by lightning."

"Wow," I said, feeling guilty and foolish in my snap judgment. A bat's wing of concern also flitted across my mind—at that moment Frank was flat in his tent, recovering. And he'd skipped dinner. "Wow."

"Yeah, the doctors say he should have been dead five years ago," Ivan said, smiling and sighing at once. "He's a warrior. He's a stubborn warrior—he won't let anything defeat him."

———

In the morning we were up at seven-thirty to ride. But the truck had to be resupplied. And there weren't enough bridles. And so on—the pluck and resource of Mongolians are matched only by their infuriating indifference to schedules. So we rode in impatient circles. Everyone was naming his horse (Buddy, Jack, Ethel), but I held off. My sorrel gelding was a three-year-old on his first long trip, and his head tossing and perpetually laid-back ears warned of a borderline personality. Also, he, like the others, was only about fourteen hands high, and I teetered in the short stirrups like a utility pole in a gale.

Finally, finally, at five P.M., the Mongolians donned their sheepskin *del* robes, sashed with yellow silk, and we stampeded northwest, leaving behind the last town we'd see. The steppe here was dotted with marmot holes, and the Mongolian trip leader Baagi's beard and ponytail were soon gray with dust from three whomping falls. This was funny but oddly disturbing, because Baagi was a huge admirer of Chinggis (Genghis) Khan; he had test-galloped all our horses and started us off by bellowing Chinggis's battle cry, "*Murindow!*"—"Mount up!" We think Chinggis a byword for mercilessness; the Mongolians consider him the thirteenth-century author of the national character, the man who banned farming and drove his cavalry to subdue the world from the Korean peninsula to the Black Sea. But Baagi's tumbles reminded me that Chinggis himself died after a fall from his horse, that fearlessness guarantees nothing.

We camped where the truck awaited, beside the black Arsa River. And after a dinner of boiled meat and potatoes—all meals were mutton or beef, boiled till it could no longer surprise the palate—Ivan and Gongor wrestled, Mongol style. The goal, as we'd seen at a festival in UB, is to put your opponent's back, knee, or elbow on the ground. Your second holds your spiked hat and periodically whacks you on the butt for encouragement. Gongor was quick and elusive—and doubtless heartened by my butt whacks—but Ivan had a rhino's wary purpose and a forty-pound advantage. He snared Gongor's left leg three minutes in and promptly gloried in the ritual winner's dance. He cradled Gongor under his arm and walked in a circle before taking squatting, mincing strides while flapping his arms like a *garuda,* the mythical bird of champions. "Attaboy, Doodle!" Frank said proudly, propped against the truck.

But the next day's ride was nine hot, fly-ridden hours in the saddle as we tried to make up ground. Trot and walk, trot and walk, in a sun-dazed dream. Frank sat rock solid but kept *thwack*ing his horse and swearing: "C'mon, you piece of shit. Move or I'll break your goddamn back." I thought he was furious, but Lynne and Ivan saw this as a good sign. Indeed, Frank had told Lynne that he loved his gelding's smooth gait and fast walk; he'd named him Evander, because his notched ear resembled Evander Holyfield's.

It was hard to guess Frank's state of mind. He didn't disclose much. I learned more later, from others: that he kept mum about his handicap among men but would tell women when he met them—rising to his feet, always, or holding the door—"I have two wooden legs, you know." (He had learned southern manners from his mother—and obstinacy, too; after an argument they wouldn't speak for days.) I learned that he never told people he read Latin and Greek and had taught himself Arabic and Spanish, or that he had written children's books that were published in Europe. That he made ingenious leather boxes and sleigh traces with giant bells for his closest friends but would leave their Christmas gifts to him unopened. And that he routinely refused payment for his harness work, growing cantankerous if pressed. Friends would guess how much the work was worth and hide money in his refrigerator, where he'd find it several weeks later among the uneaten salads and stews other friends had brought over.

He didn't eat much, didn't sleep much, and burned his lamp late into the night reading his favorites: Saki, *The Last of the Mohicans,* Lucretius, and Aristophanes. Framed above his desk was Dylan Thomas's famous valedictory, which ends, "And you, my father, there on the sad height, / Curse, bless, me now with your fierce tears I pray. / Do not go gentle into that good night. / Rage, rage against the dying of the light."

In the late afternoon, Klaus, a mad old Canadian farmer, suddenly fanned his hat and took off with a whoop. My horse's ears flew back, and I let him go as every horse surged into a cavalry charge across the rolling green steppe in a blur of crushed mint and clover. But a mule-eyed gray ridden by Mark, an amiable NASA engineer, leaped sideways in midgallop, sending him tumbling. There was a scary, arcing moment, and then Mark bounced safely on his butt, hat off and chaps flapping. The gray wheeled in its glee and stretched out toward a nearby nomad family's ger, a round felt tent. The six horses in their corral vaulted the five-foot fence, one after the other, as in motion-study photography, and followed Mark's horse toward the hills as we reined in and watched, astonished. Everything was out of control, and I suddenly felt fully, exhilaratingly present, like a child playing tag on a summer evening.

But by nine P.M., when we crept into camp, where the truck was again waiting, my saddle—a mingy Russian cavalry affair—had become a bed of rivets. Ivan and I had walked in bowlegged distress for the last two miles, our horses' heads bent like oxen's. We all limped to a pan of whitefish that Baagi had caught in the freezing Khogrog River, stuffed the sweet flesh into our mouths, and in five minutes left only a fan of bones.

—

In the next morning's thin light, I felt like the December 31 cartoons of the outgoing year—stiff, bent, feebly treading upon my long white beard. I put seven pills into my coffee—two megavitamins, two Imodium, and three Advil—and swallowed slowly. And I was one of the youngest. Kent was particularly worried about Frank. "He's not eating at all," he said. "Is that healthy for a diabetic?" He thought about this, then ambled over to Frank and Ivan's tent. Frank thanked Kent again for letting him come—"This is my dream"— then said he never ate much and was fine, aside from a sore arm from belting his horse.

Rain lowered over the mountains, heading our way. Hoping to reach the Tsaatan by nightfall—the locals had said they were probably camped some forty kilometers to the northwest—we stuffed our saddlebags and took leave of the truck for a few days, riding up out of the steppe and into the mountain taiga, through larch duff that muffled our hoofbeats to a sigh. Up and up we went, through gorse and growing patches of bog, following our tiny raisin-faced wrangler, Baldandorj, who alone knew the way. Rain fell steadily until we took a late lunch at four, when it became a biblical deluge—and then changed to hail. Drenched and bruised, we mounted again and beat our way up a long draw. My rain jacket's zipper broke, and I held it closed against the cold wet, and then my saddlebags slipped. I got off to retie them, and Baldandorj stopped without comment to hold the horse.

My numb fingers made slow work, and we fell far behind. We remounted, and Baldandorj inclined his head a little, almost slyly. Then he whipped his stallion and we were off, clods flying as my horse and I plunged ecstatically through the gorse faster than I had ever ridden, slamming blind up rises with my neck bent over his to form one prow of a scudding ship. A slight check for a brook before we dismissed it in a bound and stretched out again and again until we caught up and had to rein in and walk, shivering with pleasure as we cooled.

We camped in a clearing under a cordon of black larches. Frank was stumbling among the huge gnarled roots, so Ivan asked him to sit while he put up their tent: "It'll take two minutes for me to put it up and one and a half minutes for the two of us to put it up. Just sit there. Sit there. Will you sit there, please?"

"You've wasted thirty seconds already," Frank said, bending painfully to stab in a tent stake. This was Grandpa Tom to the word; after my grandmother died, he tottered around their Vermont farmhouse in a bewildered rage, at last driving even his children away. I had a violent urge to intervene, but I kept quiet. Everyone was exhausted, unstrung to the point that reveals true personalities. Abby, Mark's wife and, like her husband, a NASA engineer charged with weighty interplanetary matters, began clicking her heels together and capering about: "I'm a leprechaun! A leprechaun!"

As we dried our socks and mattress pads by the fire, I asked Baagi about his diet. In Mongolia, where enduring winter requires some blubber, "You're very fat" is a compliment. But Baagi was at least eighty pounds overweight. So he'd stopped eating for the last nineteen days. While the rest of us, except Frank, coveted every calorie—I'd lost eight pounds despite stuffing myself—Baagi seemed stronger than ever. Perhaps this was because he'd added a recycling element to his regimen. "As a child growing up," he said,

"I read about Chinggis Khan's men drinking their own urine to heal their wounds. But under Russian socialism we were taught that everything emerging from the human body was poison, that our old ways were wrong.

"Well, I'd tried to lose weight before by not eating, but I got so weak I couldn't do the male thing." Gongor, translating, was doing a much better job than I at keeping a straight face. "So I decided to drink my pee in the old way, 250 to 300 grams a day. For the first three days it tasted just disgusting, and for the first ten days I was still taking a big dump. After ten days, the dump began to be like chewed gum or burnt rubber—it would stick to the toilet. But now my urine has no taste, no color, and I take no more dumps and feel extremely strong. I feel like a warrior."

As I tugged my boots on damp the next morning—though the wranglers had predicted sun, the heavy rain continued—I asked Frank how he was enjoying the trip. "I wouldn't have missed it for the world," he rasped, and I thought he was being sarcastic. But his tone was reverent: "The scenery is amazing. It changes constantly, from steppes to pines to mountains to rivers to bogs—every time you look, it's a new horizon. I've never seen anything so beautiful in my life."

I liked him much better suddenly; I'll forgive almost anything for passion. And he was right. It was spectacular and wild: the only other people in these thousands of acres were the Tsaatan, if they actually existed. Left alone with food, a map, and a compass, I could have sought them for weeks in vain. The paths were too faint and braided, the landmarks too numerous.

"*Murindow!*" cried Baagi, feisty with pee, and we fell into the slow file disappearing into a field of rhubarb. Six straight hours we rode uphill through meadows of vetch and bluebells all matted by slants of rain, then down a sheer slope where the path was a brown stream and we had to lead the horses, mud and sweat flying everywhere. After climbing again through chilly pine groves, we crested above the treeline and finally spied ten white tepees at the head of a swampy draw. The Tsaatan village.

On arrival my horse was utterly knackered; I likewise. I lay supine in our tent, ignoring the friendly Tsaatan children crowded around, fairer and softer of cheek than the Mongols, and listened as Kent blew off steam. The governor of the Tsagaan-Uür district had decreed that for every photo a visitor took the Tsaatan must collect three thousand tugriks—a whopping $3.75. After some negotiation, a deal was struck, and we wandered freely, save Frank, who stuck to his tent. He was probably the only one who wasn't finding the trip much harder than expected. Yet he felt weak and kept grousing: "It's an imposition—we're just *gawking* at them." After all the *gers* we'd lounged in, Frank still didn't seem to believe that the Mongolians' warm hospitality—every visitor is greeted with snuff and fermented mare's milk and silences that allow for spiritual refreshment—was sincerely intended for him.

Abby and I ducked into the tepee of a man named Bat. Though he was one of the village's leading citizens, its liaison to the West, his only mark of splendor was a pair of eyeglasses. His family's few possessions ringed the tepee's circumference, and reindeer meat hung from a crosspole. We sat on a reindeer pelt near the central stove as Bat's daughter served us tea with reindeer milk, along with hunks of mild reindeer cheese; for our part, we lavishly admired the snuff bottle. It was all as cozy as a bear's den. But what struck me most in my weather-haunted mood was that tomorrow it would rain again. Bat conveyed the falling drops philosophically, with a fluttering of fingertips. The Tsaatan have the bundled, high-shouldered look of people who are often wet.

Then we went next door, where everyone else was crowded in, villagers and visitors alike. Gongor was translating Klaus's description of riding reindeer in his native Alberta. We learned that the Tsaatan have a shaman but no leader, that you need no training to ride a reindeer, and that they'd never heard of people with black skin.

Lynne asked if they had any questions for us. We sat expectantly, eager to explain the great world. After a long pause, the oldest man present asked, "Where did he [Klaus] ride that reindeer?"

"In Canada!" Klaus said.

Another, even longer pause. "How many reindeer do you have there?" We had come all this way to admire the reindeer, and the Tsaatan believed the world must be full of them.

Klaus began to inquire where they bury their dead, but we all frowned, having learned of the Mongolian taboo against speaking of death (it may bring it on) or the dead (it troubles their peacefully sleeping spirits).

In the morning, Bat's forecast proved as wrong as every other. The ground was blankcted in snow. We'd been behind schedule the whole trip; now we'd have to stay on another day, snowed in. Frank was secretly pleased at the news, as he'd thrown up and was feeling ropy. Kent wasn't too worried; his own stomach was rumbling from the previous night's undercooked potatoes. He asked Frank if he could take aspirin, and Frank said no, actually, because of the chemotherapy.

"Chemotherapy?" Kent said.

"You didn't know about that one, did you?" Frank said, smiling guiltily. The osteopathic sarcoma in his right shoulder—a tumor so malignant that his doctors wanted to amputate the arm—had been another secret. On his trip medical form, he'd written tersely: "Broken almost everything—all healed. Wears glasses. Diabetic on insulin. Kidney transplant. Bilateral leg amputations below the knee. Still play polo, fox hunt, ride daily." But he hadn't mentioned the cancer and how after four rounds of chemotherapy the tumor continued to thrive. The doctors had urged more chemo last winter, but Frank hated its effects so much, he'd refused.

At that point, he had been planning the Mongolia trip for several months and had persuaded Lynne to come along for help and support. Herbert Jones, a doctor friend and a fellow diabetic, repeatedly counseled Frank not to go. He pointed out that Frank's blood sugar was the most volatile he'd ever seen, ranging between 40 and 450 milligrams of glucose per deciliter—normal is 65 to 120. And that he'd seen Frank lose both prostheses playing polo and go into insulin shock after a strenuous chukker.

But Frank was determined, though the tumor made it an effort of will for him to clutch the reins. And though he had a nickel-size lesion on his left leg stump that was growing and might eventually require an amputation above the knee. And though in February he'd had a stroke that knocked him facedown in the yard. He didn't even tell his daughter, Karin, about the stroke, but he did tell his friend Louise McConnell: "I can't even make it to the mailbox and back anymore. I don't know how I'm going to make it through Mongolia."

We spent our snow day dozing in the tepees. The Tsaatan unfurled bedrolls and covered us with reindeer pelts and stirred up the fires. Lying with huskies and runny-nosed children cradled all around me, I felt elated to be so cut off from the world, so completely out of touch. Life was reduced to its simplest elements: tea, rice, dogs, a fire.

Several dozen reindeer returned from foraging in the early afternoon, grunting like pigs as they daintily clip-clopped into the tepees, seeking a handout of salt. I went outside to pee followed by two reindeer, who began butting heads for the right to drink my piss, straight from the tap: new and powerful evidence in support of Baagi's urine theories.

The next morning unveiled a snap frost that froze the tent poles and made the saddle of the mountains gleam like confectioners' sugar. Heavily swaddled, we mounted our shivering horses at dawn, hoping to reach the truck that night. We needed to, as we were out of food save a few bowls of dried ramen. Frank ate a pinch of Tsaatan bread and was led shaky legged to his horse. During the night, he'd thrown up both soup and Chinese Sprite. Several of the group had overheard him being kind—for the first time—to Lynne and were deeply alarmed. He must really be sick, they thought.

We'd noticed that Frank ragged people as a kind of entrance exam. "He hated people who didn't fight back," his friend novelist Rita Mae Brown would say later. "Being sarcastic and listing all your shortcomings was his way of getting rid of the wimps, so he didn't have to waste time." Yet Frank was devoted to those who cared to pass his tests. "When I was down about my marriage splitting up," Herbert Jones said later, "I'd go talk to Frank. He'd have his head down on the table, feeling bad, this diabetic who lived alone, but when I came he'd sit up and talk for two hours and inspire me."

"Look at that," Ivan murmured now. "He can't sit up in his tent, but he can sit straight on a horse." Frank sat tall, reins cradled in his right hand, his left hand propped on his kidney. He was the mirror image of the wranglers, who carried their knouts regally canted against their right hips.

Where the mountain shadow ended and a field of wild onions was rimed with frost so white that you couldn't look at them, Frank started swaying. Kent made a quick decision that Ivan and Frank and Batmunkh, a self-contained wrangler, should return to the Tsaatan. Gongor would remain with us, as his better English might be required if someone broke a leg riding down, which wasn't out of the question in the treacherous conditions. This all happened much too fast, as important moments do. Turning back to the shadows, Frank gave us a small sideways wave. He looked truly ill, and I had an odd, physical sense that his journey lay a different way. I felt cold, as if someone had whisked off a quilt.

But no one spoke of it; we had too many troubles of our own. Mark's horse bucked him again and became entangled in its own stirrups. Its panic infected Geoffrey's horse with wickedness— Geoffrey looked like a man tied to a lit rocket. The path was a skating rink with pockets of quicksand, and my horse did a flying face plant in the next bog. We both began watching the sloping ground ahead with winch-wire concentration, and every time we neared mud he came to a dead stop, terrified. The whole day was spent coaxing him crabwise through mud, bog after melancholy bog, and I was far behind when the steppe appeared at dusk, at last. But when we cantered the last two miles to the truck, he was so lathered and quick I forgave him everything.

Mishig was thrilled to see us. He shook everyone's hand, grinning—having had no way of knowing that we hadn't all been wiped out in an avalanche. He laid out cookies and cream that tasted as good as anything I've ever eaten in my life, and I washed them down with three warm beers that savored of nectar. I was not sick; I had not fallen; I was safe—and somewhere in all that slop I'd learned to ride. I felt happy, oh so happy, to be alive.

Up in the mountains, Frank lay in Bat's tepee with Ivan at his side. He'd passed out on returning to the Tsaatan and now was having trouble catching his breath at that altitude. As he had no fever, Frank suggested that the culprit was bad food. But it could have been sepsis—blood-borne toxins from his leg ulcer; Ivan found pus in Frank's socks. Or a surge of the cancer. Or a kidney or pancreas problem. Frank laboriously checked his blood sugar, found it high, and injected insulin. On this medical matter he was scrupulous, conscious of his debt to the dead man whose kidney he bore, of his responsibility to treat that gift, at least, well.

Not wanting to dwell on his condition, he thanked Bat for the air mattress, which was Bat's best bed. Then Frank turned to his son. Neither had ever said so, but this trip was important to them both. When Ivan had decided to come along, feeling it might be his last chance for an extended sojourn with his father, Frank was privately overjoyed. "Ivan is so big and strong," he told his friend Louise, "that if anything happens, he'll just carry me out." Frank now asked about Ivan's recent divorce, wondering if there was any hope of reconciliation. Frank and Ivan's mother had divorced when Ivan was four, and Frank wondered whether he'd provided a bad example.

The topic made Frank very sad. "He felt so bad that he didn't have a partner," Rita Mae Brown would say later. "Part of his sorrow and loneliness was that he felt he had nothing to offer a woman because he couldn't be the strong, manly protector to her. There were a couple of women who would gladly have made their lives with him, but because he felt he didn't deserve their love, he didn't see it. He didn't see it all around him."

The last thing Frank said Monday was that he was proud and touched that Baagi had told him he was a good horseman—he clung to that idea as he drifted into a fitful sleep, waking to retch every few hours. The Tsaatan bank their stoves after dinner to save wood, but Bat and his family of seven stoked the fire all night.

—

Down below we were having trouble with the satellite phone. A $5,000 briefcase-size triumph of technology, it plugged handily into a car's cigarette lighter. But our Russian truck didn't have a cigarette lighter. Nor, to everyone's great frustration, could we get it running off the truck's battery. Eventually Gongor picked up the phone, got in a jeep, and went in search of a *ger* with a generator. Late at night, far from camp, he aligned all the technologies and reached the defense minister. The minister yelled over the patchy line that none of the country's nine helicopters was available before late Wednesday, when an MI-8 transport chopper was due to pick us up anyway.

Kent gave us the grim update Tuesday morning. Our response was muted. If Frank had fallen sick early in the trip, we would have brainstormed ceaselessly, peppering Kent with questions about hospitals and airlifts. But our slow retreat from civilization had made us realize just how far out we were, how few options remained. We mounted and embarked on another long ride, west to the Boojum Lodge, at the confluence of the Tengis and Shishhid Rivers. It was a perfect spot to fish or hike, but we just lay about inside the pine cabin as evening came on.

At dinner Baagi poured out glasses of Romanian wine and toasted "that brave man, Frank." Afterward we discussed the situation in twos and threes, feeling our way along. We had shaped an identity in the mountains, a sturdy common purpose, like a spun crockery bowl, and then the bowl dropped. We couldn't quite piece it back together. I found myself sounding more cheerful than I felt, obeying the local taboo against mentioning possible bad outcomes. Kent, for his part, fully expected to see Frank come down from the mountain "as irascible as ever."

But he told me privately that he'd had a call from Frank three months before the trip. Frank was having prickings of conscience about how little he'd told Kent. He didn't disclose his cancer or his stroke, of course, but he did say, "Hey, I just want to be sure it's okay that I'm coming. If something happens to me, I don't want you to be arrested or anything." Kent, who'd been convinced by Frank's riding ability and desire—and his fudged medical form—asked for a letter from Frank's doctor saying he had approved the trip. Frank said sure, but never provided one.

Kent was beginning to kick himself for not pressing Frank, especially about what prescription drugs he was taking. Frank simply answered "yes" to the medications question without elaborating. But the prednisone he took for the transplanted kidney depressed his immune system—a danger among strange foods and viruses. For pain he often took codeine, a powerful narcotic. And no one else knew his insulin protocols.

Kent also believed that we'd relied too heavily on the miracle phone. "It creates a false sense of safety, because you believe you can just reach out for help," he would say later. "But in Mongolia it's not going to arrive. This is a remote, dangerous trip, and we have to know our limits. Next year I don't think we'll take a phone." It occurred to me that in addition to our unwarranted faith in Western technology—the phones and helicopters we'd supposedly come to Mongolia to escape—we'd also relied too heavily on keeping to the schedule, on good weather, and on our guides' judgment and expertise, including Kent's. But I didn't say that to him. It would be the same as saying we'd relied too heavily on human infallibility. Only we had.

Frank woke up Tuesday delirious. Late in the morning, after the shaman had cast his rocks and declared the helicopter would not come, Ivan took a break from scanning the skies and checked Frank's blood sugar. It was 320—quite high. He gave his father some insulin, not sure how much was enough and worried about an overdose. If only the chopper would come. In four hours Frank could be in UB, where there were at least doctors. But four hours later the chopper was nowhere in sight and Frank's blood sugar was up to 335, so Ivan gave him another shot. He found it painful and infuriating that he could do no more. Frank wasn't taking any liquid, and he'd always hated the rendered tea, even barely conscious he screwed up his face at it.

Lynne and a Tsaatan guide had started from the truck that morning and ridden back up the mountain. They arrived in Bat's tepee at seven P.M. with more insulin, some freeze-dried beef and pasta, and the news that the helicopter should come, as scheduled, the following day. But Lynne was concerned that Frank didn't even register her arrival. Ivan told her the shaman's prediction about the helicopter. "Did you ask him about Frank?" Lynne asked.

"No," Ivan said. And she knew that he hadn't wanted his hopes punctured. Bat and several other Tsaatan were very solicitous of her and kept saying, "It's going to be okay; it's going to be okay." But Batmunkh took her aside to disclose the rest of the shaman's news. His message was made starker because he hadn't the vocabulary to soft-pedal: "Frank is going to die. Everyone knows this."

That verdict didn't entirely surprise her. For months Lynne and several of Frank's other friends had been troubled by a sad suspicion. Knowing that Frank hated the idea of a further amputation that would end his riding and hated even more the looming prospect of wasting away in a hospital, they became convinced that he had decided to ride off into the sunset like a man. That he had decided to go to Mongolia, far from well-meaning interference, to die.

Frank was up all Tuesday night, agitated by some kindling inner need. At four A.M. Wednesday he began saying, "*I want to . . .*" with great urgency. "*I want to . . .*" He finally nodded off on this half-articulated wish. But I think I know what he wanted. When it came down to it, high on top of the world on those last clear mornings when the horses were kicking up their unshod hooves, prancing and nickering and blowing trumpet blasts of steam, and he was alone with his son, I think that Frank fiercely wanted to keep on living.

———

At the lodge, all we did on Wednesday was wait. Baldandorj ran out of tobacco and began chewing the foam from the sofa. Kent and Baagi had confusing sat-phone conversations with the control tower in UB: The chopper is on its way; it's in Mörön—no, sorry, Mörön is out of fuel, so it's not on its way. The rest of us gathered around the phone in a circle of sympathetic magic, wanting desperately to contribute. But all we could do was bear witness. The Tsaatan shaman's prediction about the helicopter, as we later learned, had now proven out. We went to bed at last. Thursday morning brought clear, hopeful skies, but they remained empty. Our resignation grew achingly restless: the helicopter would come when it came. But when would it come?

At midafternoon on Thursday, a big green Russian MI-8 racketed into our lost valley. At this late date it seemed unreal, almost officious, and I felt more dread than relief. Soon we'd learn. Gongor and Baagi boarded to guide the pilot up to the Tsaatan. It was a two-day ride across the sharp folds of the land but only a biscuit toss by air. An hour later, the MI-8 was back, spinning down gracefully out front. After a while, the door opened and Baagi descended alone, with his head down, and I knew.

As I later learned, very early the day before, when Frank eventually fell asleep, Lynne and Ivan also dozed exhaustedly. For several hours the tent was quiet. Lynne woke with a start at seven A.M. Frank's hands were cold. She bent her ear to his lips and heard nothing. So she let Ivan sleep, for there was no hurry now. When he woke, she took him outside to say, "Frank is gone."

Gently, but with the assurance of stagehands who have been waiting for the curtain, the Tsaatan zipped Frank completely into his sleeping bag and carried him to a ledge above the village. They rigged a green tarp over him to keep off the rain. Then they took down their tepees, hitched up the reindeer, and dragged the whole village two hundred yards downhill to confuse the dark spirits and start afresh.

Ivan was coming forward now. With his heavy stubble he looked more and more like his father. He seemed bewildered and apologetic, as if he'd somehow failed us in not bringing Frank back safe. Lynne was alongside, and we hugged them both, tears in everyone's eyes.

After a while, Ivan carried Frank out of the helicopter, his body wrapped in the green tarp, with Baagi and Gongor helping. All three would stay behind for a few days to bury him. In some unspoken way, the Mongolians had taken over Frank's care, had received him. The rest of us, heading home, were left no role but the keening.

"Frank wasn't in a hospital, and he was with his son," his daughter, Karin, said afterward, "so I can't think of a better way for him to die." Just before he left, Frank had twice gone to visit Karin and her family in Miami, which was unusual. He had asked friends to come say good-bye, which was even more unusual. And two weeks before the trip he had notarized a letter that gave Ivan "full discretion and authority as to the disposition of my remains" should he die abroad. Right before the trip he had told Ivan that if he did die, he wanted to be buried in Mongolia. But Frank had kept the letter in his own saddlebag, never believing the moment had come when he needed to hand it to his son.

Thinking of all Frank's closely held decisions and revisions and last hopes, Karin added in a burst of tears, "He loved *The Last of the Mohicans,* because he wanted to be the last and have the last word. So it seems appropriate that he's buried in Mongolia, because none of us can touch him there. He's got closure, but we don't."

The last time I saw Frank's body, he was resting by a rail fence in the steady rain. I watched his still form the whole way as the helicopter swept on a low path from the valley, thinking of my grandfather, deaf and stubborn and alone on his farm at ninety-seven. Soon he too will die, because no help can reach him; soon he too will die of remoteness.

Frank was buried in a plain pine coffin on a hillside east of the lodge, and horses now graze above him. The headstone says only FRANK KEMNER KIMBALL—JANUARY 6, 1942 TO JULY 23, 1997. There is no cause of death listed on his death certificate and no space on such a form to assess matters of intent or wisdom or courage. The form reflects only the small truth that Frank Kimball rode into Mongolia and did not ride out.

(1998)

Acknowledgments

I am greatly indebted to the original editors of these articles: Richard Alleman, Mark Bryant, Henry Finder, David Handelman, Michael Hirschorn, David Hirshey, Gerry Marzorati, Susan Morrison, Ilena Silverman, Andrew Sullivan, John Tayman, and Alice Truax. They untangled the knotted, kneaded the doughy, and furiously pruned what remained. Had they had their way entirely, each piece herein would have been whittled to a single glowing word such as "power," or "culture," or, most likely, "sex." Lusty folk, editors.

Over the years Jon Karp at Random House treated me to a number of lunches at cheap, verminous restaurants. After accustoming me to an atmosphere of dire poverty, he snapped up this collection last year for an amount roughly equal to the cost of those lunches. A few weeks afterward, Jon took a job in the film world, where he dined only with Tom Cruise and Sharon Stone. One heard of private rooms and jeroboams, of groaning platters of Kumamoto oysters, of geishas dropping truffles into the revelers' gaping mouths. Several months later, as this book was about to go to press, Jon returned to his old job at Random House. Thanks, Jon!

My agent, Binky Urban, has been trying to get me to write a book forever. At a mutual friend's wedding ten years ago, she buttonholed random guests: "Go tell Tad to get going on a book!" Binky is a force of nature, and so it was that strangers came up to me throughout the evening to explain why I owed it to the human race, or at least to Binky, to get going. A few years back she gave up on the nudging, and I discovered that I missed her tough-love bulletins:

Look, do you want to be a contender or not? You're wasting your life! Her silence proved almost as inspiring as her infectious faith and enthusiasm, and here a book is at last.

I am also obliged to Mrs. Marianne Riely, my tenth-grade English teacher. I spent that class avoiding her eye, lest she notice me and read one of my compositions aloud, with each fault announced in ringing tones. These precise and very public explanations of error were, to an adolescent, the worst imaginable torment, and we shaped up in a hurry. Mrs. Riely's hobbyhorses included—but were by no means limited to—fuzzy logic, faulty syntax, flabby vocabulary, and feeble posture. *Won't you sit up straight! Really!*

And I am particularly grateful to Mrs. Betty Maunz, a reading adviser at the Park School. When I was in the second and third grades she let me lie on her office rug and read for hours. Not what the school board had in mind, probably, but it beat sitting in class with Mrs. Merrick (indignant; an ear puller). Mrs. Maunz also took me to her house, where she fed me oatmeal cookies and more books, selected from her shelves after careful consultations: books about baseball, and wolf packs, and talkative pigs, and boys who lived in secret junkyard forts. I was living in a secret junkyard fort of my own, in those days, and she tiptoed into it. It saddens me that she is not alive to read this book. I would like to imagine her taking *Lost in Mongolia* down from a high shelf and pressing it upon her favorite sort of student: one who was small, quiet, lost, and eager to be found.

About the Author

TAD FRIEND, a staff writer for *The New Yorker,* has had his articles published in *The Best American Sports Writing* and *Goodlife: Mastering the Art of Everyday Living,* among other collections. He lives in New York City.

About AtRandom.com Books

AtRandom.com books are original publications that make their first public appearance in the world as e-books, followed by a trade paperback edition. AtRandom.com books are timely and topical. They exploit new technologies, such as hyperlinks, multimedia enhancements, and sophisticated search functions. Most of all, they are consumer-powered, providing readers with choices about their reading experience.

AtRandom.com books are aimed at highly defined communities of motivated readers who want immediate access to substantive and artful writing on the various subjects that fascinate them.

Our list features literary journalism; fiction; investigative reporting; cultural criticism; short biographies of entertainers, athletes, moguls, and thinkers; examinations of technology and society; and practical advice. Whether written in a spirit of play or rigorous critique, these books possess a vitality and daring that new ways of publishing can aptly serve.

For information about AtRandom.com Books and to sign up for our e-newsletters, visit www.atrandom.com.

Printed in the United States
by Baker & Taylor Publisher Services